The Economist

GLOBALISATION

OTHER TITLES FROM
THE ECONOMIST BOOKS

The Economist Desk Companion
The Economist Economics
The Economist Guide to Economic Indicators
The Economist Guide to the European Union
The Economist Numbers Guide
The Economist Style Guide
The Guide to Analysing Companies
The Guide to Business Modelling
The Guide to Financial Markets
The Guide to Management Ideas
The Dictionary of Economics
The International Dictionary of Finance
Business Ethics
E-Commerce
E-trends
Improving Marketing Effectiveness
Managing Complexity
Measuring Business Performance
Successful Innovation

Pocket Accounting
Pocket Advertising
Pocket Director
Pocket Economist
Pocket Finance
Pocket International Business Terms
Pocket Internet
Pocket Investor
Pocket Law
Pocket Manager
Pocket Marketing
Pocket MBA
Pocket Money
Pocket Negotiator
Pocket Strategy

The Economist Pocket Asia
The Economist Pocket Europe in Figures
The Economist Pocket World in Figures

The Economist

GLOBALISATION

THE ECONOMIST IN ASSOCIATION WITH
PROFILE BOOKS LTD

Published by Profile Books Ltd
58A Hatton Garden, London EC1N 8LX

Typeset in EcoType by MacGuru
info@macguru.org.uk

Printed in Great Britain by
St Edmundsbury Press, Bury St Edmunds

A CIP catalogue record for this book is available
from the British Library

ISBN 1 86197 348 9

Contents

Contributors

Sameena Ahmad is the consumer-industries correspondent for *The Economist*. She contributed to chapter five.

Brian Barry is *The Economist*'s Tokyo bureau chief. He contributed to chapter two.

Zanny Minton Beddoes is Washington economics correspondent for *The Economist*. She wrote all articles, save one, in chapter eight.

Matthew Bishop is the New York bureau chief of *The Economist* and the author of *Pocket Economist*. He wrote chapter four.

Frances Cairncross is *The Economist*'s management editor. Her book, *The Company of the Future: How the Communications Revolution is Changing Management*, will be published in February 2002 by Harvard Business School Press in the United States and by Profile Books in Britain. She contributed to chapter two.

Clive Crook is deputy editor of *The Economist*. He wrote chapter one and contributed to chapters two and six.

Kate Galbraith is an editor on Economist.com. She is the editor of this book.

Robert Guest is *The Economist*'s Africa editor, based in London. He wrote chapter seven.

Graham Ingham writes about economics, mainly for Global Agenda on Economist.com. He contributed to chapter eight.

Patrick Lane is an *Economist* correspondent in Frankfurt and the editor of *Economics*. He contributed to chapter two.

Marc Levinson is a former finance editor of *The Economist* and the author of *The Economist Guide to Financial Markets*. He contributed to chapter two.

Bjorn Lomborg is a statistician at the Department of Political Science, University of Aarhus, Denmark. His book, *The Skeptical Environmentalist*, is published in English by Cambridge University Press. He contributed to chapter six.

David Manasian, formerly legal-affairs editor of *The Economist*, is the editor of Global Agenda on Economist.com. He contributed to chapter five.

John Peet is the business affairs editor at *The Economist*. He wrote chapter three.

Gideon Rachman is *The Economist*'s Brussels correspondent, but perhaps better known as the wine correspondent. He contributed to chapter five.

Jeffrey Sachs is director of the Center for International Development and Galen L. Stone Professor of International Trade at Harvard University. He contributed to chapter six.

Robert Hunter Wade is Professor of Political Economy at the London School of Economics. He is the author of *Governing the Market*, a study of economic and political development in East Asia. He contributed to chapter six.

Vijay Vaitheeswaran is *The Economist*'s energy correspondent. He contributed to chapter five.

Many *Economist* editors and journalists offered advice on putting this volume together. Particular thanks are due to **Clive Crook, Anthony Gottlieb** and **John Micklethwait.**

Introduction

In *The Economic Consequences of the Peace* (1919), John Maynard Keynes wrote that:

> The inhabitant of London could order by telephone, sipping his morning tea in bed, the various products of the whole earth, in such quantity as he might see fit, and reasonably expect their early delivery upon his doorstep; he could adventure his wealth in the natural resources and new enterprises of any quarter of the world.

Keynes was recalling Europe before the first world war. Since then, of course, integration has evolved in ways he could not have imagined. The inhabitant of London can now watch events around the world as they happen, thanks to live television; he can travel by air to virtually anywhere; and he can seal business deals in an instant, via the Internet or fax machine.

All of these advances are part of globalisation – which, at its simplest, means crossing borders. Capital crosses borders; companies cross borders; whole industries cross borders; people, ideas, diseases, even governments cross borders. How many borders, and what kind of borders, and why and how successfully they are crossed, are all part of the story. Finding out who and what doesn't cross borders, and why, is just as important.

This book is a compilation of articles previously published in *The Economist* related to globalisation. They were written over a four-year period, from 1997 to 2001; and, with the exception of chapter six, all were written by *Economist* journalists.

Taken together, they convey several themes. First, globalisation is not new. Goods, ideas and people have traversed the globe for millennia. The chorus of modern technologies – the Internet in particular – has spurred talk of a "new" global economy. But the train and steamship from the 19th century were as important to global economic integration. They reduced transport costs in the same way that new technology has reduced communications costs in more recent times.

The second theme is that globalisation is good. This is a contentious point; anti-capitalist critics familiarly charge, among other things, that globalisation has served rich countries at the expense of poor ones. Since the terrorist attacks on America in September 2001, an even wider group has found such charges convenient. But economic integration has brought improvements for all. *The Economist* was founded in 1843 as an advocate of free trade; it should be no surprise that this collection argues that fewer trade barriers and fewer controls – not more – will benefit poor and rich alike. Nor does globalisation mean environmental ruin and American cultural domination – other favourite charges of anti-capitalist protestors.

Globalisation may be good, but it is not as pervasive as many people believe: that is the third theme of this book. Money and goods do not flow as easily across borders as they do within them. Labour was more mobile in the late 19th century than it is today. The extension of this idea is that globalisation is fragile. It can be stopped, or even reversed. This happened during the Great Depression; it could happen again.

This book is organised into four parts. The first part, "The case for globalisation", is the broadest and most ambitious. The opening chapter, "Globalisation and its critics", argues the liberal case for globalisation – how and why the anti-capitalist protestors have got it wrong. Chapter two, "Popular myths and economic facts", follows this up with snapshots of migration, trade, shipping, culture and multinationals.

The second part is called "The business of globalisation". It covers a range of issues that affect markets, industries and companies. "The spread of equity culture" (chapter three) looks at the rise of share-holding around the world. "Goodbye to taxpayers?", the fourth chapter, examines the implications of globalisation, and the Internet in particular, for taxpayers. Chapter five is a compilation of articles about four different industries. Together they suggest the many possible ways to address globalisation.

Problems cross borders more easily than capital does; and the third section of this book, "Rich and poor", covers development issues. This section is slightly unusual, in that the sixth chapter comprises articles by non-*Economist* writers – Robert Wade, Jeffrey Sachs and Bjorn Lomborg – that appeared in *The Economist* as signed By Invitation pieces. The seventh chapter, "The uses of technology", examines how technology can raise standards in developing countries.

The final section of the book, "Governing the global economy", looks at ways to reform the IMF and the World Bank, with two additional articles touching on recent developments.

None of the articles given here has been edited after the fact to take account of events. Such editing would inevitably be uneven, and might also obscure the author's original purpose. In the interest of space, a few articles were removed from surveys (articles published in *The Economist* as a collection). References to particular dates have also been changed in some instances to provide clarification (for example, references to September 11th might change to September 11th, 2001). In general, however, the articles in this book were selected for their ability to endure.

A final note: globalisation is not least a political phenomenon. The sweeping collapse of communism is one obvious example; the broadening reach of the United Nations is another. For reasons of space, however, this book restricts itself to the economic aspects of globalisation. I trust it will be enough.

KATE GALBRAITH
December 2001

I
THE CASE FOR GLOBALISATION

1
Globalisation and its critics

*This chapter is a polemic. It is a response to the critics of
globalisation, who have issued a host of charges – that
globalisation has hurt workers; that globalisation has undercut
governments; that globalisation has robbed voters of influence;
that the WTO, IMF and World Bank are tools of capitalist
exploitation. Clive Crook carefully considers all of these
points. He shows why they are – usually – wrong.
This chapter was published in The Economist as a survey,
shortly after the September 11 terrorist attacks on America.
Those attacks left many people discussing (some with relish)
the "end of globalisation". Indeed, a number of anti-capitalists
claimed that America had got what it deserved. This chapter
argues that such views are mistaken and that, more urgently
than ever, globalisation must go forward.*

Globalisation and its critics

Globalisation is a great force for good. But neither governments nor businesses can be trusted to make the case

THE ORIGINAL PUBLICATION of this survey in *The Economist* had been intended to coincide with the annual meetings of the World Bank and the International Monetary Fund, scheduled for September 29th–30th 2001 in Washington, DC. Those meetings, and the big anti-globalisation protests that had been planned to accompany them, were among the least significant casualties of the terrorist atrocities of September 11th.

You might have thought that the anti-capitalist protesters, after contemplating those horrors and their aftermath, would be regretting more than just the loss of a venue for their marches. Many are, no doubt. But judging by the response of some of their leaders and many of the activists (if Internet chat rooms are any guide), grief is not always the prevailing mood. Some anti-globalists have found a kind of consolation, even a cause of satisfaction, in these terrible events – that of having been, as they see it, proved right.

To its fiercest critics, globalisation, the march of international capitalism, is a force for oppression, exploitation and injustice. The rage that drove the terrorists to commit their obscene crime was in part, it is argued, a response to that. At the very least, it is suggested, terrorism thrives on poverty – and international capitalism, the protesters say, thrives on poverty too.

These may be extreme positions, but the minority that holds them is not tiny, by any means. Far more important, the anti-globalists have lately drawn tacit support – if nothing else, a reluctance to condemn – from a broad range of public opinion. As a result, they have been, and are likely to remain, politically influential. At a time such as this, sorting through issues of political economy may seem very far removed from what matters. In one sense, it is. But when many in the West are contemplating their future with new foreboding, it is important to understand why the sceptics are wrong; why economic integration is a force for good; and why globalisation, far from being the greatest cause of poverty, is its only feasible cure.

Undeniably, popular support for that view is lacking. In the developed economies, support for further trade liberalisation is uncertain; in some countries, voters are downright hostile to it. Starting a new round of global trade talks will be a struggle, and seeing it through to a useful conclusion will be harder. The institutions that in most people's eyes represent the global economy – the IMF, the World Bank and the World Trade Organisation – are reviled far more widely than they are admired; the best they can expect from opinion at large is grudging acceptance. Governments, meanwhile, are accused of bowing down to business: globalisation leaves them no choice. Private capital moves across the planet unchecked. Wherever it goes, it bleeds democracy of content and puts "profits before people".

Who will speak up for international capitalism? Governments and businesses. What a pity that is. These supposed defenders of globalisation may do more to undermine support for it than the critics.

Rich-country governments generally present economic integration to voters as an unfortunate but inescapable fact of life: as a constraint, that is, on their freedom of action. For the past ten years, this has been the favourite excuse of any government about to break an election promise.

Multinational businesses, for their part, with their enlightened mission statements, progressive stakeholder strategies, flower-motif logos and 57-point pledges of "corporate social responsibility", implicitly say that they have a case to answer: capitalism without responsibility is bad. That sounds all right; the trouble is, when they start talking about how they will no longer put profits first, people (rightly) think they are lying. If, as these defenders of economies without borders lead you to conclude, global capitalism is a cause of democratic paralysis and a cloak for old-fashioned corporate venality, even instinctive liberals ought to side with the sceptics.

With advocates like these on either side of the globalisation debate – dissembling governments and businesses in favour, angry and uncompromising protesters against – it is natural that the general public stands firmly in support of neither. It has no deep commitment to international capitalism, but it can see no plausible alternative. Certainly, the protesters do not appear to be offering one. So people are mostly puzzled, anxious and suspicious. This climate of opinion is bad for democracy and bad for economic development.

This survey offers a few suggestions for a more purposeful kind of discussion. It would be foolish to suppose that consensus will ever be possible. Some of the sceptics are opposed not just to globalisation or even to the market economy but to the very idea of economic growth.

That view has the virtue of coherence, at least, but it is unlikely in the foreseeable future to command a large following.

Nonetheless, in among all their weak arguments, dangerous good intentions and downright loony notions, the sceptics are hiding some important points. Clarifying what makes sense in the sceptics' case, and exposing the mistaken or dishonest arguments that politicians and businessmen are putting up against them, may serve some purpose. And a clearer understanding of the arguments for globalisation, of the problems it solves as well as the problems it creates, may help as well.

Good old invisible hand

The strongest case for globalisation is the liberal one. It is almost never heard, least of all from governments or businessmen. International economic integration, on the liberal view, is what happens when technology allows people to pursue their own goals and they are given the liberty to do so. If technology advances to the point where it supports trade across borders, and if people then choose to trade across borders, you have integration, and because people have freely chosen it this is a good thing. Also, again because people have freely chosen this course, you would expect there to be economic benefits as well.

By and large, theory and practice confirm that this is so. Adam Smith's invisible hand does its work. People choose what serves their own self-interest, each of them making that judgment for himself. The result is that society as a whole prospers and advances – spontaneously, not by design of any person or government.

All kinds of qualifications and elaborations are needed, obviously, to fill out the argument properly. This survey will offer some of them in due course. But it is essential to understand one point from the outset. The liberal case for globalisation is emphatically not the case for domestic or international laisser faire. Liberalism lays down no certainties about the requirements of social justice in terms of income redistribution or the extent of the welfare state. It recognises that markets have their limits, for instance in tending to the supply of public goods (such as a clean environment). A liberal outlook is consistent with support for a wide range of government interventions; indeed a liberal outlook demands many such interventions.

But the starting point for all liberals is a presumption that, under ordinary circumstances, the individual knows best what serves his interests and that the blending of these individual choices will produce socially good results. Two other things follow. The first is an initial scepticism, at least, about collective decision-making that overrides the individual kind. The other is a high regard for markets – not as a place where profits are made, it must be stressed, but as a place where society advances in the common good.

Why then are governments and business leaders rarely heard to put this case? Because for the most part they are not liberals. Perhaps it goes with the job that politicians of left and right, traditional and modern, have an exaggerated view of their ability to improve on the spontaneous order of a lightly governed society.

It would be even more naive, and contrary to all experience, to expect business itself to favour a liberal outlook. Businesses are ultimately interested in one thing: profits. The business-bashing non-governmental organisations (NGOs) are right about that. If businesses think that treating their customers and staff well, or adopting a policy of "corporate social responsibility", or using ecologically friendly stationery will add to their profits, they will do it. Otherwise, they will not.

Does that make market capitalism wrong? On the contrary, the point of a liberal market economy is that it civilises the quest for profit, turning it, willy-nilly, into an engine of social progress. If firms have to compete with rivals for customers and workers, then they will indeed worry about their reputation for quality and fair dealing – even if they do not value those things in themselves. Competition will make them behave as if they did.

Here, then, is where the anti-business NGOs get their argument completely upside down – with genuinely dangerous consequences for the causes, sometimes just, which they hope to advance. On the whole, stricter regulation of international business is not going to reduce profits: the costs will be passed along to consumers. And it is not going to diminish any company's interest in making profits. What it may well do, though, by disabling markets in their civilising role, is to give companies new opportunities to make even bigger profits at the expense of society at large.

For example, suppose that in the remorseless search for profit, multinationals pay sweatshop wages to their workers in developing countries. Regulation forcing them to pay higher wages is demanded. The biggest western firms concede there might be merit in the idea. But justice and efficiency require a level playing-field. The NGOs, the reformed multinationals and enlightened rich-country governments propose tough rules on third-world factory wages, backed up by trade barriers to keep out imports from countries that do not comply. Shoppers in the

West pay more – but willingly, because they know it is in a good cause. The NGOs declare another victory. The companies, having shafted their third-world competition and protected their domestic markets, count their bigger profits (higher wage costs notwithstanding). And the third-world workers displaced from locally owned factories explain to their children why the West's new deal for the victims of capitalism requires them to starve.

If firms ruled the world

A fashionable strand of scepticism argues that governments have surrendered their power to capitalism – that the world's biggest companies are nowadays more powerful than many of the world's governments. Democracy is a sham. Profits rule, not people. These claims are patent nonsense. On the other hand, there is no question that companies would run the world for profit if they could. What stops them is not governments, powerful as they may be, but markets.

Governments have the power, all right, but they do not always exercise it wisely. They are unreliable servants of the public interest. Sometimes, out of conviction, politicians decide to help companies reshape the world for private profit. Sometimes, anti-market thinking may lead them to help big business by accident. And now and then, when companies just set out to buy the policies they want, they find in government a willing seller. On all this, presumably, the sceptics would agree.

But they miss the next crucial step: limited government is not worth buying. Markets keep the spoils of corruption small. Government that intervenes left and right, prohibiting this and licensing that, creating surpluses and shortages – now that kind of government is worth a bit. That is why, especially in developing countries with weak legal systems, taming capitalism by regulation or trade protection often proves such a hazardous endeavour.

If NGOs succeeded in disabling markets, as many of them say they would like to, the political consequences would be as dire as the economic ones. It is because the sceptics are right about some things that they are so wrong about the main thing.

Profits over people

Critics argue that globalisation hurts workers. Are they right?

THE LIBERTY THAT makes economic integration possible is desirable in itself. In addition, advocates of globalisation argue, integration is good for people in material terms – that is why free people choose it. Sceptics disagree on both points: globalisation militates against liberty and democracy, they say, and while it makes some people who are already rich even richer, it does this by keeping the poor in poverty. After all, globalisation is merely capitalism writ large. A later part of this survey will deal with the implications of globalisation for democracy. But first, is it true that globalisation harms the poor?

In a narrow sense, the answer is yes: it does harm some of the poor. Free trade and foreign direct investment may take jobs from workers (including low-paid workers) in the advanced industrial economies and give them to cheaper workers in poor countries. Thanks to the North American Free-Trade Agreement (NAFTA), for instance, there are no tariffs or investment restrictions to stop an American manufacturer closing an old factory in the United States and opening a new one in Mexico.

Sceptics score this strategy as a double crime. The rich-country workers, who were probably on low wages by local standards to begin with, are out of work. That increase in the local supply of labour drives down other wages. Meanwhile, the poor-country workers are drawn into jobs that exploit them. How do you know that the poor-country workers are being exploited? Because they are being paid less, often much less, than their rich-country counterparts got before trade opened up – and in all likelihood they are working longer hours in shabbier premises as well. The only gain from this kind of trade, the indictment continues, accrues to the owners of the companies who have shifted their operations from low-wage factories in industrialised countries to poverty-wage factories in the south.

Some of this is true. Trade displaces workers in the industrialised countries; other things being equal, this will have some depressing effect on the wages of other workers; and pay and conditions in developing-country factories are likely to be worse than in their rich-country counterparts. But whereas the displaced rich-country workers are plainly worse off than they were before, the newly employed poor-country workers are plainly better off. They must be, because they have chosen to take those jobs.

As for profits, yes, that is the spur for moving production to a lower-wage area. But no company can expect to hang on to this windfall for long, because it will be competed away as other companies do the same thing and cut their prices. That lowering of prices is crucial in understanding the broader benefits of the change. It is what makes consumers at large – including poor consumers – better off, raising real incomes in the aggregate.

What about the rich-country workers who are not displaced, but whose wages may nonetheless come under downward pressure? It is hard to generalise. On the one hand, their wages may fall, or fail to rise as quickly as they would have done otherwise; on the other, they benefit from lower prices along with everybody else. On balance, you would expect that some will lose, some will gain, and some will be about as well off as they were before. In developing countries, the labour-market side of this process will tend to work in the other direction. The increase in demand for poor-country labour ought to push up wages even for workers who are not employed in the new trade-related jobs.

So capitalism-globalisation is not mainly concerned with shifting income from workers to investors, as the sceptics maintain. Rather, it makes some workers worse off while making others (including the poorest ones of all, to begin with) better off. And in the aggregate it makes consumers (that is, people with or without a job) better off as well. Altogether, given freer trade, both rich-country and poor-country living standards rise. That gives governments more to spend on welfare, education and other public services.

Changing gear

Note that all this counts only the so-called static gains from trade: the effects of a once-and-for-all shift in the pattern of production and consumption. Modern economics also emphasises the importance of dynamic gains, arising especially from the economies of scale that freer trade makes possible. The aggregate long-term gain for rich and poor countries alike is likely to be far bigger than the simple arithmetic would suggest.

Moreover, few displaced rich-country workers are likely to be permanently out of work. Most will move to other jobs. Also, new jobs will be created by the economic opportunities that trade opens up. Overall, trade neither reduces the number of jobs in the economy nor increases them. In principle, there is no reason to expect employment or unemployment to be any higher or lower in an open economy than in a closed economy – or, for that matter, in a rich economy as compared to a poor economy. Still, none of this is to deny that the displaced rich-country workers lose out: many, perhaps most, of those who find alternative work will be paid less than they were before.

In thinking through the economic theory of liberal trade, it is helpful to draw a parallel with technological progress. Trade allows a country to shift its pattern of production in such a way that, after exporting those goods it does not want and importing those it does, it can consume more without there having been any increase in its available resources. Advancing technology allows a country to do something very similar: to make more with less. You can think of trade as a machine (with no running costs or depreciation): goods you can make cheaply go in at one end, and goods that would cost you a lot more to make come out at the other. The logic of protectionism would demand that such a miraculous machine be dismantled and the blueprint destroyed, in order to save jobs.

No question, technological progress, just like trade, creates losers as well as winners. The Industrial Revolution involved hugely painful economic and social dislocations – though nearly everybody would now agree that the gains in human welfare were worth the cost. Even in far milder periods of economic transformation, such as today's, new machines and new methods make old skills obsolete. The Luddites understood that, which made them more coherent on the subject than some of today's sceptics, who oppose integration but not technological progress. Logically, they should oppose both or neither.

Politically, of course, it is essential to keep the two separate. Sceptics can expect to win popular support for the view that freer trade is harmful, but could never hope to gain broad backing for the idea that, so far as possible, technological progress should be brought to a halt. Still, it might be better if the sceptics concentrated not on attacking trade as such, but on demanding help for the workers who suffer as a result of economic progress, whether the cause is trade or technology.

Winners and losers

So much for the basic theory. What does the evidence say? For the moment, concentrate on the prospects for workers in rich countries such as the United States (the next section will look in more detail at workers in poor countries). By and large, the evidence agrees with the theory –

though things, as always, get more complicated the closer you look.

A first qualification is that most outward foreign direct investment (FDI) from rich countries goes not to poor countries at all, but to other rich countries. In the late 1990s, roughly 80% of the

Where the money goes		1
America's stock of direct investment overseas, 2000		
	$bn	% of total
High-income countries	982.8	81.0
Middle-income countries	218.1	18.0
Low-income countries	12.2	1.0
All countries	1,213.1	100.0

Sources: Edward M. Graham, Institute for International Economics; *The Economist*

stock of America's outward FDI was in Canada, Japan and Western Europe, and nearly all of the rest was in middle-income developing countries such as Brazil, Mexico, Indonesia and Thailand. The poorest developing countries accounted for 1% of America's outward FDI (see table 1). Capital is hardly flooding to the world's poorest countries – more's the pity, from their point of view.

The notion that outward FDI reduces the demand for labour in the sending country and increases it in the receiving one needs to be revised as well. It was based on the assumption that when rich-country firms invest in poor countries, rich-country exports (and jobs) are replaced by poor-country domestic production. In fact, evidence from the United States and other countries suggests that outward FDI does not displace exports, it creates them: FDI and exports are, in the jargon, net complements. This is because the affiliates of multinationals trade with each other. Figures for 1995 show that America's exports to its foreign-owned affiliates actually exceeded its imports from them (see table 2).

Before FDI, the companies exported finished goods. After FDI, they ship, let us suppose, a mixture of finished goods and intermediate goods. The intermediate goods will be used to make finished goods in the FDI-receiving country. The corresponding increase in exports of intermediate goods outweighs the fall, if any, in exports of finished goods. Overall, then, exports from the FDI-sending country rise. At the same time, the sending country's imports rise as well, partly because the affiliate sells goods back to the sending country. Exports rise, which increases the demand for labour; and imports rise, which decreases the demand for labour.

What does all this mean for the labour markets of the rich, FDI-sending countries? Jobs are created in exporting industries which will tend to be relatively high-paying, but overall employment will not rise, for reasons explained earlier. For every job created, another one somewhere

Keeping it in the family 2

American exports to, and imports from,
American-owned affiliates abroad, 1995, $bn

	Intra-company	Inter-company	Total
All countries			
Exports	145.5	24.5	170.0
Imports	123.9	19.4	143.3
Balance	21.6	5.1	26.7
High-income countries			
Exports	129.0	20.8	149.9
Imports	94.0	15.1	109.1
Balance	35.0	5.7	40.7
Middle-income countries			
Exports	28.9	5.4	34.3
Imports	31.5	1.9	33.4
Balance	-2.6	3.5	0.8
Low-income countries			
Exports	1.6	0.2	1.8
Imports	1.8	0.4	2.2
Balance	-0.2	-0.2	-0.4

Source: Edward M. Graham, Institute for International Economics

else will be destroyed. The jobs that go will tend to be in industries that compete with imports. On average, studies suggest, those jobs pay lower wages.

On balance, then, you could say that the economy has gained: it now has more higher-paying jobs and fewer lower-paying jobs. A policy which attempted to resist a shift like that would be difficult to defend on its merits. Unfortunately, though, the people getting the higher-paying jobs are not necessarily the ones who have lost the lower-paying jobs. Because of the boost to exports, the overall effect of outward FDI on jobs and wages in the sending country is more benign than the simple theory suggests – but some people still lose.

Another implication of the shift in the demand for labour in the rich, FDI-sending countries is a possible widening of income inequality. In a country such as the United States, the combined action of trade and capital flows is likely to raise the demand for relatively skilled labour and lower the demand for relatively unskilled labour. Some hitherto low-wage workers may succeed in trading up to higher-paid jobs, but many others will be left behind in industries where wages are falling. In this scenario, high and average wages may be rising, but wages at the bottom may be falling – and that means greater inequality.

You would expect to see a similar pattern in an economy that was undergoing rapid technological change. So in the United States, which fitted that description better than most in the 1990s, you could say that economic integration may have added to the already powerful pressures that were acting to increase inequality. Since those same pressures were raising living standards in the aggregate – not just for the very rich – it would be a misleading summary, but not a false one.

Explaining inequality

Of these two unequalising forces, economic integration and technological progress, which is likely to be more powerful? If it were the latter, that would raise doubts over the sceptics' focus on globalisation as the primary cause of social friction. The evidence suggests that technology is indeed much the more powerful driver of inequality. One study, by William Cline, estimated that technological change was perhaps five times more powerful in widening inequality in America between 1973 and 1993 than trade (including trade due to FDI), and that trade accounted for only around six percentage points of all the unequalising forces at work during that period. That is just one study, but it is not unrepresentative. The consensus is that integration has exerted a far milder influence on wage inequality than technology.

Getting less equal 3

Illustrative sources of increase in the ratio of skilled to unskilled wages in the United States 1973–93, %

A. Equalising forces	
Increase in stock of skilled relative to unskilled labour	-40
B. Unequalising forces	
Trade:	7
Lower transport and communication costs	3
Liberalisation	3
Outsourcing	1
Immigration	2
Falling minimum wage	5
Deunionisation	3
Skill-biased technological change	29
Other unexplained	29
TOTAL	**97**
C. Net effect	**18**

Note: Percentages for unequalising forces must be chained, not added, to equal total unequalising effect. Similarly, "A" and "B" must be chained to calculate "C".
Source: William R. Cline, Institute for International Economics

Mr Cline's study in fact deserves a closer look. It found to begin with that the total increase in the ratio of skilled to unskilled wages in the two decades to the early 1990s was 18%. This was the net result of opposing influences. An increase in the supply of skilled labour relative to the supply of unskilled labour acted to equalise wages, by making unskilled labour relatively scarce. By itself, this would have driven the wage ratio down by 40% (see table 3). But at the same time a variety of unequalising forces pushed the ratio up by 97%, resulting in the net increase of 18%. These unequalising forces included not just trade and technology, but also immigration, reductions in the real value of the minimum wage and de-unionisation.

Two things strike you about the numbers. First, trade has been relatively unimportant in widening income inequality. Second, this effect is overwhelmed not just by technology but also by the main force operating in the opposite, equalising, direction: education and training.

This means that globalisation sceptics are missing the point if they are worried mainly about the effect of integration on rich-country losers: trade is a much smaller factor than technology. Some people in rich countries do lose out from the combination of trade and technology. The remedy lies with education and training, and with help in changing jobs. Spending in those areas, together perhaps with more generous and effective help for people forced to change jobs by economic growth, addresses the problem directly – and in a way that adds to society's economic resources rather than subtracting from them, as efforts to hold back either technological progress or trade would do.

Grinding the poor

折磨

Sceptics charge that globalisation especially hurts poor workers in the developing countries. It does not

FOR THE MOST part, it seems, workers in rich countries have little to fear from globalisation, and a lot to gain. But is the same thing true for workers in poor countries? The answer is that they are even more likely than their rich-country counterparts to benefit, because they have less to lose and more to gain.

Orthodox economics takes an optimistic line on integration and the developing countries. Openness to foreign trade and investment should encourage capital to flow to poor economies. In the developing world, capital is scarce, so the returns on investment there should be higher than in the industrialised countries, where the best opportunities to make money by adding capital to labour have already been used up. If poor countries lower their barriers to trade and investment, the theory goes, rich foreigners will want to send over some of their capital.

If this inflow of resources arrives in the form of loans or portfolio investment, it will supplement domestic savings and loosen the financial constraint on additional investment by local companies. If it arrives in the form of new foreign-controlled operations, FDI, so much the better: this kind of capital brings technology and skills from abroad packaged along with it, with less financial risk as well. In either case, the addition to investment ought to push incomes up, partly by raising the demand for labour and partly by making labour more productive.

This is why workers in FDI-receiving countries should be in an even better position to profit from integration than workers in FDI-sending countries. Also, with or without inflows of foreign capital, the same static and dynamic gains from trade should apply in developing countries as in rich ones. This gains-from-trade logic often arouses suspicion, because the benefits seem to come from nowhere. Surely one side or the other must lose. Not so. The benefits that a rich country gets through trade do not come at the expense of its poor-country trading partners, or vice versa. Recall that according to the theory, trade is a positive-sum game. In all these transactions, both sides – exporters and importers, borrowers and lenders, shareholders and workers – can gain.

17

What, if anything, might spoil the simple theory and make things go awry? Plenty, say the sceptics.

First, they argue, telling developing countries to grow through trade, rather than through building industries to serve domestic markets, involves a fallacy of composition. If all poor countries tried to do this simultaneously, the price of their exports would be driven down on world markets. The success of the East Asian tigers, the argument continues, owed much to the fact that so many other developing countries chose to discourage trade rather than promote it. This theory of "export pessimism" was influential with many developing-country governments up until the 1980s, and seems to lie behind the thinking of many sceptics today.

A second objection to the openness-is-good orthodoxy concerns not trade but FDI. The standard thinking assumes that foreign capital pays for investment that makes economic sense – the kind that will foster development. Experience shows that this is often not so. For one reason or another, the inflow of capital may produce little or nothing of value, sometimes less than nothing. The money may be wasted or stolen. If it was borrowed, all there will be to show for it is an insupportable debt to foreigners. Far from merely failing to advance development, this kind of financial integration sets it back.

Third, the sceptics point out, workers in developing countries lack the rights, legal protections and union representation enjoyed by their counterparts in rich countries. This is why, in the eyes of the multinationals, hiring them makes such good sense. Lacking in bargaining power, workers do not benefit as they should from an increase in the demand for labour. Their wages do not go up. They may have no choice but to work in sweatshops, suffering unhealthy or dangerous conditions, excessive hours or even physical abuse. In the worst cases, children as well as adults are the victims.

Is trade good for growth?

All this seems very complicated. Can the doubters be answered simply by measuring the overall effect of openness on economic growth? Some economists think so, and have produced a variety of much-quoted econometric studies apparently confirming that trade promotes development. Studies by Jeffrey Sachs and Andrew Warner at Harvard, by David Dollar and Aart Kraay of the World Bank, and by Jeffrey Frankel of Harvard and David Romer of Berkeley, are among the most frequently cited. Studies such as these are enough to convince most economists that trade does indeed promote growth. But they cannot be said to settle the matter. If the application of econometrics to other big, complicated questions in economics is any guide, they probably never will: the precise economic linkages that underlie the correlations may always be too difficult to uncover.

This is why a good number of economists, including some of the most distinguished advocates of liberal trade, are unpersuaded by this kind of work. For every regression "proving" that trade promotes growth, it is too easy to tweak a choice of variable here and a period of analysis there to "prove" that it does not. Among the sceptics, Dani Rodrik has led the assault on the pro-trade regression studies. But economists such as Jagdish Bhagwati and T.N. Srinivasan, both celebrated advocates of trade liberalisation, are also pretty scathing about the regression evidence.

Look elsewhere, though, and there is no lack of additional evidence, albeit of a more variegated and less easily summarised sort, that trade promotes development. Of the three criticisms just stated of the orthodox preference for liberal trade, the first and most influential down the years has been the "export pessimism" argument – the idea that liberalising trade will be self-defeating if too many developing countries try to do it simultaneously. What does the evidence say about that?

Pessimism confounded

It does not say that the claim is nonsense. History shows that the prediction of persistently falling export prices has proved correct for some commodity exporters: demand for some commodities has failed to keep pace with growth in global incomes. And nobody will ever know what would have happened over the past few decades if all the developing countries had promoted trade more vigorously, because they didn't. But there are good practical reasons to regard the pessimism argument, as applied to poor-country exports in general, as wrong.

The developing countries as a group may be enormous in terms of geography and population, but in economic terms they are small. Taken together, the exports of all the world's poor and middle-income countries (including comparative giants such as China, India, Brazil and Mexico, big oil exporters such as Saudi Arabia, and large-scale manufacturers such as South Korea, Taiwan and Malaysia) represent only about 5% of global output. This is an amount roughly equivalent to the GDP of Britain. Even if growth in the global demand for imports were somehow capped, a concerted export drive by those parts of the developing world not already engaged in the effort would put no great strain on the global trading system.

In any event, though, the demand for imports is not capped. In effect, export pessimism involves a fallacy of its own – a "lump-of-trade" fallacy, akin to the idea of a "lump of labour" (whereby a growing population is taken to imply an ever-rising rate of unemployment, there being only so many jobs to go round). The overall growth of trade, and the kinds of product that any particular country may buy or sell, are not preordained. As Mr Bhagwati and Mr Srinivasan argued in a recent review of the connections between trade and development, forecasts of the poor countries' potential to expand their exports have usually been too low, partly because forecasters concentrate on existing exports and neglect new ones, some of which may be completely unforeseen. Unexpected shifts in the pattern of output have often proved very important.

Pessimists also make too little of the scope for intra-industry specialisation in trade, which gives developing countries a further set of new opportunities. The same goes for new trade among developing countries, as opposed to trade with the rich world. Often, as developing countries grow, they move away from labour-intensive manufactures to more sophisticated kinds of production: this makes room in the markets they previously served for goods from countries that are not yet so advanced. For example, in the 1970s, Japan withdrew from labour-intensive manufacturing, making way for exports from the East Asian tigers. In the 1980s and 1990s, the tigers did the same, as China began moving into those markets. And as developing countries grow by exporting, their own demand for imports rises.

It is one thing to argue that relying on trade is likely to be self-defeating, as the export pessimists claim; it is another to say that trade actually succeeds in promoting growth. The most persuasive evidence that it does lies in the contrasting experiences from the 1950s onwards of the East Asian tigers, on one side, and the countries that chose to discourage trade and pursue "import-substituting industrialisation" (ISI) on the other, such as India, much of Latin America and much of Africa.

Years ago, in an overlapping series of research projects, great effort went into examining the developing countries' experience with trade policy during the 1950s, 60s and early 70s. This period saw lasting surges of growth without precedent in history. At the outset, South Korea, for instance, was a poor country, with an income per head in 1955 of around $400 (in today's prices), and such poor economic prospects that American officials predicted abject and indefinite dependence on aid.

Within a single generation it became a mighty exporter and world-ranking industrial power.

Examining the record up to the 1970s, and the experience of development elsewhere in East Asia and other poor regions of the world, economists at the OECD, the World Bank and America's National Bureau of Economic Research came to see the crucial importance of "outward orientation" – that is, of the link between trade and growth. The finding held across a range of countries, regardless of differences in particular policies, institutions and political conditions, all of which varied widely. An unusually impressive body of evidence and analysis discredited the ISI orthodoxy and replaced it with a new one, emphasising trade.

The trouble with ISI

What was wrong with ISI, according to these researchers? In principle, nothing much; the problems arose over how it worked in practice. The whole idea of ISI was to drive a wedge between world prices and domestic prices, so as to create a bias in favour of producing for the home market and therefore a bias against producing for the export market. In principle, this bias could be modest and uniform; in practice, ISI often produced an anti-export bias both severe and wildly variable between industries. Managing the price-rigging apparatus proved too much for the governments that were attempting it: the policy produced inadvertently large and complex distortions in the pattern of production that often became self-perpetuating and even self-reinforcing. Once investment had been sunk in activities that were profitable only because of tariffs and quotas, any attempt to remove those restrictions was strongly resisted.

ISI also often had an even more pernicious consequence: corruption. The more protected the economy, the greater the gains to be had from illicit activity such as smuggling. The bigger the economic distortions, the bigger the incentive to bribe the government to tweak the rules and tilt the corresponding pattern of surpluses and shortages. Corruption and controls go hand in hand. ISI is not the only instance of this rule in the developing countries, but it has proved especially susceptible to shady practices.

Today, developing-country governments are constantly, and rightly, urged to battle corruption and establish the rule of law. This has become a cliché that all sides in the development debate can agree on. But defeating corruption in an economy with pervasive market-suppressing controls, where the rewards to illegality are so high, is extraordinarily hard. This is a connection that people who favour closed or restricted markets prefer to ignore. Limited government, to be sure, is not necessarily clean; but unlimited government, history suggests, never is.

Remember, remember

On the whole, ISI failed; almost everywhere, trade has been good for growth. The trouble is, this verdict was handed down too long ago. Economists are notoriously ignorant of even recent economic history. The lessons about what world markets did for the tigers in the space of a few decades, and the missed opportunities of, say, India (which was well placed to achieve as much), have already been forgotten by many. The East Asian financial crisis of 1997–98 also helped to erase whatever lessons had been learned. And yet the prosperity of East Asia today, crisis and continuing difficulties notwithstanding, bears no comparison with the economic position of India, or Pakistan, or any of the other countries that separated themselves for so much longer from the international economy.

By and large, though, the governments of many developing countries continue to be guided by the open-market orthodoxy that has prevailed since the 1980s. Many want to promote trade in particular and engagement with the world economy in general. Even some sceptics might agree that trade is good for growth – but they would add that growth is not necessarily good for poor workers. In fact, it is likely to be bad for the poor, they argue, if the growth in question has been promoted by trade or foreign capital.

Capital inflows, they say, make economies less stable, exposing workers to the risk of financial crisis and to the attentions of western banks and the International Monetary Fund. Also, they argue, growth that is driven by trade or by FDI gives western multinationals a leading role in third-world development. That is bad, because western multinationals are not interested in development at all, only in making bigger profits by ensuring that the poor stay poor. The proof of this, say sceptics, lies in the evidence that economic inequality increases even as developing countries (and rich countries, for that matter) increase their national income, and in the multinationals' direct or indirect use of third-world sweatshops. So if workers' welfare is your main concern, the fact that trade promotes growth, even if true, is beside the point.

Yet there is solid evidence that growth helps the poor. Developing countries that have achieved sustained and rapid growth, as in East

Asia, have made remarkable progress in reducing poverty. And the countries where widespread poverty persists, or is worsening, are those where growth is weakest, notably in Africa. Although economic policy can make a big difference to the extent of poverty, in the long run growth is much more important.

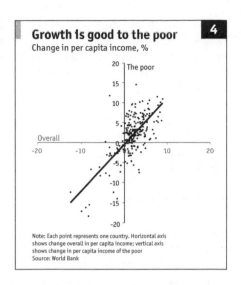

Growth is good to the poor 4

Change in per capita income, %

Note: Each point represents one country. Horizontal axis shows change overall in per capita income; vertical axis shows change in per capita income of the poor
Source: World Bank

It is sometimes claimed that growth is less effective in raising the incomes of the poor in developing countries than in rich countries. This is a fallacy. A recent study confirms that, in 80 countries across the world over the past 40 years, the incomes of the poor have risen one for one with overall growth (see chart 4).

If all this is true, why does global income inequality seem to be widening? First, the evidence is not at all clear-cut. Much depends on how you make your comparisons. An overall comparison of country aggregates – comparing rich countries with poor countries – is generally more encouraging than a comparison of the richest 10% of people in the world with the poorest 10%. In 1975, America's income per head was 19 times bigger than China's ($16,000 against $850); by 1995, the ratio had fallen to six ($23,000 against $3,700). On the other hand it is true that Africa's income per head is rising more slowly than America's: as a result, their income-gap ratio has increased, from 12 in 1975 to 19 in 1995. But it would be odd to blame globalisation for holding Africa back. Africa has been left out of the global economy, partly because its governments used to prefer it that way. China has embraced the global economy with a vengeance – and see how well it has done.

Better than nothing

Statistical difficulties aside, suppose it were true that global inequality is increasing. Would that be a terrible indictment of globalisation, as sceptics seem to suppose? Perhaps not. It would be disturbing, and extremely surprising, if poor countries engaged in globalisation were failing to catch up – but they aren't, as China and many other avid glob-alisers show. It would also be disturbing if inequality across the world as a whole were rising because the incomes of the poorest were falling in absolute terms, rather than merely in relative terms – but this is extremely rare. Even in Africa, which is doing so badly in relative terms, incomes have been rising and broader measures of development have been getting better. It may be too little, but it is not nothing, merely because other countries have been doing better.

The sceptics are right to be disturbed by sweatshops, child labour, bonded labour and the other gross abuses that go on in many poor countries (and in the darkest corners of rich ones, too). But what makes people vulnerable to these practices is poverty. It is essential to ask if remedial measures proposed will reduce poverty: otherwise, in attack-ing the symptoms of the problem, you may be strengthening their underlying cause. It is one thing for the sceptics to insist, for instance, that child labour be prohibited; it is quite another to ensure that the chil-dren concerned go to school instead, rather than being driven to scrape a living in even crueller conditions.

The barriers to trade that many sceptics call for seem calculated to make these problems worse. Some sceptics want, in effect, to punish every export worker in India for the persistence of child labour in parts of the Indian economy. This seems morally indefensible as well as counter-productive in economic terms. The same goes for the campaign to hobble the multinationals. The more thoroughly these companies penetrate the markets of the third world, the faster they introduce their capital and working practices, the sooner poverty will retreat and the harder it will be for such abuses to persist.

This is not to deny that the multinationals are in it for the money – and will strive to hire labour as cheaply as they can. But this does not appear to be a problem for the workers who compete to take those jobs. People who go to work for a foreign-owned company do so because they prefer it to the alternative, whatever that may be. In their own judgment, the new jobs make them better off.

But suppose for the moment that the sceptics are right, and that these workers, notwithstanding their own preferences, are victims of exploitation. One possibility would be to encourage foreign firms to pay higher wages in the third world. Another course, favoured by many sceptics, is to discourage multinationals from operating in the third world at all. But if the aim is to help the developing-country workers, this second strategy is surely wrong. If multinationals stopped hiring in the third world, the workers concerned would, on their own estimation, become worse off.

Compared with demands that the multinationals stay out of the third world altogether, the idea of merely shaming them into paying their workers higher wages seems a model of logic and compassion. Still, even this apparently harmless plan needs to be handled cautiously.

The question is, how much more is enough? At one extreme, you could argue that if a multinational company hires workers in developing countries for less than it pays their rich-country counterparts, it is guilty of exploitation. But to insist on parity would be tantamount to putting a stop to direct investment in the third world. By and large, workers in developing countries are paid less than workers in rich countries because they are less productive: those workers are attractive to rich-country firms, despite their lower productivity, because they are cheap. If you were to eliminate that offsetting advantage, you would make them unemployable.

Of course you could argue that decency merely requires multinationals to pay wages that are "fair", even if not on a par with wages in the industrial countries. Any mandatory increase in wages runs the risk of reducing the number of jobs created, but you could reply that the improvement in welfare for those who get the higher pay, so long as the mandated increase was moderate and feasible, would outweigh that drawback. Even then, however, two difficult questions would still need to be answered. What is a "fair" wage, and who is to decide?

What fairness requires

A "fair" wage can be deduced, you might argue, from economic principles: if workers are paid a wage that is less than their marginal productivity, you could say they are being exploited. Some sceptics regard it as obvious that third-world workers are being paid less than this. Their reasoning is that such workers are about as productive as their rich-country counterparts, and yet are paid only a small fraction of what rich-country workers receive. Yet there is clear evidence that third-world workers are not as productive as rich-country workers. Often they are working with less advanced machinery; and their productivity also depends on the surrounding economic infrastructure. More tellingly, though, if poor-country workers were being paid less than their marginal productivity, firms could raise their profits by hiring more of them in order to increase output. Sceptics should not need reminding that companies always prefer more profit to less.

The lure of multinationals

5

Average wage paid by foreign affiliates and average domestic manufacturing wage
by host-country income, 1994

	All countries	High-income	Middle-income	Low-income
Average wage paid by affiliates, $'000	15.1	32.4	9.5	3.4
Average domestic manufacturing wage, $'000	9.9	22.6	5.4	1.7
Ratio	1.5	1.4	1.8	2.0

Source: Edward M. Graham, Institute for International Economics

Productivity aside, should "good practice" require, at least, that multi-nationals pay their poor-country employees more than other local workers? Not necessarily. To hire the workers they need, they may not have to offer a premium over local wages if they can provide other advantages. In any case, lack of a premium need not imply that they are failing to raise living standards. By entering the local labour market and adding to the total demand for labour, the multinationals would most likely be raising wages for all workers, not just those they hire.

In fact, though, the evidence suggests that multinationals do pay a wage premium – a reflection, presumably, of efforts to recruit relatively skilled workers. Table 5 shows that the wages paid by foreign affiliates to poor-country workers are about double the local manufacturing wage; wages paid by affiliates to workers in middle-income countries are about 1.8 times the local manufacturing wage (both calculations exclude wages paid to the firms' expatriate employees). The numbers come from calculations by Edward Graham at the Institute for International Economics. Mr Graham cites other research which shows that wages in Mexico are highest near the border with the United States, where the operations of American-controlled firms are concentrated. Separate studies on Mexico, Venezuela, China and Indonesia have all found that foreign investors pay their local workers significantly better than other local employers.

Despite all this, you might still claim that the workers are not being paid a "fair" wage. But in the end, who is to make this judgment? The sceptics distrust governments, politicians, international bureaucrats and markets alike. So they end up appointing themselves as judges, overruling not just governments and markets but also the voluntary preferences of the workers most directly concerned. That seems a great deal to take on.

Is government disappearing?

Not as quickly as one might wish

ECONOMISTS ARE OFTEN accused of greeting some item of news with the observation, "That may be so in practice, but is it true in theory?" Sceptics too seem much more interested in superficially plausible theories about the diminishing power of the state than in the plain facts.

In practice, though perhaps not in theory, governments around the world on average are now collecting slightly more in taxes – not just in absolute terms, but as a proportion of their bigger economies – than they did ten years ago. This is true of the G7 countries, and of the smaller OECD economies as well (see chart 6). The depredations of rampant capitalists on the overall ability of governments to gather income and do good works are therefore invisible. These findings are so strange in theory that many economic analysts have decided not to believe them.

Tax burdens vary a lot from country to country – something else which is wrong in theory. Despite the variations, governments in all the advanced economies are well provided for. The United States is invoked by some European anti-globalists as the land of naked capitalism, the nadir of "private affluence and public squalor" to which other countries are being driven down. Well, its government collected a little over 30% of GDP in taxes in 2000: an average of some $30,000 per household, adding up to roughly $3 trillion. This is a somewhat larger figure than the national income of Germany, and it goes a long way if spent wisely.

At the other extreme is Sweden, despite its celebrated taxpayer revolt of the early 1990s. In 2000 its taxes came to 57% of GDP, a savage reduction of three percentage points since 1990. Next comes Denmark, on 53%, fractionally higher than in 1990. And here's a funny thing. Sweden and Denmark are among the most open economies in the world, far more open than the United States. Denmark's ratio of imports to national income is 33%, compared with America's 14%. And in common with other advanced economies, neither of these Scandinavian countries has capital controls to keep investment penned in.

Harvard's Dani Rodrik, one of the more careful and persuasive globalisation sceptics, has written: "Globalisation has made it exceedingly difficult for government to provide social insurance ... At

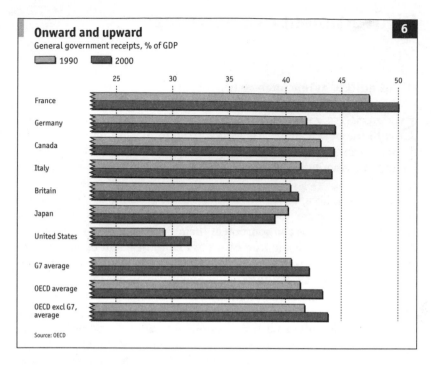

Onward and upward

General government receipts, % of GDP

1990   2000

6

Source: OECD

present, international economic integration is taking place against the background of receding governments and diminished social obligations. The welfare state has been under attack for two decades." Sweden, admittedly, is reeling, its government now able to collect only 57% of GDP in tax. But plucky Denmark is resisting these attacks well, and so is most of the rest of Europe.

Money isn't everything

Even if taxes were falling precipitously, it would be absurd to claim, as many globalisation sceptics do, that companies are nowadays more powerful than governments. It is routine to be told, as in *The Silent Takeover*, a book by a Cambridge University academic, Noreena Hertz (Heinemann, 2001), things like this: "51 of the 100 biggest economies in the world are now corporations." Quite what that implies is never explained: readers are invited to draw their own conclusion about the relative power of governments and companies.

Before you even think about whether it makes sense to weigh corporate power against state power, you can see that this particular comparison, which measures the size of companies by their sales, is bogus. National income is a measure of value added. It cannot be compared with a company's sales (equal to value added plus the cost of inputs). But even if that tiresome, endlessly repeated error were corrected, there would be no sense in comparing companies with governments in terms of their power over people.

The power of even the biggest companies is nothing compared with that of governments – no matter how small or poor the country concerned. The value added of Microsoft is a little over $20 billion a year, about the same as the national income of Uruguay. Does this make it remotely plausible that Bill Gates has more sway over the people of Uruguay than their government does? Or take Luxembourg – another small economy with, presumably, a correspondingly feeble state. Can Microsoft tax the citizens of Luxembourg (whose government collected 45% of GDP from them in 2000), conscript them if it has a mind to, arrest and imprison them for behaviour it disapproves of, or deploy physical force against them at will? No, not even using Windows XP.

But those are specious comparisons, you might reply. Of course Bill Gates is less powerful than the government of Uruguay in Uruguay, but Mr Gates exercises his power, such as it is, globally. Well then, where, exactly, is Mr Gates supposed to be as powerful in relation to the government as the alarming comparison between value added and national income implies? And if Bill Gates does not have this enormous power in any particular country or countries, he does not have it at all. In other words, the power that Mr Gates exercises globally is over Microsoft. Every government he ever meets is more powerful than he is in relation to its own citizens.

In a war between two countries, national income is relevant as a measure of available resources. If companies raised armies and fought wars, their wealth would count for something. But they don't, and couldn't: they lack the power. Big companies do have political influence. They have the money to lobby politicians and, in many countries, to corrupt them. Even so, the idea that companies have powers over citizens remotely as great as those of governments – no matter how big the company, no matter how small or poor the country – is fatuous. Yet it is never so much as questioned by anti-globalists.

Any power to tax, however limited, gives a country more political clout than Microsoft or General Electric could dream of. But how can a small, exceptionally open economy such as Denmark manage to collect more than 50% of GDP in taxes, in utter defiance of the logic of global capitalism? The answer seems inescapable: Denmark no longer exists, and questions are starting to be asked about the existence of many other European countries. At least, that is how it looks in theory; in practice, the theory needs to be looked at again.

The limits of government

The alleged squeeze on government arises from the fact that, in a world of integrated economies, again in Mr Rodrik's words, "owners of capital, highly skilled workers, and many professionals ... are free to take their resources where they are most in demand". The people Mr Rodrik refers to have high incomes. Through the taxes they pay, they make an indispensable contribution to the public finances. If economic integration allows capital and skills to migrate to low-tax jurisdictions, the tax base will shrink. Governments will find themselves unable to finance social programmes, safety nets or redistribution of income. Anticipating this flight of capital and skills, governments have to cut taxes and dismantle the welfare state before the migration gets under way. Markets triumph over democracy.

That is the theory. Experience largely refutes it, but it is not entirely wrong. In a variety of ways, economic integration does put limits on what governments can do. However, some of those constraints are eminently desirable. Integration makes it harder to be a tyrant. Governments have been known to oppress their subjects. Oppression is more difficult with open borders: people can leave and take their savings with them. In such cases, global markets are plainly an ally of human rights.

The affinity of totalitarianism and economic isolation was obvious in the case of the Soviet Union and communist Eastern Europe; it is still plain today in the case of North Korea, say. But democracies are capable of oppression too. It would therefore be wrong to conclude that integration is undesirable merely because it limits the power of government, even if the government concerned is democratic. One needs to recognise that some constraints on democracy are desirable, and then to ask whether the constraints imposed by markets are too tight.

These issues are rarely, if ever, addressed by the critics of globalisation: it is simpler to deplore the notion of "profits before people". The sceptics either insist, or regard it as too obvious even to mention, that the will of the people, democratically expressed, must always prevail. This is amazingly naive. Even the most elementary account of democracy recognises the need for checks and balances, including curbs on the majoritarian "will of the people". Failing those, democracies are capable of tyranny over minorities.

The sceptics are terribly keen on "the people". Yet the idea that citizens are not individuals with different goals and preferences, but an undifferentiated body with agreed common interests, defined in opposition to other monolithic interests such as "business" or "foreigners", is not just shallow populism, it is proto-fascism. It is self-contradictory, as well. The sceptics would not hesitate to call for "the people" to be overruled if, for instance, they voted for policies that violated human rights, or speeded the extermination of endangered species, or offended against other values the sceptics regard as more fundamental than honouring the will of the majority.

The possibility that people might leave is not the only curb that economic integration puts on government. The global flow of information, a by-product of the integration of markets, also works to that effect. It lets attention be drawn to abuses of all kinds: of people especially, but also of the environment or of other things that the sceptics want to protect. Undeniably, it also fosters a broader kind of policy competition among governments. This works not through the sort of mechanical market arbitrage that would drive down taxes regardless of what citizens might want, but through informing voters about alternatives, thus making them more demanding.

The fashion for economic liberalisation in recent years owes something to the remarkable success of the American economy during the 1990s: a success which, thanks to globalisation, has been seen and reflected upon all over the world. Growing knowledge about the West helped precipitate the liberation of Eastern Europe. But information of this kind need not always favour the market. For instance, the failure of the American government to extend adequate health care to all its citizens has been noticed as well, and voters in countries with universal publicly financed health care systems do not, on the whole, want to copy this particular model. The global flow of knowledge creates, among other things, better-informed voters, and therefore acts as a curb on government power. This does nothing but good.

The anti-globalists themselves, somewhat self-contradictorily, use the information-spreading aspect of globalisation to great effect. Organising a worldwide protest movement would be much harder without the World Wide Web, but the web itself is merely one dimension of globalisation. The economic integration that sceptics disapprove of is in many ways necessary for effective resistance to the more specific things they object to – not all of which, by any means, are themselves the products of globalisation.

Still, all this is to acknowledge that economic integration does limit the power of government, including democratic government. The question is whether it limits it too much, or in undesirable ways. So far as public spending is concerned, the answer seems clear. Given that even in conditions of economic integration people are willing to tolerate tax burdens approaching 60% of GDP, and that tax burdens of between 40% and 55% of GDP are routine in industrial economies other than the United States, the limits are plainly not that tight. These figures say that democracy has plenty of room for manoeuvre.

The mystery of the missing tax cut

One puzzle remains: why are taxes not coming down? There are several answers. One is that international integration is far from complete, and is likely to remain so. Technology has caused distance to shrink, but not to disappear. National borders still matter as well, even more than mere distance, and far more than all the interest in globalisation might lead you to expect. For all but the smallest economies, trade and investment are still disproportionately intranational rather than international. Especially in the developed world, borders still count not so much because of overt protectionist barriers, but because countries remain jurisdictionally and administratively distinct. This is not likely to change in the foreseeable future.

For instance, if a supplier defaults on a contract to sell you something, it is much easier to get legal redress if your seller is in the same country (and subject to the same legal authority) than it would be if you had to sue in a foreign court. Because of these difficulties in contracting, trading across borders still calls for much more trust between buyers and sellers than trading within borders – so much so as to rule out many transactions. This remains true even in systems such as the European Union's, where heroic efforts have been made to overcome inadvertent obstacles to trade, suggesting that they will prove even more durable everywhere else.

You would expect the international mobility of capital to be especially high, given that the costs of physical transporting the stuff are virtually zero, yet it is surprising just how relatively immobile even capital remains. In the aggregate, the flow of capital into or out of any given country can be thought of as balancing that country's saving and investment. If the country invests more than it saves (that is, if it runs a current-account deficit), capital flows in; if it saves more than it invests (a current-account surplus), the country must lend capital to the rest of the world. Perfect capital mobility would imply that, country by country, national saving and investment would move freely in relation to each other. Very large inflows or outflows of capital in relation to national income would be the order of the day. In fact they are not. Nowadays, a surplus or deficit of just a few percentage points of GDP is regarded as big.

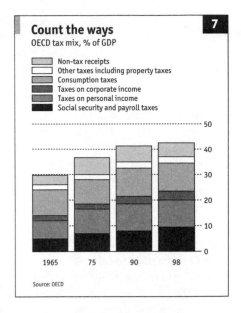

Count the ways
OECD tax mix, % of GDP

- Non-tax receipts
- Other taxes including property taxes
- Consumption taxes
- Taxes on corporate income
- Taxes on personal income
- Social security and payroll taxes

1965   75   90   98

Source: OECD

Still, capital is much more mobile than labour – and mobile enough, to be sure, to have given rise to some tax competition among governments. So far this competition has affected the structure of tax codes rather than overall tax burdens; total yields have been unaffected. In an effort to attract inflows of capital, and especially inflows of foreign direct investment, governments have been lowering their tax rates for corporate income and raising them for personal income, or relying more on a variety of indirect taxes, or both (see chart 7). But it is easy to exaggerate the extent even of this structural shift, never mind the effect on total taxation. This is because taxes on corporate income were small to begin with, so not much was at stake. In fact, heavy reliance on corporate taxes is bad policy even in a closed economy. Indeed, in a closed economy, you can make a respectable case on efficiency grounds for excluding corporate income from taxes altogether.

Taxes on company profits, the argument goes, are taxes on shareholders' income – ultimately, that is, taxes on a particular category of personal income. In the end, although it is politically convenient to pretend otherwise, "the people" pay all the taxes: companies are mere intermediaries. There is no reason to tax the income people receive as shareholders any differently from the income they receive as owners of bank deposits or as workers. In a closed economy, you might as well abolish the corporate income tax and instead tax profits when they turn up as dividends in the incomes of individual taxpayers: it is simpler, and it is less likely to affect investment decisions in unintended ways.

In an open economy, however, company ownership is to some extent in the hands of foreigners, not just the citizens of the country where the company is based. This makes it more tempting to tax corporate income, because this allows the government to bring foreigners within the scope of its tax base. Seen this way, it is odd to blame globalisation for downward pressure on corporate tax rates. Were it not for globalisation, there would be no reason to have corporate taxes in the first place. But it is true that once you are collecting corporate taxes, greater capital mobility limits your take. Economic integration rationalises, and at the same time limits, reliance on corporate income taxes. The issue is subtler than it seems.

Staying put

But what matters far more than corporate tax policy is that most people, skilled as well as unskilled, are reluctant to move abroad. Since workers tend to stay put, governments can tax them at surprisingly high rates without provoking flight. In all but extreme cases, the democratic constraint (the need to secure a broad measure of popular support for tax increases) binds governments long before the economic constraint imposed by international integration (the risk that groups facing very high taxes will leave). In the case of taxes on profits, it is true that the economic constraint will bind before the democratic one, and that globalisation serves to tighten the economic constraint further – but this does not matter. There is no need for high taxes on profits if people are willing to hand over 50% or more of what they produce in the form of taxes on income and consumption.

To simple-minded believers in the most desiccated branch of neoclassical economics, all this may seem surprising. Their theories regard people as "rational economic men", narrow utility-maximisers with no ties to family, place or culture. Presumably, these ciphers would shop around for low-tax jurisdictions. Oddly, the same benighted view of human nature must be shared by many globalisation sceptics – otherwise, why would they fear taxpayer flight on a scale sufficient to abolish the European welfare state? But in real life, it is better to take a fuller, broader view of the human condition. Since people seem to choose to be tied down, indeed to relish it, governments, within broad limits, can carry on taxing them regardless of globalisation. If it seems prudent to cut taxes on profits in order to attract inflows of foreign investment, no problem. Taxes on people will still be sufficient to finance generous public spending of every kind.

Be very afraid

Many anti-globalists have strangely little confidence in the merits of the policies they are anxious to sustain. Fearing what may be lost if globalisation continues uncurbed, Mr Rodrik writes:

> If it was the 19th century that unleashed capitalism in its full force, it was the 20th century that tamed it and boosted its productivity by supplying the institutional underpinnings of market-based economies. Central banks to regulate credit and the supply of liquidity, fiscal policies to stabilise aggregate demand, antitrust and regulatory authorities to combat fraud and anti-competitive behaviour, social insurance to reduce lifetime risk, political democracy to make the above institutions accountable to the citizenry – these were all innovations that firmly took root in today's rich countries only during the second half of the 20th century. That the second half of the century was also a period of unprecedented prosperity for Western Europe, the United States, Japan and some other parts of East Asia is no coincidence. These institutional innovations greatly enhanced the efficiency and legitimacy of markets and in turn drew strength from the material advancement unleashed by market forces ... The dilemma that we face as we enter the 21st century is that markets are striving to become global while the institutions needed to support them remain by and large national ... The desire by producers and investors to go global weakens the institutional base of national economies.

The argument, presumably, is that international capital will flow away from countries with the high public spending and taxes that these highly developed institutions involve. One answer is that international investment, as already noted, is much less important in most countries than domestic investment. But a more fundamental question is this: why should foreign capital flow away from countries that have equipped themselves with these institutions, if, as Mr Rodrik emphasises, those arrangements have "boosted ... productivity" and "greatly enhanced the efficiency ... of markets" – so much so that the most ambitious period of national institution-building was also a time of growing and "unprecedented" prosperity for the nations that joined in?

If public spending boosts productivity, then competition among governments for inward investment is likely to favour more public spending (and the taxes needed to pay for it), not less. Suppose, as seems plausible, that public spending on education raises productivity by increasing the supply of skilled workers. Then you would expect international investment to be drawn to countries that invest heavily in top-quality schools and universities. Suppose, as may also be true, that public spending on social programmes such as health and welfare raises productivity, by producing a healthier and more contented workforce, with better labour relations and greater labour mobility. If so, again international capital will be drawn to countries that spend money on those things. Globalisation, surely, will not frown on policies whose net effect is to foster productivity and efficiency.

But what about policies that do not serve those goals? Many would argue, for instance, that welfare policies, especially if too generous, encourage idleness and reduce economy-wide productivity. Suppose that is true. Also suppose that, knowing it to be true, most people want such policies anyway. You might feel that they are entitled to that opinion, and in a democracy they are entitled to get their way. Another example might be policies to limit working hours. Suppose that they reduce productivity, but that people vote for them anyway. Must globalisation overrule democracy?

Globalisation v democracy

The answer even in this case is no – and to see why is to understand why so many of the fears about globalisation and democracy are groundless. Policies that reduce productivity do, in the first instance, cut a country's feasible standard of living, narrowly defined in terms of GDP per head. But what happens after that? If a country that is open to international trade and capital flows adopts some such policies, perhaps on the ground that they will raise living standards according to some broader definition, wages and profits will fall relative to what they would otherwise have been. Next, investment will fall and the capital stock will shrink, again compared with what they would otherwise have been. This will continue until the scarcity of capital drives the rate of profit back up, at the margin, to the rate prevailing in the global capital market.

All this time the economy will grow more slowly than if the policies had not been followed. Once the economy has adjusted, however, it remains as "competitive" as it was at the outset: lower wages have restored labour costs per unit of output, and a smaller stock of capital has restored the return on capital. The economy has grown more slowly for a spell. It is less prosperous than it would have been. But in due course, once wages and profits have adjusted, the economy will again be as attractive, or unattractive, to foreign investors as it was at the outset. The government's adoption of policies that compromise efficiency is not punished by excommunication from the global economy, or with an accelerating spiral of decline; the only penalty is compromised efficiency and lower measured incomes, which is what the country chose in the first place.

Would the economy have fared any better without globalisation? Had it been closed to international flows of goods and capital, could it have adopted those productivity-cutting policies and paid no price at all? The answer is no. Even in a closed economy, policies that reduce productivity would cause wages and profits to fall, as in the open-economy case. The return on capital would be lower, so saving and investment would decline, relative to what they would have been (there would be no cross-border capital flows in this case, so saving and investment must always be equal). The capital stock would shrink and growth would be held back until the scarcity of capital drove the return back up. As in the open-economy case, the result would be a spell of slower growth and a standard of living permanently lower than it would otherwise have been.

The main difference is probably that in the closed-economy case, the losses would be subtracted from an economy that is already very much poorer than its open-economy counterpart, because it is closed. Conceivably, this would make further losses politically easier to sustain. But that is the most you can say in defence of the view that globalisation forbids social policies which jeopardise productivity. "Stay poor, because once you start to get rich you may find that you like it." Not exactly compelling, is it?

You might well conclude from all this that globalisation, if anything, will lead to higher rather than lower social spending. As argued earlier, globalisation raises aggregate incomes but at the same time increases economic insecurity for certain groups. Both of these consequences tend to raise social spending. Generous social spending is a "superior good": as countries grow richer, they want to spend more of their incomes on it, and can afford to. At the same time, quite separately, greater economic insecurity directly spurs demand for social spending.

Given that globalisation increases the demand for social spending; given that it does not rule out any decision to increase such spending which harms productivity, any more than a closed economy would; given that increases in social spending which raise productivity will be rewarded with inflows of capital; given all this, should globalisation and the generous social spending that democracies favour not go hand in hand? They should, and indeed rising social spending alongside faster, deeper globalisation is exactly what the figures for the past several decades show.

Governments in rich countries need to look again at their social policies, partly to make sure that temporary and longer-term losers from globalisation, and from economic growth in general, get well-designed help. But there is no reason whatever to fear that globalisation makes social policies more difficult to finance. In the end, by raising incomes in the aggregate, it makes them easier to finance. It creates additional economic resources, which democracies can use as they see fit.

A crisis of legitimacy

People are fed up with politics. Do not blame globalisation for that

IT WOULD BE wrong to say that economic integration neuters democracy or, more specifically, places any real constraints on the welfare state. Yet the view that globalisation is hollowing out politics seems to be almost universal among the economic and political commentariat. The fears expressed go wider than the implications of globalisation for the welfare state. Opinion polls in western democracies show disaffection with the political process. That, the columnists say, is because globalisation has made politics much less important. Fewer people are turning out to vote in elections these days. It hardly seems worth bothering, the argument runs, now that multinational companies rather than elected governments are calling the shots. True or false?

In his best-selling book on globalisation, *The Lexus and the Olive Tree* (Anchor Books/Doubleday, 2000), Thomas Friedman of the *New York Times* makes much of the "Golden Straitjacket". That is what he calls the policies which, according to the current orthodoxy, are necessary to establish the markets' confidence in any particular economy and its government: balanced budgets, moderate taxes, light regulation, privatisation and so forth. Once a country puts on the Golden Straitjacket, Mr Friedman says:

> Two things tend to happen: your economy grows and your politics shrinks ... The Golden Straitjacket narrows the political and economic choices of those in power to relatively tight parameters. That is why it is increasingly difficult these days to find any real differences between ruling and opposition parties in those countries that have put on the Golden Straitjacket. Once your country puts on the Golden Straitjacket, its political choices get reduced to Pepsi or Coke – to slight nuances of policy, slight alterations in design to account for local traditions, some loosening here or there, but never any major deviation from the core golden rules.

This argument is widely quoted and almost universally accepted. There can be no denying that the world has seen a striking convergence of economic ideology in the past decade or two. That makes Mr Friedman's argument seem plausible. But something else about it ought to arouse suspicion: advocates of globalisation and sceptics alike go along with it. Enthusiasts for globalisation (Mr Friedman among them) by and large think that the policies of the Golden Straitjacket are the right ones, and agree that your economy will indeed grow faster if you adopt them. Many sceptics are willing to concede this second point. The Golden Straitjacket may indeed make your economy grow faster – by the flawed and inequitable measures of free-market economics, at any rate – but in their view this gain cannot outweigh the loss of political sovereignty and democratic legitimacy that the straitjacket also entails.

The policies favoured by current orthodoxy do involve restraint – that much is true, and it makes the straitjacket metaphor apt. Balancing the budget is usually more difficult than letting public spending run ahead of taxes. From the government's point of view, deregulation, privatisation and so forth are also restricting rather than liberating: they mean doing less, whereas day-to-day political pressures usually urge governments to do more. But the crucial question that Mr Friedman's analysis leaves aside is whether or not these constraints are being imposed legitimately.

To talk of the narrowing of choices and the "shrinking of politics" implies that the process is anti-democratic. It need not be so. Voters everywhere may have come to prefer balanced budgets, moderate taxes, privatisation and the rest on their merits. If they have, the shrinking of politics around the current orthodoxy does not represent any weakening of democracy. If the voters decide to choose Pepsi or Coke, you might say, their choice has narrowed to Pepsi or Coke, until they choose next time.

On the other hand, questions of legitimacy certainly do arise if voters would rather not have balanced budgets, moderation in public spending and taxes, privatisation and so on – but are getting those policies anyway. And they also arise, you might argue, even if voters accept the straitjacket policies reluctantly, and only because forces more powerful than their governments have narrowed the range of choices before the electorate even comes to decide.

What about the voters?

Critics of globalisation make both arguments. The first, which says that voters are simply ignored, is unpersuasive. It is difficult to believe that if voters really did want big budget deficits, higher taxes, more public ownership of industry and so on, political parties would not seek to get elected – and succeed in getting elected – by offering those things. The second argument, which says that voters support the policies favoured by current orthodoxy but wish they did not have to, has real weight. The straitjacket policies are supported by most voters, it seems, but not with much enthusiasm. There is a recurring sense of bowing down to forces more powerful than liberal democracy – the markets, the multinationals, the WTO and the IMF. That disenchantment is in itself a kind of democratic failure.

Where does the blame for this lie? For the most part, not with globalisation as such – not with economic integration, not with markets, not with institutions like the Fund and the WTO – but with politicians. In all kinds of ways, again and again, governments and their political opponents have used the supposed demands of globalisation to deny responsibility. If you tell people you are helpless often enough, they will start to believe you.

One of the principal themes in western politics of the past ten or 15 years has been the "modernisation" of the left. Ex-socialist and moderate left-of-centre parties alike have moved to the centre, and in some cases past it. They have renounced outright egalitarianism, no longer advocate public ownership as an end in itself, seek opportunities for "partnership" with the private sector, prefer "conservative" macroeconomic policies, and favour moderation in taxes and public spending. Tony Blair's Labour government in Britain is probably the clearest case, but it is by no means unique in Europe. And something similar happened to America's Democrats under Bill Clinton. It was Mr Clinton, New Democrat, who duly signed the legislation "ending welfare as we know it" – terminating the federal government's commitment of 61 years' standing to provide cash assistance to the poor.

This realignment of the left has coincided over the past decade or so, it is pointed out, with an acceleration of economic integration. It is tempting to see, like Mr Friedman, a connection between the two trends – especially since the modernising left itself insists that there is one. "The world has changed," Tony Blair tells his party's traditional supporters, "but our values have not." In other words, if only we could, we would still like to do all the things leftist parties have traditionally done. We cannot, because the world now follows different rules. Today, governments need the co-operation of the global capital markets. Competition is fiercer than it has ever been before. We have to sound more like our conservative opponents – and the reason is globalisation.

But is it really? It seems unlikely. Globalisation may or may not be accelerating, but no particular turning point, so far as economic integration is concerned, coincides with the rather sudden repositioning of America's Democratic Party and the virtual disappearance, at about the same time, of Europe's classical left.

An embarrassing coincidence

Another event did coincide with these changes: the collapse of communism. However much the left in the West disavowed or even despised Soviet communism, that system had stood as a living, breathing alternative to the capitalist paradigm: a reminder that an alternative did exist. When that standard was torn down, it was a severe embarrassment. When, thanks to glasnost, the West found out exactly how disgusting communism in practice had been, the embarrassment deepened so much that most of the left's political vocabulary was discredited. These world-historical events were especially badly timed for the left: they seemed to seal the success that strident, iconic, right-of-centre governments in America, under Ronald Reagan, and Britain, under Margaret Thatcher, had already achieved.

The left was humiliated by association, found its values rendered deeply suspect, and suffered a monumental crisis of confidence. Also, it went out of fashion. Subtle repositioning in America's case, outright reinvention in Britain's, and something in-between elsewhere in Western Europe, became a domestic political necessity. No doubt many of the reformers welcomed this opportunity to recast their parties along lines closer to their own beliefs. But for most of the party members and long-time supporters it was an extremely reluctant conversion.

How were the leaders to present – to market, as they now might say – their newly realigned parties, both to the members and to voters? Grand empty talk of a new "third way" was a telling sign of desperation. The leaders of the new left could hardly expect to retain the loyalty of traditionalists if they came out and said: "Most of what we used to assert is wrong. Now that we have been found out, we are going over to the other side. From now on we stand for a kinder, gentler, more compassionate sort of conservatism." Instead, to appeal to centrist voters, while at the same time flattering traditionalists into believing that their ideas still prevailed, they put it another way: "The world has changed, our values have not."

Was this nothing but a ruse? Globalisation, as already noted, has left the capacity of governments to gather taxes and pay for public spending essentially undiminished. But there are other kinds of constraint. It is often argued, for instance, that global capital markets nowadays stop governments running big budget deficits. Global capital will no longer tolerate public ownership of utilities or other monopolistic enterprises, it is said. And the need to keep companies internationally competitive leaves governments no choice but to dismantle health and safety regulation, or to ease up on environmental rules.

In reality, the global capital market makes it easier to run big budget deficits, because there is an infinitely larger pool of funds to tap. As for public ownership, on balance global capital doesn't much care. Investors lending to publicly owned enterprises may see advantages, in fact, notably government guarantees of the debt. China has many state-owned enterprises, and seems to have no trouble attracting inward investment.

Race to the bottom?

What about the regulatory race to the bottom? There has lately been a good deal of economic deregulation, it is true, aimed at spurring competition in finance especially. And deregulation of this sort, once you start, has a habit of leading to more deregulation. In this area, governments might be forgiven for feeling sometimes that they have started something they cannot stop or any longer control. But questions such as whether banks should be allowed to sell insurance, or how exactly financial institutions should be supervised, are not deeply ideological. Important as they are, these are technical issues.

Other kinds of regulation – for example, of health and safety in the workplace, terms of employment, product and environmental standards – have far more ideological content. Has globalisation led to a race to the bottom in this kind of regulation? There is little sign of it. The clear trend in rich and poor countries alike is for ever tighter regulation of this sort. If globalisation has started a race in these areas, it is to the top, not the bottom.

Where formerly left-of-centre parties have adopted soft-conservative policies – moderation in taxes and spending, "fiscal responsibility" and the rest – the reason cannot be globalisation. The reason, in fact, is democracy. These policies, for the moment, are popular. Globalisation has been a useful subterfuge for the left – and, it should be noted, for the right as well, albeit to a smaller extent. Conservatives too can compete for support in the centre by prating on about how such and such a tax must be cut for the sake of preserving competitiveness, rather than because low taxes are good in themselves. Just as the left has found, there is advantage in claiming that a policy you propose must be adopted because there is no choice.

If you believe that the realignment of the left was a good thing, you might feel that the globalisation subterfuge is a small price to pay for moving the parties intact to the centre, where they can do more good. But there is a price, and it may be higher than anybody realised. The denial of responsibility, the pretence that policies are dictated by global markets rather than chosen by elected governments, the refusal to consider alternatives – all these are profoundly corrosive of democracy.

The ex-left has repeated countless variations on its new slogan – the world has changed, our values have not – all over the industrialised world. Often, the right has joined in. This was bound to persuade many people that conventional politics is indeed a waste of time. That, in effect, is exactly what political leaders are saying.

When anti-capitalist protesters tried to disrupt a meeting of European Union leaders in 2001, Tony Blair was especially scathing, calling the rioters mindless thugs. No doubt he was right about many of them, but his contempt was nonetheless ironic. The protesters say that people have been disempowered by global capitalism. They are wrong, but politicians themselves played a large part in devising that specious theory. It seemed an innocent deception at the time, but the protesters' rage, and the support they receive from large parts of the public, suggest that it was a dangerous move for democracy.

A plague of finance

Anti-globalists see the "Washington consensus" as a conspiracy to enrich bankers. They are not entirely wrong

WHEN THEY CRITICISE globalisation, sceptics are not just talking about economic integration across borders, or about the particular economic policies, such as liberal rules on trade and international investment, that directly facilitate it. They have in mind a much larger set of economic nostrums and institutions: the policies of the "Washington consensus", as it is known, and the international bodies, notably the International Monetary Fund and the World Bank, that strive to put it into effect.

The term "Washington consensus" was coined by the economist John Williamson in 1989. He called it that because of the support it enjoyed from the American government and (not coincidentally) from the Fund and the Bank, the big Washington-based institutions. He said it stood for ten policies. Measures to promote trade and FDI were high on the list, but the new orthodoxy, as he described it, also ran to the following: fiscal discipline (ie, smaller budget deficits), fewer subsidies, tax reform, liberalised financial systems, competitive exchange rates, privatisation, deregulation and measures to secure property rights.

In the view of many sceptics, this broad "neo-liberal" agenda has been deliberately designed to serve the needs of the rich at the expense of the poor. The sceptics' thinking on trade and foreign investment has already been discussed; their view of the rest of the formula is just as scathing. Fiscal discipline, curbs on subsidies and increases in taxes – measures long emphasised by the IMF in its dealings with distressed developing-country borrowers – directly hurt the poor, they say. Privatisation, financial liberalisation and industrial deregulation work to the same effect, by delivering windfall profits to domestic and foreign speculators, by stripping the state of its assets and by weakening rules that protect consumers and workers from abuse.

These policies are forced on poor-country governments regardless of their own views and priorities, incidentally undermining democracy in the third world. In the longer term, this kind of development – in effect, on terms dictated by the rich countries – saddles the developing countries with crippling debts. It also exposes them to the crazy fluctuations of the global business cycle. East Asia, one-time exemplar of the Washington model, discovered that to its cost; now Argentina, another darling of the Washington development establishment, is on the rack for the same reason. Insupportable debts and chronic instability worsen the developing countries' dependence on aid, and allow the IMF to tighten the screws even more vigorously next time, at the direction of American bankers. In every way, sceptics believe, the Washington consensus is a calculated assault on the weak.

Extreme as this caricature may be when taken as a whole, it contains some truths – which is why, for all its absurdity, it is recognisable. The idea that the Washington establishment is engaged in a deliberate conspiracy to oppress the third world may be nonsense, but there have been mistakes, big and small, and unintended consequences aplenty. The problem is that the valid criticisms are buried under a heap of error, muddle and deliberate distortion. The IMF, the Bank and America's Treasury Department would all feel much more threatened if the shards of intelligent criticism could be filtered from all the rubbish and gathered together.

Beware foreign capital

One of the clearest lessons for international economics in the past few decades, with many a reminder in the past few years, has been that foreign capital is a mixed blessing. This stricture does not apply so much to FDI because, unlike debt, FDI does not need to be serviced and cannot flee at short notice. As a result, providers of FDI themselves bear most of the financial risk attached to the investment, but this advantage comes at a price. Over the long term, FDI is a more expensive form of finance than debt because the outflow of remitted profits usually gives this kind of investor a bigger return than a foreign bank or bondholder could expect to receive. All the same, FDI is not only less risky for the host country, it is also more productive, as noted earlier, because of the technology and techniques that come with it. It is expensive from the host country's point of view, but good value.

Other forms of foreign capital, and especially short-term bank debt, have led many a developing country into desperate trouble. Because of the debt crisis, the 1980s were a lost decade for Latin America; today, in different ways, Argentina and Brazil are both in difficulty again because of debt. The financial crisis of the late 1990s set back even the East Asians, up to then the best-performing of all the developing countries. Why has this happened – and why so often?

Borrowers, obviously, have to take their share of the blame for borrowing too much, though that is rarely the whole explanation. Governments that borrow heavily in order to finance recklessly large budget deficits are plainly at fault. There was a lot of that in the 1970s and early 1980s. The case of corporate borrowers in developing countries is more complicated. They may sometimes borrow amounts which seem individually prudent given certain macroeconomic assumptions – such as no devaluation of the currency – but which become collectively insupportable if those assumptions turn out to be wrong. This happened in East Asia in the 1990s, with the further complication that much of the borrowing was channelled through domestic banks, meaning that the ultimate borrowers were unaware of the system-wide exchange-rate risk.

Sometimes, therefore, developing-country banks have been at fault as well – and their governments too, for failing to regulate them effectively. Some governments have also allowed, or actively encouraged, too much foreign borrowing by firms, with or without the intermediation of domestic banks and other financial institutions. Even some governments that have taken care to keep their own borrowing in check have been guilty of these failures of regulation and oversight.

But at least as much of the blame for the developing world's recurring debt traumas lies with rich-country lenders and, at one remove, rich-country governments. Modern banking operates, notoriously, under the persistent influence of moral hazard. This arises because deposit-taking banks are intrinsically fragile operations – and because governments are reluctant to let them fail. Banks are fragile because they promise depositors to repay deposits on demand and in full, even though they are unable to keep that promise if a significant number of depositors decide to exercise their right all at once. To avoid the risk of bank runs, which is high given the design of the contract with depositors, governments arrange deposit-insurance schemes, and other forms of assurance, including the doctrine of "too big to fail".

There are good reasons for this. If a bank fails, it may take other banks and enterprises, not to mention depositors' savings, with it; the broader payments system may also be imperilled. Historically, bank failures are associated with economy-wide recessions; for example, they helped to bring on the Depression of the 1930s (which was the inspiration for the modern deposit-insurance model). But the upshot is that banks are systematically protected from the consequences of their reckless behaviour.

Modern banks keep a far smaller fraction of their deposits as reserves than their historical forebears. Depositors have no incentive to supervise the banks by keeping an eye on reserves or by withdrawing money from the ones that are taking too many risks: their deposits are protected in any case. And banks have a correspondingly big incentive to compete aggressively for deposits which they can lend at high interest rates to risky projects. It is a formula for ruin – and, despite the efforts of regulators to measure and curb those risks, it keeps on working exactly as you would expect. In almost every case of spectacular boom and bust in recent years, in rich and poor countries alike, an exaggerated cycle of banking greed and fear has been a principal cause.

Too big to fail

So when sceptics accuse rich-country governments of being mainly concerned with bailing out western banks when financial crisis strikes in the third world, they have a point. The pernicious logic of "too big to fail" applies in the international context as well as the domestic one. If you are going to go bust, make sure you are a big developing country rather than a small one, with debts large enough to threaten catastrophic damage to America's financial system. That way you can be assured of prompt attention.

Until the intractable dilemmas of global bank regulation have been resolved – supposing they ever can be – the hazards of borrowing from abroad do argue for greater caution than poor-country borrowers have often used, or been advised to use by the IMF and the World Bank. The confidence with which the Fund and the Bank advised, or required, countries to abolish capital controls now looks misplaced in many cases.

The policy was doubtless well-intended. There is no question that moderate inflows of debt can speed development. This is why a good credit standing is a valuable asset for a developing country, and why too ready a willingness to default on debt usually proves self-defeating. But if bank regulation in rich countries leaves much to be desired, in many poor countries it is even worse. No doubt it would be best to bring financial regulation in developing countries up to the standard, such as it is, of regulation in America and Europe. But that is easier said than done. In the meantime, taxes or controls on short-term foreign-currency inflows, of the kind Chile has used with success, may well be better for some poor countries than the alternatives of, on the one hand, no inflows at all and, on the other, completely unrestricted inflows intermediated by a weakly or corruptly regulated domestic financial system.

In many other respects, however, the sceptics' attacks on the Fund and the Bank are ill-conceived. The IMF, especially, is criticised for sending its experts into developing countries and commanding governments to balance the budget in ways that assault the poor – by cutting spending on vital social services, ending subsidies or raising taxes on food and fuel, levying charges for use of water, and so on down the list of shame.

Measures to curb budget deficits are often unavoidable by the time the Fund is called in. The only way to reduce a budget deficit is to raise taxes or cut public spending. In many developing countries, where tax systems are narrowly based and unsophisticated, governments may have few options in deciding how to go about it. It would not be in the political interests of the Fund or the Bank to recommend measures that fall heavily on the poor if there were an obvious alternative.

However, the Fund, especially, may have invited much of the criticism it receives in this respect because it specifies policy changes in such detail. The IMF should strenuously avoid letting itself be seen as running the country, giving the government instructions and telling workers and voters to get lost. On the other hand, many sceptics seem to be under the impression that all was well in the countries concerned until the Fund barged in. The Fund turns up only when things have already gone very wrong indeed – and only when the government in question has asked for its help. That last point is surely worthy of more attention than the sceptics pay to it. If governments find the Fund's conditions so oppressive, they always have the option of refraining from asking for its help.

Governments know that the alternative to the Fund's intervention would usually be an even sharper contraction of public spending (including on social services) and/or an increase in taxes (including on things the poor need to buy). By the time the IMF is called in, the question whether to curb government borrowing is not so much a matter of weighing, as sceptics suppose, the case for laisser faire against the demands of social justice. Often, in the good-faith judgment of the IMF's officials, it is just an inescapable necessity if the economy is to be stabilised. And at times of impending economic collapse, stabilisation is very much in the interests of the poor, who suffer most during slumps.

In fact, most of the policies of the Washington consensus serve, or are capable of serving, the interests of the poor directly, not merely by promoting growth. If governments have been at fault in defending that agenda, it has mainly been in failing to emphasise this. The centrepiece of these policies, fiscal discipline, is sometimes necessary to avert an economic calamity; but even in more normal times, the alternative to steady control of government borrowing is usually high inflation. That, all the evidence shows, hurts the poor more than anyone else.

As noted by Mr Williamson back in 1989, the consensus called not just for fewer subsidies, but for new priorities in public spending, especially more effective support for industry and more spending on education and health – priorities intended to help the poor which the Bank has tried hard to put into practice. The need to broaden the tax base, so as to support additional public spending without destabilising the economy, is another idea that favours the poor, because there is no other way to provide the resources necessary to pay for effective safety nets. Deregulation and improved property rights can also make a real difference to the poor. As the work of Hernando de Soto has shown, it is the poor who suffer most from obstacles to small-scale enterprise and insecure titles to land.

Many sceptics might warm to the Fund and the Bank if they paid more attention to the criticisms directed at the two institutions from the political right. Conservatives worry not so much because the Fund is too mean, or the Bank too keen on market economics, but rather the opposite: they complain that both are engaged in throwing good money after bad. Worse than that, critics on the right argue, the two institutions reward the bad policies that got the patients into trouble in the first place, thereby creating their own kind of moral hazard.

If the Fund and the Bank were simply shut down, as many sceptics and many conservatives would wish, the flow of resources to the developing countries would certainly diminish, at least in the short term. The world economy would be a harsher place for the poor countries. The conservatives argue, in effect, that this would be good for them in the longer term. Those sceptics who favour slower economic growth for the third world would also be gratified, presumably, if the Fund and the Bank packed up. But it is hard to see what those who are not opposed to development as such see in this course.

Trying to get it right

The IMF and the Bank have certainly made mistakes. They have had spells of over-confidence, though they cannot be accused of that at the moment. Noted scholars such as Joseph Stiglitz, a former chief economist at the World Bank, have criticised them for technical incompetence, and for theological devotion to discredited economic theories; but other economists have argued in their defence, saying, plausibly, that they have done their best in difficult circumstances. They have certainly neglected the importance of allowing governments to "own", and take responsibility for, their policies – a mistake which supplicant governments, anxious to deny responsibility, have usually been keen to encourage. But the Fund and the Bank are aware of this criticism, and are trying to do something about it.

Other improvements in the way the international financial institutions work are surely called for. Many different panels of experts have produced countless proposals, big and small, and some of these are being taken up. Overall, a shift of emphasis is needed. Now that many developing countries have access, for good or ill, to the global capital markets, the Bank needs to focus on disseminating knowledge rather than money. And for both political and economic reasons it would be better if the Fund, for its part, specialised in providing liquidity during emergencies rather than development finance, subject to simple financial conditions rather than immensely detailed policy blueprints.

The institutions themselves have gone far to acknowledge their mistakes, and the need for reform. In view of this, the ability of the sceptics to maintain their hysterical animosity toward the institutions is surprising. In its way, it demands a measure of respect.

ed the WTO?

The WTO is no would-be tyrant. It is democratic to a fault, and has few powers of its own

UNSURPRISINGLY, SCEPTICS EXTEND many of the criticisms they make of the IMF and the World Bank to the World Trade Organisation as well. If anything, they detest the WTO even more. Perhaps this is because, unlike the Fund and the Bank, the WTO brings what many critics regard as the most objectionable aspects of globalisation home to the rich countries, where most of those critics live.

The IMF undermines democracy in the developing world, the charge goes, which is bad enough; the WTO does the same thing in America and Europe as well, which is worse. The IMF and the Bank bring financial ruin to the poor countries that turn to them for help; but in the long term, the WTO inflicts even worse damage than that on all countries, rich and poor alike, solvent or otherwise. It does this, sceptics say, not through onerous borrowing conditions but by force of international law. Its prohibitions undermine efforts to protect the environment and eviscerate safeguards developed over decades to protect the health and well-being of consumers and workers.

On top of all this, of course, the specific mandate of the WTO is to promote trade, which many sceptics regard as a bad thing in itself. According to the anti-globalists' world view, it is only logical that much of the threat posed by the WTO to democracy springs from its dedication to trade. As noted earlier, many sceptics regard a liberal regime of international trade and investment as intrinsically hostile to democracy, because it promotes a competition for profits that overrides voters' political preferences.

This is the "race to the bottom" argument once more. The counter-arguments to this mistaken idea so far as it applies to taxes and the welfare state have already been rehearsed earlier in this survey. In the regulation of products and processes, with respect either to safety or to environmental impact, signs of a race to the bottom are equally hard to find. All the movement is the other way. Everywhere, the adoption of more demanding environmental standards gathers pace as incomes rise.

But sceptics are also making a separate point that is less easy to dismiss. They say that the WTO is anti-democratic not merely indirectly,

because of its devotion to trade, but also directly, as a matter of institutional design. This anti-democratic character, it is alleged, is a deliberate
part of the organisation's working methods – and that is unacceptable,
full stop.

According to sceptics, the WTO takes powers away from elected governments and grants them to faceless bureaucrats. It can tell America
and Europe that rules to protect endangered species or to keep food free
of dangerous chemicals are illegal, and that they must abandon these
policies. It can stop governments in poor countries providing cheap
generic medicines to their people because that would hurt the profits of
the drug companies. The sick must pay over the odds for patent-pro-
tected branded drugs, or do without – either is fine with the WTO.

In all these cases, sceptics say, the interests of multinational corporations happen to be in conflict with the democratically expressed wishes
of the people. Whenever that occurs, the WTO rules against democracy.
Moreover, the critics continue, its unaccountable and unrepresentative
bureaucrats arrive at their outrageous edicts in secret: the hidden mas-
ters of globalisation are not even required to explain themselves. The
WTO is a kind of embryonic world government, but with none of the
checks and balances that true democratic government requires. In short,
it is an embryonic world tyranny. That is why, in the view of many
sceptics, it is the most dangerous of all the institutions of globalisation.

True in part

As before, this indictment combines error, gross exaggeration and
apparently deliberate distortion – but, as before, it also contains particles
of truth.

The WTO's anti-democratic powers are held to reside mainly in the
organisation's new dispute-resolution procedures. The strengthening of
these arrangements was one of the notable achievements of the
Uruguay Round of trade talks which concluded in 1994; they constitute
one of the main differences between the WTO and its predecessor, the
General Agreement on Tariffs and Trade (GATT). Under the new rules,
governments cannot block the findings of a WTO dispute panel: once
they have exhausted their right of appeal, countries held to have broken
WTO rules must either change their policies so as to comply, or pay
compensation to the injured party, or face trade sanctions. This apparent ability to overrule governments lies at the centre of the sceptics'
objections to the new system.

It is true that the system is no longer, if it ever was, a mere bundle of

procedure for arbitration should disputes arise. Even
angements were adopted, the GATT had developed a
as opposed to strictly rule-clarifying, character: the
a bit further in that direction. Even so, it remains highly
misleading to talk of the WTO "taking powers" or forcing governments
to ignore voters' wishes.

Despite its developing quasi-judicial role, the WTO remains an unambiguously intergovernmental, rather than supragovernmental, entity.
Changes to the organisation's rules are proposed by member governments and adopted "by consensus" – which in practice means they
require unanimity. As the WTO likes to say, far from being anti-democratic, it is actually hyper-democratic. No government ever had to accept
a new WTO rule because it was outvoted, as might happen in the European Union; every one of the organisation's 142 members has a veto.

If the WTO involves any pooling of sovereignty, therefore, it is only
in an extremely limited sense. When a dispute arises, the quarrel may be
over exactly what a rule means, or how it should be applied in particular, possibly unforeseen, circumstances; a government can never be
compelled to obey a rule that it opposed in the first place. This applies to
the new dispute-settlement rules as much as to anything else: every
member government has agreed to them as well.

Moreover, the idea that the WTO enforces obedience by punishing
violators is itself a distortion. Its principal role, once a dispute is under
way, is still to act as referee while two or more governments fight it out.
Consider a favourite example of European sceptics: the continuing dispute between the European Union and the United States over hormone-
treated beef.

Europe first banned imports of such beef from America in 1989, citing
health concerns. The United States has taken the matter to the WTO's
dispute-settlement body. Although sceptics often claim otherwise, the
WTO's rules (which, to repeat, both Europe and the United States have
freely agreed to) do allow countries to ban imports to protect consumers
from dangerous products. But they also require governments to show
reputable scientific evidence in support of their controls, and insist that
measures do not discriminate between suppliers, rather than favouring
one country's exports over another's, or domestic production over
imports. Without these provisos, countries could ban imports at will,
something which the signatories to the agreement presumably considered undesirable.

At present, to the sceptics' horror, Europe is deemed to have violated the rules. This is not because health concerns are routinely set at naught by the WTO, as is often falsely claimed, nor even because the beef-import ban itself has been ruled illegal: the issue never got that far. It is because the EU elected to produce scientific evidence in support of its ban and then failed to do so. In due course, the WTO may authorise the United States to impose retaliatory trade sanctions of its own. In the face of that threat, the European Union may or may not give way and lift its ban.

In either case, to say that the WTO is trying to force Europe to open its markets seems odd. It is the United States, surely, which is doing the forcing. Every case that comes before the WTO is first and foremost a dispute between governments, not a dispute between a government and the organisation itself. Also, whatever the merits of the beef-and-hormones case, America's government claims to be serving its citizens' interests, just as the EU's authorities claim to represent the voters of Europe. So it is hardly a matter of the WTO against democracy, as sceptics would have it; rather, it is a question of one democracy against a union of other democracies – with the WTO in the middle, taking the brickbats for trying to calm things down.

What if the WTO did not exist, as most sceptics seem to wish? Would the EU ban have been sustained without objection, assuring the primacy of health and environmental standards worldwide, and everywhere peace and light? Plainly not. The same trade dispute would simply have been prosecuted through other means: instead of a mediated dispute conducted under agreed rules, there would have been a naked trial of strength between the EU and the United States.

In such a contest, who knows whether Europe's view on beef and hormones would prevail? To make peace in due course, it might have to abandon its present position. What is certain is that the costs of conducting the dispute this way, rather than through the WTO's procedures, would be very much greater. And although the EU might be able to stand up for its interests in an economic fight with America, a small country in a dispute with a much bigger one would have a less good chance. That is why the governments of poor countries have been so eager in recent years to join first the GATT and then the WTO. They understand that in trade policy, unless attitudes change a lot, the alternative to the WTO is not "democracy prevails" but "might is right".

Doing good by stealth?

As in other areas, the sceptics' overall case against the WTO is deluded –

but some of their points, lost in the fog of rage, are fair. In trade policy, their strongest argument is about the system's culture of secrecy. They are right about much of this. The reasons go deeper than they may know, or governments may care to acknowledge.

The multilateral approach to trade liberalisation, pursued first through the GATT and now through the WTO, does have a horrible flaw. It espouses the idea that lowering trade barriers is a concession you make to your trading partners; a sacrifice for which you require compensation, or "reciprocity", in the jargon. This mercantilist view of trade – exports are good, imports are bad – is an economic fallacy. Politically – and this is to endorse a point made by sceptics – it serves to enthrone producer interests, neglecting all others. Trade agreements go forward when exporters on all sides tell their governments that they see something in it for them; the interests of importers (that is, workers and consumers at large) are implicitly regarded as politically insignificant.

This has a further consequence. Most governments insist that the grubby details of trade negotiations be kept secret; this is their idea, not the WTO's. At the end of any round of trade talks, a triumphant breakthrough backed by all sides can be announced. In the meantime, as you might expect, governments prefer to keep their negotiators' craven submission to corporate interests under wraps.

The justification for this pact with the devil is that by setting one country's producer interests against another's, it has mobilised big business in support of freer trade, helping to neutralise protectionist sentiment; as a result, trade has in fact been liberalised. Exporters have been pleased with the outcome, to be sure, but that is not the point. Liberal trade is good because it raises the incomes of consumers and workers at large, and especially because it improves the prospects of the poorest countries. It could be argued that this great prize has been well worth the cost in intellectual dishonesty and political stealth.

But whether or not the mercantilist pact can be justified in that way, its terms will probably have to change. Wrong as they are about most things, the sceptics may be right about that. Governments have no persuasive reply to the demand that trade policy should be conducted in public, and that the WTO's dispute-settlement machinery, especially, should work in plain sight. Proponents of liberal trade can no longer expect trade policy to be sheltered, in the interests of "effectiveness", from the demands for honest, open and accountable governance that are regarded as compelling in other areas.

If the mercantilist pact breaks down under public scrutiny, as it may, there is a risk that the cause of liberal trade will be set back. Certainly that is what anti-globalists are hoping. But there is also another, more encouraging, possibility. If governments still want to promote liberal trade – and rising incomes, other things being equal, are popular with voters – they could try to do so on its economic merits. Being honest would be inconvenient, and after all these years would certainly seem peculiar. Exporters would be displeased to find that governments were listening to them less avidly. But governments would find it easier to be straightforward about the case for trade. Perhaps they could even convince themselves, and enough voters to make the difference, that unilateral, uncompensated trade liberalisation is the best way to serve the public interest.

If they could do that – but only then – the WTO in its present form would no longer be needed at all, and liberals could join sceptics in celebrating its demise. But given the demands this would place on government, that day will not dawn just yet.

A different manifesto

If sceptics could learn to love capitalism, they would still have plenty to complain about

SOME SCEPTICS HAVE recently started to argue that the movement against globalisation dwells too much on what it is against; it must grow up, and start to say what it is for. This is a worthy thought, but tactically ill-advised.

The main things holding the anti-globalist coalition together are a suspicion of markets, a strongly collectivist instinct and a belief in protest as a form of moral uplift. Once upon a time this combination would have pointed to socialism as a coherent alternative to "the system". But socialism, after the unfortunate experiences of the 20th century, is not quite ready yet for release back into the community. The attitudes that support it are still out there, as evidenced by the protesters, and by the sympathy they arouse among the public. But for the moment, as a programme for government, socialism lacks sufficiently broad appeal.

What else is there? The protest coalition can hang together only if it continues to avoid thinking about what it might be in favour of – a challenge it is all geared up to meet. All the same, it seems a pity.

Meanwhile, the champions of globalisation – governments and big business – are also giving a deeply unimpressive account of themselves. Intellectually, their defence of globalisation ("it's good for our exporters and creates jobs") is a disgrace. And governments deserve fierce criticism for many of their policies, not least in areas of particular concern to anti-globalists.

Rich countries' trade rules, especially in farming and textiles, still discriminate powerfully against poor countries. Rich countries' subsidies encourage wasteful use of energy and natural resources, and harm the environment. It is at least arguable that rich countries' protection of intellectual property discriminates unfairly against the developing world. And without a doubt, rich countries' approach to financial regulation offers implicit subsidies to their banks and encourages reckless lending; it results, time and again, in financial crises in rich and poor countries alike.

All these policies owe much to the fact that corporate interests exercise undue influence over government policy. Sceptics are right to deplore this. But undue influence is hardly new in democratic politics; it has not been created by globalisation forcing governments to bow down. On the contrary, special-interest politics is easier to conduct in closed economies than in open ones. If allowed to, all governments are happy to seek political advantage by granting preferences.

It is dispiriting to watch as big companies work out how to maintain their influence nationally and extend it to the global arena, using "civil society" and "corporate social responsibility" as levers. Naturally, in the light of the protesters' concerns, the multinationals are willing to sit down with governments and NGOs – they have lots of ideas for collecting extra subsidies, and piling punitive taxes and regulation on their less responsible competitors.

Barking up the wrong tree

The protesters' main intellectual problem is that their aversion to capitalism – that is, to economic freedom – denies them the best and maybe the only way to attack and contain concentrations of economic and political power. The protesters do not need to embrace laisser-faire capitalism. They need only to discard their false or wildly exaggerated fears about the mixed economy; that is, about capitalism as it exists in the West, with safety-nets, public services and moderate redistribution bolted on.

Under this form of capitalism, economic growth does not hurt the poor, as sceptics allege; indeed, for developing countries, capitalist growth is indispensable if people are ever to be raised out of poverty. Growth in mixed economies is compatible with protecting the environment: rich countries are cleaner than poor ones. And if prices are made to reflect the costs of pollution, or allowed to reflect the scarcity of natural resources, growth and good stewardship go hand in hand. Above all, free trade does not put poor countries at a disadvantage: it helps them.

Try this for size

If some of the protesters could accept these tenets of mixed-economy capitalism, a narrower but far more productive protest manifesto would come into view. Its overriding priority would be to address the scandal of third-world poverty. To that end, it would demand that rich-country governments open their markets to all developing-country exports, especially to farm goods and textiles. (Concerns about displaced workers would be met not by holding down the poorest countries, but by spending more on training and education in rich countries, and by cushioning any losses in income there.) It would insist that western governments increase spending on foreign aid, taking care that the benefits flow not to rich-country banks or poor-country bureaucrats, but to the poor, and especially to the victims of disease. To protect the environment, it would call for an end to all subsidies that promote the wasteful use of natural resources, and for the introduction of pollution taxes, including a carbon tax, so that the price of energy reflects the risk of global warming.

This programme to accelerate globalisation and extend the reach of market forces – although at first it might be better to put it another way – would also have a good-governance component. Under that rubric, "trade policy" should ideally be abolished outright: governments have no business infringing people's liberty to buy goods where they will, least of all when the aim is to add to corporate earnings. Short of instant abolition, trade policy should at least be brought into the light so that corporate interests find it harder to dictate its terms. Governments should hold themselves accountable to voters at large, not to companies, industry associations, special interests or indeed to any kind of non-governmental organisation, whatever its ideology or dress code.

Among other things, accountability means accepting rather than denying responsibility. Corrupt or incompetent governments in the developing countries deny responsibility when they blame the IMF or the World Bank for troubles chiefly caused by their own policies. Rich-country governments, notably America's, also use the Fund, the Bank and the WTO – institutions which in practice could never defy their wishes – to deflect blame. Worst of all, governments everywhere deny responsibility when they explain broken promises, failures of will or capitulations to special interests as the unavoidable consequences of globalisation. That is no harmless evasion, but a lie that rots democracy itself. Critics of economic integration should be striving to expose this lie; instead, they greet it as a grudging endorsement of their own position.

The crucial point is that international economic integration widens choices – including choices in social provision – because it makes resources go further. Policies to relieve poverty, to protect workers displaced by technology, and to support education and public health are all more affordable with globalisation than without (though not even globalisation can relieve governments of the need to collect taxes to pay for those good things). When governments claim that globalisation ties their hands, because politically it makes their lives easier, they are conning voters and undermining support for economic freedom. Whatever else that may be, it is not good governance.

Whenever governments use globalisation to deny responsibility, democracy suffers another blow and prospects for growth in the developing countries are set back a little further. Anti-globalists fall for it every time, seeing the denials as proof of their case. They make plenty of other mistakes, but none so stupid as that.

Sources

This survey has drawn on the work of many authors. A full list of sources and suggestions for further reading appears alongside the version of the survey published on *The Economist*'s website, www.economist.com. The parts of the survey that deal with multinationals in the developing countries owe a particular debt to *Fighting the Wrong Enemy: Anti-Global Activists and Multinational Enterprises* by Edward Graham, published by the Institute for International Economics.

The material on pages 5–61 first appeared in a survey written by Clive Crook in *The Economist* in October 2001.

2
Popular myths and economic facts

These articles were first published in The Economist *in late 1997 as part of a critical series on globalisation. They look at particular aspects of globalisation: migration; trade; container ships; culture; and multinational companies. Taken together, they serve a single purpose: to show that globalisation is neither as all-encompassing, nor as demonic, as it is often made out to be. The articles have endured well because they consider globalisation in its historical context. The case they make rings true today.*

Workers of the world

Is migration increasing? What drives it, and how does it affect national economies?

FROM THE BEGINNING, migration has been one of the most conspicuous features of human history. Humanity did not appear simultaneously all over the earth but, according to the current scientific consensus, first evolved in Africa, and from there spread far and wide.

Even after mankind had populated most of the planet, migration continued to play a decisive role in history down the centuries, as people contended for territory and the resources that go with it.

In many of history's biggest movements of people, the migrants were not volunteers. In the 17th and 18th centuries 15m people were taken as slaves from Africa and shipped to Brazil, the Caribbean and North America. In the 19th century, between 10m and 40m indentured workers ("coolies", often no better than slaves) were sent in vast numbers around the world, mainly from China and India.

In the 20th century, wars in Europe and Asia displaced millions more. But perhaps the most intense episode of migration-under-duress in modern times occurred after the partition of India in 1947, when 7m Muslims fled India for the new state of Pakistan and 7m Hindus fled in the opposite direction.

As individuals, not merely as members of races or religions in flight, people have always travelled in search of a better life. Between the middle of the 19th century and the start of the second world war 60m people left Europe and moved overseas – to the United States (which received 40m of them), Canada, Latin America, Australia, New Zealand and South Africa. Much of this movement was guided by economic calculation. Most modern migration is of this kind, though nowadays the pull is high wages rather than cheap land.

For the past century or so, the pattern of migration has shifted a good deal, with changes in government policy playing a key role. Until 1914 governments imposed almost no controls. This allowed the enormous 19th-century movement of migrants from Europe to North America. The United States allowed the entry of anybody who was not a prostitute, a convict, a "lunatic" – or, after 1882, Chinese.

Travel within Europe was largely uncontrolled: no passports, no work-permits. Foreign-born criminals could expect to be deported, but that was the extent of immigration policy. The only questions were whether migrants could afford the journey and, having arrived, be better off than at home.

Between 1914 and 1945, partly reflecting security concerns, migration was curtailed. Many countries excluded immigrants – including refugees from Hitler's Germany – on openly racist grounds. America's Congress passed laws aiming to preserve the country's racial and religious make-up.

After 1945 came another great change. Many European countries faced labour shortages. Their immigration laws by and large were not repealed, but were enforced much more liberally. Governments actively recruited immigrants for jobs in their expanding industries. Migration surged again, now not mainly from Europe to North America but from the developing countries to the rich ones.

The next big change came in the 1970s. The rich countries were no longer growing quickly and struggling with labour shortages. Recession came to Europe and America, and immigration rules were tightened again. This more restrictive regime continues to apply.

Counting heads

It is difficult to say how much migration is going on. Official definitions of "migrant" vary, and migrants on any definition are difficult to count.

However, according to estimates in *The Work of Strangers*, a study by Peter Stalker published by the International Labour Organisation in 1994, roughly 80m people live in countries they were not born in. Another 20m live in foreign lands as refugees from natural disasters or political oppression. Each year sees another 1.5m or so emigrate perma-nently, and perhaps another 1m seek temporary asylum abroad. By his-torical standards, these numbers are large in absolute terms, but small in relation to the now much larger populations of the receiving countries (see chart 1).

The United States remains much the world's biggest recipient. It gets about as many permanent immigrants as every other country in the world added together: 720,000 in 1995, down from a peak of nearly 2m in 1991. Germany, easily the main receiving country in Europe, had roughly 800,000 immigrants in both 1994 and 1995, but its definition of "immigrant" is much broader than America's and includes many tem-porary workers.

The underlying trend of economic migration reflects two countervail-

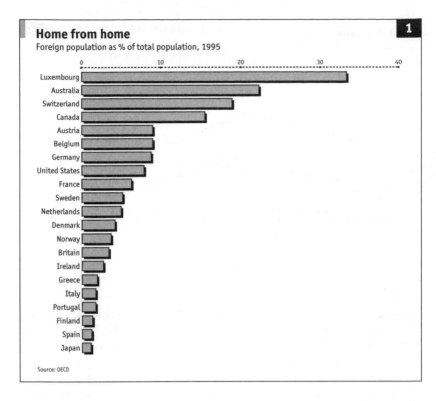

Home from home
Foreign population as % of total population, 1995

Source: OECD

ing forces. As the cost of travel drops and incomes rise in developing countries, migration becomes easier. On the other hand, in poor countries with fast-rising incomes the incentive to move shrinks. The net effect in the early years of industrialisation tends to be higher migration. Despite the tightening of rules in many rich countries during the 1970s, immigration did increase somewhat during the 1980s and early 1990s. New restrictions have slowed this expansion (see chart 2).

Has there ever been a global market for labour? During the 19th century, arguably there was. Otherwise, the United States could not have expanded at anything like the rate it did. Nowadays, there is no real market, such is the severity of restrictions in force. The interplay of these rules and other factors gives rise to complicated migratory patterns. Each receiving country has its own sources: the links are often historical as well as economic or geographical. Earlier generations of migrants form networks that help new ones to overcome legal obstacles; and today's tighter rules tend to confine immigration to family members of

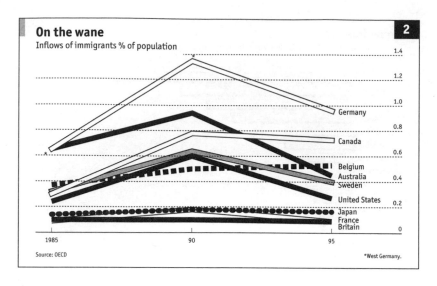

On the wane
Inflows of immigrants % of population

2

Germany
Canada
Belgium
Australia
Sweden
United States
Japan
France
Britain

1985   90   95

Source: OECD
*West Germany.

earlier "primary" migrants.

Mexico is the main source of migrants to the United States, with about 90,000 permanent (legal) settlers in 1995. But the former Soviet Union and the Philippines, taken together, supplied even more during that year – 55,000 and 51,000 respectively (see table 3).

Citizens of European Union countries are free to work anywhere within the EU. This is presumably promoting the flow of economic migrants within the EU, but it is difficult to be sure of the effect (see chart 4). The proportion of EU citizens in each member-country's foreign-born population varies widely – from 25% in the Netherlands to 89% in Luxembourg – and any tendency for this share to rise has been overshadowed by the influx of new immigrants from Central and Eastern Europe.

Another new trend is a worldwide shift towards migration of highly skilled workers. Again this reflects the interplay of economics and regulation. As multinational companies expand, they develop their own internal markets for skilled workers. The expansion of trade also creates opportunities for skilled migrants, both directly (in trade-related occupations) or indirectly (by changing attitudes towards "abroad"). Governments also prefer high-income arrivals, so immigration rules favour those with skills.

The growth of the multinational enterprise seems likely to spur the next big development in the history of migration. Big companies want

Melting pots

3

Country of origin of immigrants '000, 1995

Australia		Britain		Canada	
New Zealand	12.3	Pakistan	6.3	Hong Kong	31.7
Britain	11.3	India	4.9	India	16.2
China	11.2	United States	4.0	Philippines	15.1
Ex-Yugoslavia	7.7	Bangladesh	3.3	China	13.3
Hong Kong	4.4	Nigeria	3.3	Sri Lanka	8.9
India	3.7	Australia	2.0	Taiwan	7.7
France		**Japan**		**United States**	
Algeria	8.4	China	38.8	Mexico	89.9
Morocco	6.6	Philippines	30.3	Ex-Soviet Union	54.5
Turkey	3.6	United States	27.0	Philippines	51.0
United States	2.4	South Korea	18.8	Vietnam	41.8
Tunisia	1.9	Brazil	11.9	Dominican Rep.	38.5
Ex-Yugoslavia	1.6	Thailand	6.5	China	35.5

Source: OECD

the freedom to shift employees from country to country, and to use citizens of one country to alleviate skills shortages in another. This will be not so much a quantitative change (which governments would resist in any case) but a qualitative one – namely, greater migration of workers-plus-skills, or "human capital". If a truly global market for labour ever reappears, it is likely to be for highly skilled workers only.

Migration may not be new, but it has become more controversial than for many years. On the face of it, immigration brings a variety of benefits to the receiving country. An important one for many rich countries is demographic. The average age of the advanced economies' populations is rising. Immigration tends to lower it, because most migrants are young. This improves the ratio of active workers to retired people, so taxes can be lower than otherwise.

Against this, a common view is that immigrants compete for jobs which would otherwise have gone to nationals, reducing wages and/or employment prospects for the indigenous workers. This sounds plausible – surely an increase in the supply of labour must reduce wages or increase unemployment? The truth is more complicated.

Jobs and wages

Immigrants are consumers as well as producers, so they create jobs as

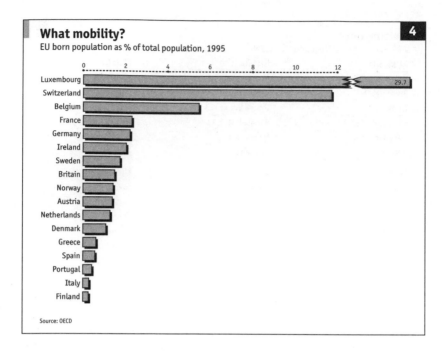

What mobility?
EU born population as % of total population, 1995

Source: OECD

well as taking them. And the work they do need not be at the expense of native workers. Immigrants often hold jobs (as domestic servants, for instance) that natives are unwilling to accept at any feasible wage.

Also, immigrants sometimes help to keep industries viable that would otherwise disappear altogether, causing employment to fall. This was the conclusion, for instance, of a study of the Los Angeles garment industry in the 1970s and 1980s. And when immigrants working for low wages do put downward pressure on natives' wages, they may raise the (real) wages of natives in general by keeping prices lower than they otherwise would be.

In theory, then, the net effect of immigration on native wages is uncertain. Unfortunately, most of the empirical research on whether immigrants make natives worse off in practice is also inconclusive – except that the effect, one way or the other, seems small. Most of this research has been done in America: if there were any marked influence on wages, that is where you would expect to find it, given the scale of immigration and the tendency of the newcomers to concentrate in certain areas. But most studies have found that the impact, if any, is slight.

Many studies have compared wages and employment in areas with many immigrants to wages and employment in areas with few. For instance, one examined the impact of the sudden and notorious inflow of refugees to Miami from the Cuban port of Mariel in 1980. Within the space of a few months, 125,000 people had arrived, increasing Miami's labour force by 7%. Yet the study concluded that wages and employment among the city's natives, including the unskilled, were virtually unaffected.

Another study examined the effect of immigration on wages and employment of those at the bottom of the jobs ladder – unskilled blacks and hispanics. It found that a doubling of the rate of immigration had no detectable effect on natives (although the wages of the previous group of immigrants, presumably those in closest competition with the newcomers, saw their relative wages fall by 2.5%).

The most recent work, admittedly, has tended to question these findings. This new strand of research is linked to recent work on the effects of trade on wages, and especially on wage inequality. Using more detailed statistics and more sophisticated methods than the earlier studies, this work has tended to find that immigrants' wages take longer to rise to the level of natives' wages than had been supposed. This implies a more persistent downward pressure on the host economy's labour market.

Typically, these studies find that immigration does depress unskilled natives' wages – to a small extent. But even these new results (which are by no means unchallenged) need to be kept in perspective. Nearly all economists would agree that the effects of immigration are insignificant in relation to other influences.

In his book *Trade and Income Distribution* (Institute for International Economics, 1997), William Cline reviews the literature on globalisation and wages. In general, Mr Cline's estimates tend to the pessimistic end of the range. Nonetheless he finds that of all the forces acting to lower unskilled wages relative to skilled, immigration is the weakest.

According to his estimates, immigration would by itself account for a fall of two percentage points in the ratio of unskilled to skilled wages in America between 1973 and 1993. Technological change, acting to reduce the demand for unskilled labour, and a category called "unidentified factors" pushing the same way would each account for a much greater fall of nearly 30 percentage points.

It seems safe to conclude, despite the uncertainties, that fears over the economic effects of immigration are much exaggerated.

The material on pages 65–71 first appeared in a Schools Brief in *The Economist* in November 1997.

Trade winds

Why does it make sense for countries to trade goods and services? How much trade do they do? And why are there obstacles to freer trade?

TIME WAS WHEN trade flows were of interest mainly to economic experts and executives of big corporations. But the movement of goods and services across national boundaries has become the subject of intense public attention all over the world. To the public at large, trade is the most obvious manifestation of a globalising world economy.

Measured by the volume of imports and exports, the world economy has become increasingly integrated in the years since the second world war. A fall in barriers to trade has helped stimulate this growth. The volume of world merchandise trade is about 16 times what it was in 1950, while the world's total output is only five-and-a-half times as big (see chart 1). The ratio of world exports to GDP has climbed from 7% to 15% (see chart 2).

Virtually all economists, and most politicians, would agree that freer trade has been a blessing. However, the economists and politicians would probably give quite different reasons for thinking so.

Politicians, by and large, praise greater trade because it means more

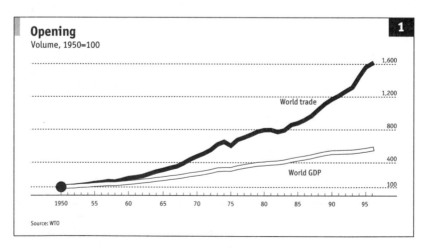

Opening · · · **1**
Volume, 1950=100

World trade

World GDP

1,600
1,200
800
400
100

1950 55 60 65 70 75 80 85 90 95

Source: WTO

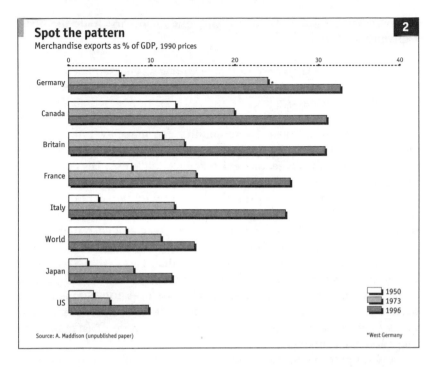

Spot the pattern

Merchandise exports as % of GDP, 1990 prices

2

Source: A. Maddison (unpublished paper)   *West Germany

exports. This, in turn, purportedly means more jobs – and, if the exports involve sophisticated products such as cars or jet engines, more "good" jobs. The American government, zealous to promote exports, has even produced estimates that try to show how many new jobs are created by each $1 billion of American sales abroad.

This is misleading. A big export order may well cause an individual company to add workers, but it will have no effect on a country's total employment, which is determined mainly by how fast the economy can expand without risking inflation and by microeconomic obstacles, such as taxes that deter employers from hiring or workers from seeking jobs. America, where exports are a relatively small fraction of GDP, has fuller employment than Germany, where exports loom larger.

Gains from trade

To economists, the real benefits of trade lie in importing rather than in exporting. Politicians frequently urge consumers to favour domestically made goods, and portray a widening trade deficit as a Bad Thing. But economists know that the only reason for exporting is to earn the wherewithal to import. As James Mill, one of the first trade theorists, explained in 1821:

The benefit which is derived from exchanging one commodity for another, arises, in all cases, from the commodity received, not the commodity given.

This benefit arises even if one country can make everything more cheaply than all others. The basic theory that explains this, the principle of comparative advantage, has existed since Mill's day. His contemporary, David Ricardo, usually gets the credit for expounding it.

To see how this theory works, think about why two countries – call them East and West – might gain from trading with one another. Suppose, for simplicity, that each has 1,000 workers, and each makes two goods: computers and bicycles.

West's economy is far more productive than East's. To make a bicycle, West needs the labour of two workers; East needs four. To make a computer, West uses ten workers while East uses 100. Suppose that there is no trade, and that in each country half the workers are in each industry. West produces 250 bicycles and 50 computers. East makes 125 bikes and five computers.

Now suppose that the two countries specialise. Although West makes both bikes and computers more efficiently than East, it has a bigger edge in computer making. It now devotes most of its resources to that industry, employing 700 workers to make computers and only 300 to make bikes. This raises computer output to 70 and cuts bike production to 150 (see table 3). East switches entirely to bicycles, turning out 250. World output of both goods has risen. Both countries can consume more of both if they trade.

At what price? Neither will want to import what it could make more cheaply at home. So West will want at least five bikes per computer; and East will not give up more than 25 bikes per computer. Suppose the terms of trade are fixed at 12 bicycles per computer and that 120 bikes are exchanged for ten computers. Then West ends up with 270 bikes and 60 computers, and East with 130 bicycles and ten computers. Both are better off than they would be if they did not trade.

This is true even though West has an "absolute advantage" in making both computers and bikes. The reason is that each country has a different "comparative advantage". West's edge is greater in computers than in bicycles. East, although a costlier producer in both industries, is a relatively

Gains from trade   3

	Output and consumption under autarky		Output after specialisation		Consumption after trade	
	Bicycles	Computers	Bicycles	Computers	Bicycles	Computers
East	125	5	250	0	130	10
West	250	50	150	70	270	60

less-expensive maker of bikes. So long as each country specialises in products in which it has a comparative advantage, both will gain from trade.

Fair deal

Some critics of trade say that this theory misses the point. They argue that trade with developing countries, where wages tend to be lower and work hours longer than in Europe and North America, is "unfair", and will wipe out jobs in high-wage countries.

It is generally accepted that trade with poor countries has been one of the factors reducing the wages of unskilled workers, relative to skilled ones, in the United States. That said, the threat to rich-country workers from developing-country competition is often overstated.

For a start, it is important not to confuse absolute and comparative advantage. Even if developing countries were cheaper producers of everything under the sun, they could not have a comparative advantage in everything. There would still be work for people in high-wage countries to do.

Moreover, it is not true that countries with cheap labour always have lower costs. Wage differences generally reflect differences in productivity; companies in low-wage countries often need far more labour to produce a given amount of output, and must deal with less efficient communications and transportation systems. In most cases hourly wages are not decisive in determining where a product is made.

Suppose that the "fair traders" succeed in eradicating international differences in production costs, so that a given product cost precisely the same to make in different countries. In that case, no country would have a comparative advantage, and hence there would be no trade. Rich-country workers, who are also consumers, would lose.

At first blush, real-world trade patterns would seem to challenge the theory of comparative advantage. Most trade occurs between countries which do not have huge cost differences. America's biggest trading partner, for instance, is Canada. Well over half the exports from France,

Germany and Italy go to other European Union countries. Moreover, these countries sell similar things to each other: cars made in France are exported to Germany, while German cars go to France, dependent largely upon consumers' differing tastes rather than differences in costs.

The importance of geography and the role of similar but different products appealing to diverse tastes expand our understanding of why trade occurs. But they do not overturn the fundamental insight of the theory of comparative advantage. The agricultural exports of Australia, say, or Saudi Arabia's reliance on oil, clearly stem from their natural resources. Poorer countries tend to have relatively more unskilled labour, so they tend to export simple manufactures, such as clothing. So long as relative production costs differ between countries, there are gains to be had from trade.

Enter the state

What is confusing, perhaps, is that comparative advantage is often the product of history and chance, not of differences in natural resources or workers' skills. A stark example is America's civil-aircraft industry. There is no God-given reason why the production costs of jumbo jets, relative to other goods and services, should be lower in America than in Japan. But they are: America's early embrace of airmail, its large purchases of military aircraft and the great public demand for air travel in a large country all helped American plane makers get big early on, allowing them to achieve per-plane costs lower than those of foreign competitors.

A logical question follows: if comparative advantage can be created, why should governments not help create it? The idea is that through subsidies, such as those given by several European nations to finance the European-made Airbus passenger jets, governments can promote their own national champions and hobble foreign rivals. Since the late 1970s, a stream of theoretical research has shown that governments can use such "strategic trade policy", in principle, to make their own citizens better off.

The theoretical work, however, has shed little light on how, in practice, governments can select which industries to subsidise – and which to tax in order to finance the subsidy – so that, in the end, the country's welfare is improved. And then there is the matter of politics: once the government has agreed to support "strategic" industries, every industry will assert its strategic importance in order to share in the pie. Under real-world political pressures, the allure of strategic trade policy fades quickly.

Governments' intervention in trade is not limited to fine calculations of strategy. There is plenty of aid to politically sensitive industries, such as agriculture. And governments often rush to obstruct "unfair" competition from abroad.

Anti-dumping duties are a case in point. In theory, these are intended to keep foreign producers from "dumping" goods abroad at less than their cost of production, by subjecting the goods to extra import duties. In practice, they are a politically neat method of protecting a particular industry. Once the favoured weapon of rich-world governments, anti-dumping duties have been been taken up eagerly by developing countries (see table 4).

Despite such machinations, world trade flows more freely than it used to. This is due mainly to international agreements under which governments agree to forswear trade barriers – most notably, the General Agreement

Anti-trade		4
Summary of anti-dumping actions, 1996		
	New measures	Actions in force*
South Africa	30	31
Argentina	23	30
EU	23	153
United States	21	311
India	20	15
Australia	17	47
Brazil	17	24
Korea	13	14
Indonesia	8	na
Israel	6	na
Canada	5	96
Peru	5	4
New Zealand	4	27
Chile	3	0
Mexico	3	95
Venezuela	3	3
Malaysia	2	na
Colombia	1	7
Guatemala	1	na
Thailand	1	1
Japan	0	3
Singapore	0	2
Turkey	0	37
Total	206	900
Source: WTO		*31 December 1996.

on Tariffs and Trade (GATT). All told, there have been eight rounds of GATT talks since 1947, in which countries have cut their import tariffs. Tariffs on manufactured goods are now down to around 4% in industrial countries.

The Uruguay GATT round ended in 1993. It did much more than cut tariffs on goods. It heralded a big institutional change, creating the World Trade Organisation (WTO), which now boasts 132 members, as a successor to GATT. It also made three big changes to the rules of world trade. First, it began the process of opening up the most heavily protected industries, agriculture and textiles.

Second, the Uruguay round vastly extended the scope of international trade rules. The rules were extended to cover services, as well as goods. New issues, such as the use of spurious technical barriers to keep out imports and the protection of foreigners' "intellectual property", such as patents and copyrights, were addressed for the first time.

Of these new agreements, the one in services is especially interesting. A lot of trade no longer involves putting things into a crate and sending them abroad on ships. Many services can be traded internationally: a British construction firm can build an airport in Japan, and an American insurance company can sell its products in Germany.

Lots to talk about

The WTO estimates that commercial-service trade was worth $1.2 trillion in 1996, around one-quarter of the value of trade in goods. The services agreement, plus a deal on telecommunications trade, should ease the barriers that limit such trade.

The third change wrought by the Uruguay round was the creation of a new system for settling disputes. In the past, countries could (and sometimes did) break GATT rules with impunity. Under the new system, decisions can be blocked only by a consensus of WTO members. Once found guilty of breaking the rules (and after appeal), countries are supposed to mend their ways. This system seems to be working better than the old one, and is helping to build up the new institution's credibility.

Despite these advances, there are plenty of difficulties ahead. China, the world's second-biggest economy, and its 11th-biggest exporter, is not yet a member of the WTO, and talks on its accession have been difficult. [It is scheduled to join in December 2001.] Some countries, such as America and France, would like to see the WTO address itself to the relationships between trade, labour standards and the environment. Others, notably India and Malaysia, are opposed. In 1996 the WTO's members agreed to study the issues, but there is no agreement about whether the WTO should go further.

The material on pages 72–78 first appeared in a Schools Brief in *The Economist* in November 1997.

Delivering the goods

The vast expansion in international trade owes much to a revolution in the business of moving freight. Here is how it happened

IF SHOP WINDOWS everywhere seem to be filled with imports, there is a reason. International trade has been growing at a startling pace. While the global economy has been expanding at a bit over 3% a year, the volume of trade has been rising at a compound annual rate of about twice that. In 1996 some $5.2 trillion of goods was sent from one country to another, up from $2 trillion a decade earlier. Foreign products, from meat to machinery, play a more important role in almost every economy in the world, and foreign markets now tempt businesses that never much worried about sales beyond their nation's borders.

What lies behind this explosion in international commerce? The general worldwide decline in trade barriers, such as tariffs and import quotas, is surely one explanation. The economic opening of countries that have traditionally been minor players in the world economy, such as China and Mexico, is another. But one force behind the import-export boom has passed all but unnoticed: the rapidly falling cost of getting goods to market.

In the world of trade theory, shipping costs do not matter. Goods, once they have been made, are assumed to move instantly and costlessly from place to place. The real world, however, is full of frictions. Exporting Italian steel to Britain may be good business if freight costs £20 ($34) a tonne and impractical if it costs £100 a tonne. Cheap labour may make Chinese clothing competitive in America, but if delays in shipment tie up working capital and cause winter coats to arrive in April, trade may lose its advantages. Freight costs, in short, can have a huge impact on both the overall volume of trade and on individual countries' trade patterns.

They are a far less daunting obstacle than they used to be. This reflects two notable economic trends. First, the world economy has become far less transport-intensive than it once was. Second, the transportation industry has changed in remarkable ways, making it far cheaper and easier to ship goods around the world.

Neighbourly   **1**
Leading world exporters, 1996

	Biggest export market*
United States	Canada (21.3)
Germany	EU (56.4)
Japan	US (27.5)
France	EU (62.6)
Britain	EU (52.7)
Italy	EU (55.4)
Netherlands	EU (78.1)
Canada	US (82.3)
Belgium-Lux.	EU (70.4)
China	Hong Kong (21.8)
South Korea	US (16.7)
Singapore	US (18.4)
Taiwan	Hong Kong (39.6)
Spain	EU (79.0)

Source: IMF   *% of total exports.

Brawn and brains

At the turn of the 20th century, agriculture and manufacturing were the two most important sectors almost everywhere. Together, they accounted for about 70% of total output in Germany, Italy and France, and 40–50% in America, Britain and Japan.

International commerce was therefore dominated by raw materials, such as wheat, wood and iron ore, or processed commodities, such as meat and steel. In 1900 "crude materials" and "crude food" made up 41% of America's exports, by value, and 45% of its imports. The story in Britain was similar. Basic materials and foodstuffs, both processed and unprocessed, accounted for 75% of imports and 20% of exports. These sorts of products are heavy and bulky. The cost of transporting them is relatively high, compared with the value of the goods themselves, so transport costs had much to do with the volume of international trade.

Countries still trade disproportionately with their geographic neighbours (see chart 1). Over time, however, world output has shifted into goods whose value is unrelated to their size and weight. Finished manufactured products, not raw commodities, dominate the flow of trade (see chart 2). And thanks to technological advances, such as light-weight composites to replace steel and microprocessors to do the job of huge control panels, manufactured goods themselves have tended to become lighter and less bulky. As a result, less transportation is required for every dollar's worth of imports or exports.

To see how this influences trade, consider the business of making disk drives for computers. Most of the world's disk drive manufacturing is concentrated in South-East Asia. This is possible only because disk drives, while valuable, are small, light and so cost little to ship. Computer manufacturers in Japan or Texas will not face hugely bigger freight bills if they import drives from Singapore rather than buying them domestically. Distance therefore poses no obstacle to the

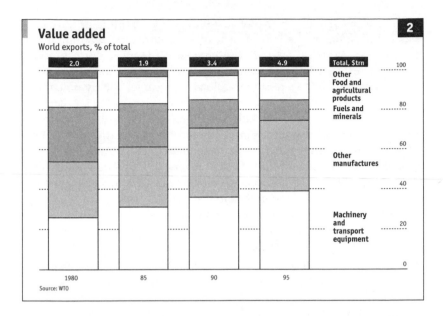

Value added
World exports, % of total

globalisation of the disk-drive industry.

This is even more true of the fast-growing information industries. Films and compact discs cost little to transport, even by aeroplane. Computer software can be "exported" without ever loading it on to a ship or a cargo plane, simply by transmitting it over telephone lines from one country to another. In such cases, freight rates and cargo-handling schedules become insignificant factors in deciding where to make the product.

The trend towards less transport intensity is clearly visible in trade statistics. The average dollar value of a unit of exported manufactured goods rose at an annual rate of 2% from 1990 to 1995, according to the World Trade Organisation. As that unit of exports is worth more and more, the cost of shipping it matters less and less. Businesses can locate based on other considerations, such as the availability of labour and good airline service for peripatetic employees, while worrying less about the cost of delivering their output.

At the same time, the cost of shipping itself has fallen sharply. In many countries, deregulation has helped to drive the process along. But behind the scenes, a series of technological innovations, known broadly as "containerisation" and "intermodal transportation", has led to swift productivity improvements in cargo-handling – and, in the process, has lowered one of the biggest obstacles to trade.

Forty years ago, the very physical process of exporting or importing was arduous. Imagine a European textile manufacturer wanting to sell its wares in America. First, at the company's loading dock, workers would have lifted bolts of fabric into the back of a lorry. The lorry would have headed to a port and unloaded its cargo, bolt by bolt, into a dockside warehouse.

As a ship prepared to set sail, longshoremen would have removed the bolts from the warehouse and hoisted them into the hold, where other longshoremen would have stowed them in place. At the American end, the process would have been reversed: dockers would have hoisted the cloth out of the hold, carried it to storage and then, eventually, placed it into a lorry that would take it to its destination.

Simply arranging this sort of shipment was a complex task. The repeated cargo-handling and storage would have been expensive, and the cloth would have spent days, or even weeks, sitting in warehouses. As likely as not, portions of the shipment would have been damaged or stolen along the way. Add in high customs duties and importing was a costly affair.

Smoother sailing

That first began to change in 1955, when an American road-hauling magnate named Malcom McLean hit upon a more efficient way to ship goods. Under his original scheme, a lorry body, wheels and all, was unhitched from the driver's cab and lifted on to the deck of a ship, eliminating the need for dockworkers to handle the individual items inside the cargo compartment. This method soon gave way to the use of metal containers that could be separated from the lorry's chassis and wheels. With the chassis left at dockside, the containers could be stacked several high aboard the ship.

Mr McLean's first ship, an oil tanker called the *Ideal-X*, made its initial voyage from New York to Houston in 1956 with lorry bodies on its deck. In 1965 ships with containers on board began crossing the Atlantic. Ports were forced to adapt, as narrow piers in urban centres were replaced by large docks on the edge of town, alongside patios to hold thousands of containers.

The container crane, a new invention, made it possible to load and unload containers without capsizing the ship. The adoption of standard container sizes allowed almost any box to be transported on any ship. By 1967 dual-purpose ships, carrying loose cargo in the hold and containers on the deck, were giving way to all-container vessels that moved

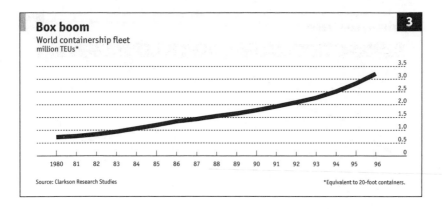

Box boom
World containership fleet
million TEUs*

Source: Clarkson Research Studies   *Equivalent to 20-foot containers.

hundreds – and now thousands – of boxes at a time.

Containerisation had huge consequences for world trade. The most obvious was that the cost of shipping fell precipitously, as ships could be loaded by a few dozen longshoremen rather than hundreds, and as pilferage was much reduced. The need to build wooden crates to protect individual items was eliminated, making it feasible to ship consumer goods such as toys and stereo systems halfway around the world. International shipping capacity soared (see chart 3), driven by large increases in the volume of goods shipped.

Mixing modes

The shipping container transformed ocean shipping into a highly efficient, intensely competitive business. But getting the cargo to and from the dock was a different story. National governments, by and large, kept a much firmer hand on lorry and railroad tariffs than on charges for ocean freight. Almost everywhere, rates were either set by state bureaucrats or were subject to their approval. New companies could enter the freight business only with great difficulty, and were subject to tight restrictions.

This started changing in the mid-1970s, when America began to deregulate its transportation industry. First airlines, then road hauliers and railways, were freed from restrictions on what they could carry, where they could haul it and what price they could charge. Lorries were no longer forced to run empty because they were licensed to carry goods on only one leg of a round-trip journey. Railways were no longer obliged to maintain unprofitable branch lines, but could focus on moving freight in large volumes over long distances.

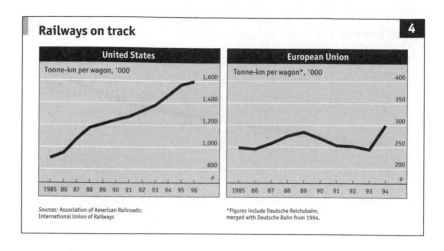

Railways on track | **4**

Sources: Association of American Railroads; International Union of Railways

*Figures include Deutsche Reichsbahn, merged with Deutsche Bahn from 1994.

Big productivity gains resulted (see chart 4). Between 1985 and 1996, for example, America's freight railways dramatically reduced their employment, their trackage, and their fleets of locomotives and freight wagons – while increasing the amount of cargo they hauled. Europe's railways have also shown marked, albeit smaller, productivity improvements. Road hauliers have also been able to improve utilisation of their fleets, thanks to measures ranging from satellite tracking of vehicles, which enables more precisely timed pick-ups and deliveries, to soliciting back-haul cargoes to fill vehicles that formerly returned empty to their home bases.

These advances have benefited shippers, as tariffs for both road freight and rail freight have fallen sharply (see chart 5). This made it feasible for companies located well inland to rely on imported components and to export, giving world trade yet another push. Impressed by the results, Japan and many emerging economies began to deregulate freight transport in the 1990s.

This freight revolution accelerated in the 1980s, as deregulation and new technology broke down the boundaries between different modes of transportation. For the first time, a manufacturer in, say, South Korea could ask a shipping line to deliver its exports to the American mid-west. The shipping line might strike a deal with a railway to haul the container from Los Angeles to Chicago; hire a road hauler to transport it from Chicago to South Bend; take responsibility for meeting delivery schedules at every stage of the journey; and send a single invoice for the entire shipment.

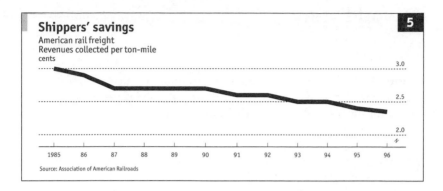

Shippers' savings **5**
American rail freight
Revenues collected per ton-mile
cents

Source: Association of American Railroads

Intermodalism has given rise to cargo companies, such as FedEx and UPS, which specialise in using a combination of aircraft and lorries to deliver freight fast. It has led railway companies to build tracks at dockside, so containers can be moved directly from ships on to trains. And it has led to partnerships that would have been unthinkable a decade ago.

In Chicago, for example, lorries can pull into a railway marshalling yard, where overhead cranes can lift their containers on to waiting flatcar trains at the rate of one every 30 seconds. Two days later, having stopped en route only to change crews, the train arrives at a precise time in Los Angeles, nearly 2,000 miles away. Such careful management is squeezing yet more costs out of the transport system, making trade all the easier.

In America, the period of huge productivity gains in transportation may be almost over after two decades of deregulation. But in most other countries, the process still has far to go. Although trade itself has been liberalised, transportation has been slow to follow. State ownership of railways and airlines, regulation of freight rates and toleration of anti-competitive practices, such as ocean-shipping cartels and cargo-handling monopolies, all keep the cost of shipping unnecessarily high and deter international trade. Bringing these barriers down would help the world's economies grow even closer.

The material on pages 79–85 first appeared in a Schools Brief in *The Economist* in November 1997.

A world view

Culture is local. So why are the news media and the entertainment industry increasingly global? And does it matter if we all watch the same shows and listen to the same songs?

IN MOST CORNERS of the world, the name of Mickey Mouse will elicit at least a glimmer of recognition. Walt Disney's most famous creation was one of the first stars with a global name. Now, Mickey has become a symbol – of the influence the United States has on global media, and particularly on television. Flick a remote control almost anywhere on earth, and you will see American products: Hollywood films, the CNN news channel, television shows such as "Friends" or "The X-Files".

Until recently, globalisation and Americanisation have gone hand in hand. But now the media business, and especially television, are becoming increasingly multinational. That trend is inextricably linked with another: an activity that was once mainly state-owned and monopolistic is becoming privatised and competitive. Both developments are driven partly by technological change, which has both increased the production and distribution capacity of media companies, and reduced some of their costs.

For the moment, the scale of America's role in global media, both as exporter and investor, is unique. Other countries are big producers of entertainment: India, for instance, makes more films each year than America (see chart 1), and the Mexican Televisa network is helping to launch digital television in South America. But the giants of American media, such as Time Warner, Walt Disney and Viacom, dominate entertainment export markets and lead joint ventures which are creating new television businesses around the world. Although some of the world's largest book and newspaper publishers are based elsewhere, America is home to most of the world's largest audio-visual companies.

Governments have not fostered the globalisation of media. Instead, even more than in other industries, they resist foreign investment. Most countries restrict foreign ownership of television channels. In continental Europe in particular, some politicians want to go further, and ration imports of foreign television. But do such measures make sense? Is the globalisation of media really a threat to local cultures? And what forces are driving it?

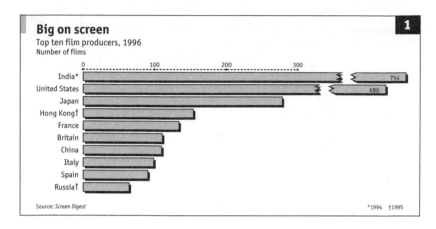

Big on screen `1`
Top ten film producers, 1996
Number of films

India*			754
United States			686
Japan			
Hong Kong†			
France			
Britain			
China			
Italy			
Spain			
Russia†			

Source: *Screen Digest*   *1994 †1995

Tuning in

The globalisation of television is essentially a consequence of the transition of broadcasting from a medium in scarce supply to one of plentiful capacity. For most of the 20th century, the limitations of spectrum
restricted the number of television and radio channels. That is why, in
most countries, the state has owned and run broadcasting – sometimes
at arm's length, as in Britain and Japan, sometimes directly. Even where,
as in the United States, broadcasting has been a commercial and competitive business from the start, it has been heavily regulated.

The transition to plenty began in the United States. The sheer size of
the country, and the absence of public subsidies for transmission facilities, has meant that the quality of over-the-air television signals has
been worse than in other rich countries. So most American homes have
long had the option of television delivered by cable. As even quite rudimentary cable can carry many more channels of television than can be
broadcast over the air, America has long had far more television channels than other countries.

In the 1980s multichannel television began to spread around the
world. The main driver was the falling cost of launching communications satellites: the technology that had once allowed the Soviet Union
and America to spy on each other became an inexpensive way to transmit television signals. Initially, only cable companies could afford the
huge antennas required to capture those signals, which they would then
retransmit to fee-paying subscribers. In the late 1980s, miniaturisation
made it possible for individuals to pick up those signals directly with
dishes small enough to be mounted on the roof of a home.

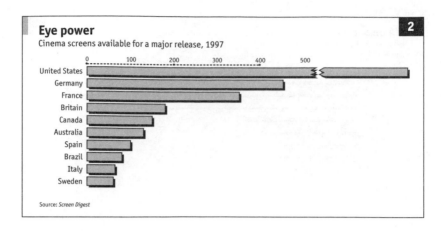

Eye power 2

Cinema screens available for a major release, 1997

Source: *Screen Digest*

The result was a big increase in the capacity of broadcasting systems. What could fill that capacity? National television industries tended to be geared to filling the limited number of slots on domestic channels – and their output was often unadventurous or just plain dull.

American media groups, though, had off-the-peg channels such as CNN, Nickelodeon and MTV to offer. They were also used to producing for a competitive market; they had the world's most successful film industry; and they had huge libraries of cartoons, elderly soap operas, classic films and other programmes ripe for reuse.

This material has been the basis of the expansion of global media, an expansion that is now accelerating with the arrival of digital television. Digital compression typically allows between eight and 12 channels to occupy the same capacity required by a single analogue channel. Starting with satellite, but moving on to cable and over-the-air broadcasting, the ability to transmit television programmes will thus become eight to 12 times greater – and the number is rising.

Two other factors have helped to create a market for American exports. One is language and culture; the other, the curious economics of the business.

Well before the birth of multi-channel television, American films dominated world cinema. True, in the 1950s and 1960s, they competed with those made in Europe. But by the 1970s European film-making was moribund. And American films have always been more successful at tapping a global mass market than any others.

The average investment for a theatrical feature film is $12.3m in the United States, compared with $6m in Britain and less than $5m in

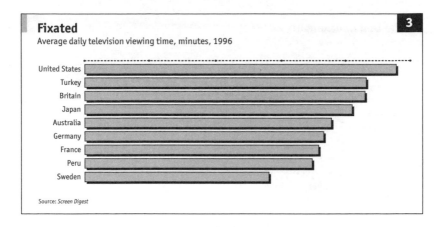

Fixated **3**

Average daily television viewing time, minutes, 1996

United States
Turkey
Britain
Japan
Australia
Germany
France
Peru
Sweden

Source: *Screen Digest*

France. In addition, the American culture that they package seems to have a universal appeal that may have something to do with America's melting pot or simply with Hollywood's commercial cunning. And English has become, thanks to the combination of British colonialism and American commercialism, a global tongue. All these factors give the American entertainment industry advantages that Japan, say, or Germany cannot easily emulate.

Add to this set of cultural strengths a second factor: the huge advantages brought by the size of the American domestic market for entertainment. According to *Screen Digest*, a British trade magazine, a major film release in the United States is typically shown on 1,300 screens, compared with 450 in Germany and even fewer in other rich countries (see chart 2).

Television shows enjoy a similarly vast home market (see chart 3). This is important, because television production is a fixed-cost business. It costs little more to bring the "Oprah Winfrey" show to its first audience than to its millions of viewers around the world. The main expense is Ms Winfrey. The producers of such shows can cover their costs at home, and then sell around the globe at prices that local programmers find hard to match. Most European broadcasters find that the programming they make costs between two and five times as much as programming bought from outside (see chart 4). Imports are thus the cheapest way to fill the airwaves.

Side by side with the increasing import of foreign programming, there has been a growth of foreign – again, mainly American – investment in media. Once more, television has been the chief focus. Usually, investment takes the form of joint ventures, often of labyrinthine com-

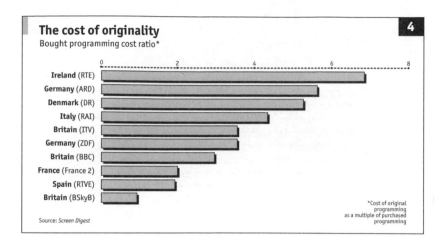

The cost of originality
Bought programming cost ratio*

	0	2	4	6	8
Ireland (RTE)					
Germany (ARD)					
Denmark (DR)					
Italy (RAI)					
Britain (ITV)					
Germany (ZDF)					
Britain (BBC)					
France (France 2)					
Spain (RTVE)					
Britain (BSkyB)					

*Cost of original programming as a multiple of purchased programming

Source: *Screen Digest*

4

plexity. This is because restrictions on foreign ownership make it hard for foreigners to buy local stations and networks, and because cultural differences make it useful to have a local guide.

The switch to digital is creating new opportunities for foreign participation. Partly, this reflects the falling cost of distribution, as digitisation has cut annual operating costs. In addition, governments that would never allow foreigners to buy an over-the-air analogue channel seem willing to let them experiment with digital channels. The same applies to the mobile-telephone business, where governments have been more willing to allow competition with digital than with analogue telephones.

Go home, Mickey Mouse

But television is not telephony. When foreign companies buy into local media groups, or foreign shows appear on television screens, people often feel much more concerned than they do about other sorts of foreign investment and imports.

That is understandable. Media and entertainment play special roles in society. The fact that, say, Rockefeller Centre in New York is bought by a Japanese company may be galling but has few political repercussions. In Britain, where one-third of newspaper circulation is controlled by a single foreign company (Rupert Murdoch's News Corp, based in Australia), many people resent what they see as foreign influence on national politics. Some worry that this foreign invasion will destroy local cultures. Others fear the homogenisation of distinctive national and regional tastes.

Last, some countries fret about the economics of globalised media. European broadcasters in particular have become huge markets for imported television programming. According to *Screen Digest*, Germany, France and Britain each spends more on such imports than Australia, Canada and Japan combined.

More than half their spending goes on American imports, with the result that the continent runs a large and growing deficit on this account. All told, Europe buys about $2 billion a year of American television programmes; Britain, the only European country with sizeable programme exports, sells a meagre $85m-worth to the entire North American market.

Some European governments therefore advocate quotas on the proportion of foreign programming that national channels can show. After a long debate, the European Union agreed in 1997 to a directive called "Television without Frontiers". Its aim was to keep frontiers in place, by insisting that half the programming shown on European television be made within the EU. In the face of intense opposition, led by Britain, the words "where practicable" were added, rendering the provision ineffectual.

Do attempts to restrict foreign influence in the media make sense? Take, first, controls on foreign ownership of broadcasting. When spectrum was extremely scarce, it was defensible for governments to allocate it. Once many homes have access to hundreds of digitally compressed channels, the logic diminishes.

It is, of course, undesirable for one company, foreign or local, unduly to dominate a market; but big is not necessarily bad. A single television group producing several channels with different viewpoints is surely preferable to several groups with almost identical channels. In a world with many channels, television may well become a more differentiated product, more akin to the multiplicity of magazines than the narrow market for national newspapers.

Indeed, foreign ownership may sometimes be a way to ensure diversity. In countries where excessive domination by one group is a problem (such as Italy, where virtually all commercial networks are owned by a company controlled by Silvio Berlusconi, the problem is more likely to be too little foreign investment than too much.

Foreign ownership does not necessarily reinforce the tendency to buy foreign programming. In television, as everywhere else, companies usually seek to provide the goods their customers seem to want. In Asia, Rupert Murdoch's plan for a pan-regional satellite channel has been a failure: instead, he has been forced to develop channels to suit local tastes. Almost everywhere, the programmes audiences like to watch the most are their own country's.

Look at the top-rated shows in almost any country, and most or all will be local products. Audiences watch imports only as a second choice – and American television channels increasingly repackage their shows when they take them abroad to give them a local presenter and a local feel. In China, for example, Shanghai TV is making a Chinese version of "Sesame Street", backed by America's General Electric, to show its 100m viewers.

In fact, the technological change that makes it less expensive to distribute American programming around the world will sometimes help to reinforce local culture. True, global competition threatens the survival of the high-cost programming that many state-owned broadcasters in Europe produce. But technology will cut the cost of producing cheap-and-cheerful local programming. It will also be less expensive to distribute minority programming to scattered audiences around the world.

In 1997, for example, a group of Taiwanese investors launched Space TV Systems, a group of eight digital direct-to-home channels, in Chinese, Vietnamese, Japanese and Korean, for Asians in North America and Australia. In this way, the globalisation of media may underwrite a globalisation not merely of Mickey Mouse, but of the many cultures valued by people who are separated by distance from their geographic or ethnic origins.

The material on pages 86–92 first appeared in a Schools Brief in *The Economist* in November 1997.

Worldbeater, Inc

What role do multinational corporations play in integrating the world's economies?

MULTINATIONAL CORPORATIONS STAND at the heart of the debate over the merits of global economic integration. Their critics portray them as bullies, using their heft to exploit workers and natural resources with no regard for the economic well-being of any country or community. Their advocates see multinationals as a triumph for global capitalism, bringing advanced technology to poorer countries and low-cost products to the wealthier ones.

Both of these stereotypes have some truth to them. But it would be wrong to portray the multinational corporation as either good or evil. Companies become multinational in many different ways and for many different reasons. Their impact on the global economy is far from simple to determine.

There is no doubting that multinationals matter. They are one of the main conduits through which globalisation takes place. In 1995, multi-nationals cranked out some $7 trillion in sales through their foreign affiliates – an amount greater than the world's total exports. Multinational firms' sales outside their home countries are growing 20–30% faster than exports.

Multinationals also play an important role in global investment. At the end of 1996, the total stock of foreign direct investment – plants, equipment and property owned by businesses outside their home countries – stood at over $3 trillion. Worldwide, foreign direct investment has been growing three times as fast as total investment (see chart 1), although it still accounts for only 6% of the annual investment of rich industrial economies. In addition, the UN's 1997 World Investment Report estimated that 70% of all international royalties on technology involve payments between parent firms and their foreign affiliates, showing that multinationals play a key role in disseminating technology around the globe.

Few companies, even the most familiar household names (see table 2), are truly global. The average multinational produces more than two-thirds of its output and locates two-thirds of its employees in its home country. Although both operate worldwide, the culture of General

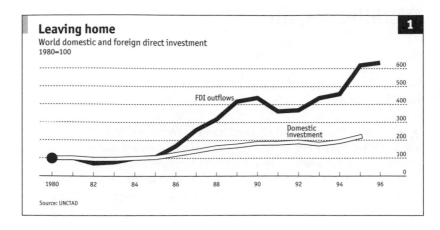

Leaving home   **1**
World domestic and foreign direct investment
1980=100

FDI outflows

Domestic
investment

Source: UNCTAD

Motors is distinctively American, that of Volkswagen identifiably German. Yet there is no denying that multinationals are the main force behind worldwide flows of capital, goods and services.

Scale and scope

In the public mind, globalisation and multinational corporations are closely related. The stereotype has giant companies shifting production from one country to another in search of the cheapest sources of labour, without regard for the well-being of either the high-wage workers who stand to lose their jobs or the low-paid ones who will be hired. Yet globalisation could just as easily make multinational companies less necessary.

Why? As transport costs and trade barriers fall, it becomes easier to serve foreign markets by exporting, rather than establishing factories and research centres around the world. And as capital markets become more integrated and liquid, it is easier for single-country firms to raise money by selling bonds or shares. Big American, Japanese or European firms, which have benefited from their ready access to capital, should therefore be losing one of their main advantages.

This suggests that the economic logic of the multinational company lies elsewhere. Some explanations appear more valid than others, but none fully clarifies why multinationals became so prominent at the end of the 20th century.

The most common explanation for multinationals' growth is economies of scale. In certain industries, the argument goes, firms can become more efficient by becoming bigger and producing more. What

At a location near you
Top 15 TNCs by foreign assets, 1995

Company	Industry	Foreign assets as % of total	Foreign sales as % of total	Foreign employment as % of total
Royal Dutch/Shell	Energy	67.8	73.3	77.9
Ford	Automotive	29.0	30.6	29.8
General Electric	Electronics	30.4	24.4	32.4
Exxon	Energy	73.1	79.6	53.7
General Motors	Automotive	24.9	29.2	33.9
Volkswagen	Automotive	84.8	60.8	44.4
IBM	Computers	51.9	62.7	50.1
Toyota	Automotive	30.5	45.1	23.0
Nestlé	Food	86.9	98.2	97.0
Bayer	Chemicals	89.8	63.3	54.6
ABB	Electrical equipment	84.7	87.2	93.9
Nissan	Automotive	42.7	44.2	43.5
Elf Aquitaine	Energy	54.5	65.4	47.5
Mobil	Energy	61.8	65.9	52.2
Daimler-Benz	Automotive	39.2	63.2	22.2

Source: UNCTAD

better way to accomplish this than by serving a global market?

Upon further inspection, however, the notion that economies of scale force companies to become multinationals does not hold up. Consider aircraft manufacturing, an industry in which a big producer has enormous cost advantages over a small one. This industry is dominated by two firms, Boeing and Airbus Industrie. Boeing assembles almost all of its aircraft in the United States, although it buys components from subcontractors around the world. Airbus, which is made up of four separate firms in four different European countries, manufactures only in those countries and relies on exports to sell its aircraft elsewhere. The mere existence of significant scale economies has not forced either to become a true multinational.

Firms may, however, find economies of scale at a level other than that of the factory floor. Coca-Cola is a case in point. Scale is not a huge advantage on the manufacturing side of its business, which involves blending water, gas and a special syrup. Scale economies come into play in other areas, such as reinforcing its brand by making a global marketing effort and helping its bottlers, most of whom are independent, learn from the experiences of their counterparts in other countries. These scale effects have driven Coca-Cola to become a highly multinational company.

Another explanation for the growth in multinationalism is vertical integration. In some industries, the interdependence of suppliers and users of a particular resource makes it difficult for such firms to co-operate at arm's length, since there is always the risk that one will try to undermine the other. This is the reason many firms integrate vertically, buying up their suppliers or their customers. Sometimes, those suppliers or customers will be abroad, turning the acquiring firms into a multinational.

A third reason for the spread of multinationals is that they tend to be successful. In any business, inefficient firms will eventually fold, giving way to those that can earn higher profits. As the world economy becomes more integrated, it is to be expected that the companies most adept at crossing borders are those that prosper. It should come as no surprise that firms from richer countries do this best. As a rule, they have been exposed to more competition in their home markets and are therefore well equipped for international competitive battles.

There is yet one other reason for firms to operate as multinationals: because everyone else is doing it. Many companies exist to serve other companies, rather than household consumers. If multinational car manufacturers want to use the same headlights in cars assembled in different countries, then headlight manufacturers must become multinational, too. This is why consulting firms and accountancies have been falling over one another to build seamless global networks. Although deregulation and privatisation have had a big effect on the telecoms industry, the demands of corporate customers are helping propel the globalisation of that industry.

Credit the critics

The reasoning above suggests that the growth of multinational companies is fairly benign. But that is not always the case.

For one thing, multinationals' size and scale can make it possible for them to exert power in an exploitative way. A company whose facilities are located in a single country has no alternative but to comply with that country's laws and social norms, unless it wishes to import products made by others rather than making them itself. A multinational, however, can move production: if America's worker-safety law is too restrictive, the company can move its factory to Mexico. It can also lower its tax bill by using internal pricing to shift profits from high-tax countries to low-tax ones.

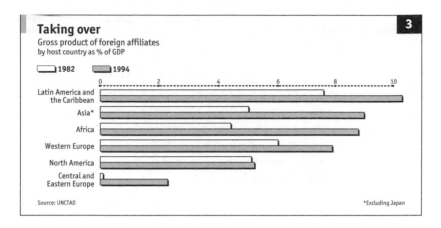

Taking over `3`
Gross product of foreign affiliates
by host country as % of GDP

1982   1994

Latin America and the Caribbean
Asia*
Africa
Western Europe
North America
Central and Eastern Europe

Source: UNCTAD   *Excluding Japan

This flexibility may make it harder for governments to raise revenue, protect the environment and promote worker safety. Critics fear an undesirable "race to the bottom", with governments reducing desirable social protections to attract investment by multinationals.

Others point out that the race can be healthy in so far as it forces governments to be careful before imposing costly regulations and taxes. Certainly, many developing countries are eager to be "exploited" by as many multinationals as possible.

Another common criticism is that multinationals are exporting jobs to low-wage countries. This may be true in some industries, such as textiles and electronics. But in most cases it is exaggerated. Labour costs now make up only 5–10% of production costs in OECD countries, down from 25% in the 1970s. Multinationals tend to be motivated more by the other considerations that have been mentioned, rather than simple wage-cutting exercises.

Although the social impacts are often misstated, some multinational expansions are indeed unequivocally bad, with no offsetting benefits. Since most company bosses gain esteem (and, studies show, more pay) from operating a bigger outfit, it is no surprise that they expand at every opportunity, whether it is through a merger or a direct foray into a new market. As globalisation takes hold, these adventures are increasingly of a multinational nature. In some cases they represent a wasteful use of shareholders' capital.

Today, as for many years, roughly three-fifths of all foreign direct investment goes into wealthy countries and two-fifths into "developing" countries. Those two fifths, however, are not flowing into the same

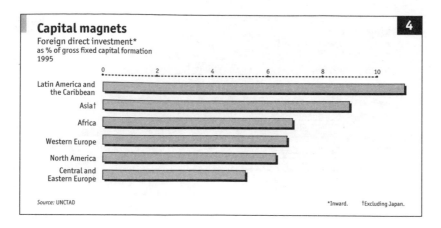

Capital magnets 4
Foreign direct investment*
as % of gross fixed capital formation
1995

	0	2	4	6	8	10
Latin America and the Caribbean						
Asia†						
Africa						
Western Europe						
North America						
Central and Eastern Europe						

Source: UNCTAD   *Inward.   †Excluding Japan.

countries; China, now the leading recipient of foreign investment among developing countries, received almost none in the 1980s.

In those days, a large share of direct investment in developing countries went into the extraction of natural resources, especially oil, for shipment abroad. Now, however, a much bigger share of it aims to tap local markets. As they become wealthier, people are able to buy more cars, computers and other consumer products. This is why car makers are racing to build plants in countries such as Thailand and Brazil: not to export to Japan and America, but to meet rising demand within South-East Asia and South America. Multinationals are more prominent in these developing economies than in richer ones (see chart 3).

The flows to developing countries, therefore, are going directly to regions with the highest growth prospects (see chart 4). In 1996 Asia, excluding Japan, captured $80 billion, around two-thirds of the developing-country total; Latin America pulled in another $39 billion. In Eastern Europe, which enjoyed huge inflows in 1994–95, the tap was suddenly shut off in 1996, as governments sold fewer state-owned companies. Africa, despite its rich natural resources, receives almost no foreign direct investment, because few in the region can afford rich-world consumer products.

Size isn't everything

Around half of all foreign direct investment involves mergers and acquisitions. These deals help companies to achieve economies of scale in marketing and distribution, for example, and they allow well-managed firms to take over poorly managed ones. Many of those mergers have also been between firms which supply other multinationals with professional services, telecommunications and air travel, in an effort to develop global networks. For all of these reasons, such cross-border M&A activity occurs disproportionately among firms based in rich countries. This is why, for all the interest in developing countries, the United States was the world's biggest recipient of foreign direct investment in 1996.

In certain industries and for certain products, the importance of multinational companies is increasing quickly. But the trend is easy to overstate. Most economic activity – cutting hair, driving taxi cabs, renovating houses – is still performed on a small scale. Most industries operate, if not at the level of the town or neighbourhood, then on a national basis. Even in manufacturing, speed, innovation and proximity to customers can matter more than sheer size. Being multinational is no guarantee of success.

The material on pages 93–9 first appeared in a Schools Brief in The Economist in November 1997.

II
THE BUSINESS OF GLOBALISATION

3
The spread of equity culture

This chapter looks at the rapid rise of equity culture around the world – the impact of its spread, and the means by which it could be made to spread further (and more effectively) still. Writing this survey in May 2001, John Peet looked ahead to the effects of a downturn on investors. The period after the terrorist attacks in America will continue to put markets to the test.

The rise and the fall

The fall in global equity markets has delivered a salutary shock to investors. But it should not stop the spread of an equity culture around the world

THE FIRST FEW months of 2001 were tragic in a classical sense: the hubris engendered by the long rise in most of the rich world's equity markets was duly followed by the nemesis of their sharp fall. Now the world is gloomily contemplating the possibility of the first sustained, globally shared, bear market for a quarter of a century. All those who have spent the past five years predicting a crash, even as the markets attained ever giddier heights – including, it should be confessed at once, *The Economist* – are feeling belatedly vindicated.

There have been other sharp falls in equity prices, and indeed several genuine bear markets, within living memory: in the 1970s, for example, or, even more painfully, over the past decade in Japan. But most of today's investors have never experienced them. Some may even have begun to assume that, perhaps thanks to the benign influence of America's Federal Reserve, it was normal for share prices to keep going up and up. Yet, historically, what is truly unprecedented is not the arrival of a bear market. It is the extraordinary two decades of rising share prices that ran until late 2000.

It is worth putting the figures on record before the bears stamp out the memory altogether. At the start of 1982 the Dow Jones Industrial Average stood at 875; the index for the exuberant and then newish Nasdaq stockmarket was 196. Eighteen years later, at the start of 2000, after the longest and strongest bull market in history, the two indices stood at 11,497 and 4,069, respectively. That meant they had run up average annual real increases over that period of 11.7% and 14.6%, respectively. And this included, among several other dips, the great crash of October 19th 1987, when the Dow fell by 23% in a single day.

The markets have now fallen back sharply, with the fall picking up speed as company profit warnings and worries about a recession have spread. The broad S&P 500 index has fallen by well over 20% from its January 2000 peak (a 20% fall is widely, if unofficially, regarded as defining a bear market). The Dow has fallen by less, but it too is well off

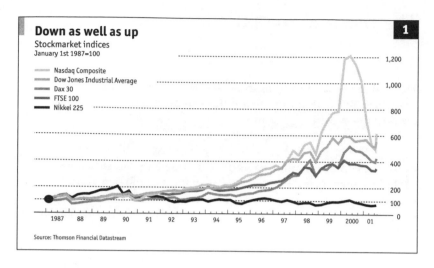

Down as well as up   **1**
Stockmarket indices
January 1st 1987=100

- Nasdaq Composite
- Dow Jones Industrial Average
- Dax 30
- FTSE 100
- Nikkei 225

Source: Thomson Financial Datastream

its peak. As for the technology-heavy Nasdaq stockmarket, it is down some 60% from its peak in March 2000. Plenty of blood-curdling figures have been hurled around. Some $3 trillion has been wiped off the nominal value of America's stockmarkets, equivalent to (though not comparable to: one is a stock, the other a flow) a third of the country's GDP. Around the world the paper loss amounts to as much as $7 trillion.

As chart 1 shows, Europe's stockmarkets have mostly followed a similar path to America's, with a slightly less dramatic rise followed by an equally sharp decline. Europe's smaller technology markets have seen an even bigger short-term boom and bust than the Nasdaq. Among rich countries' markets, only Japan's has followed an essentially different path, reaching a peak at the end of 1989 from which it crashed, and has since stagnated as worries about the economic outlook have increased. All in all, it seems safe to conclude that, whether or not the bear market persists, the long bull market is well and truly over.

Bulls and bears

What caused markets to put in such an unprecedentedly strong performance in the first place? Many things, not least two broadly successful decades of macroeconomic performance, with mostly low inflation and steady growth (except in Japan). Yet equity valuations, as we shall see, are a matter of huge controversy, and markets have a pronounced tendency to get out of line with economic fundamentals,

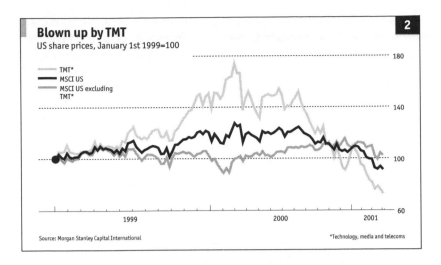

Blown up by TMT

US share prices, January 1st 1999=100

Source: Morgan Stanley Capital International

*Technology, media and telecoms

producing froth or even bubbles. The sharpness of the fall into a bear market, at a time when the real economy has done little more than slow down, suggests that this may have been happening in the 1990s.

It is the now notorious technology, media and telecoms (TMT), or "new economy", bubble that was largely responsible for the heady rise in the markets, and it is its deflation that was responsible for a big part of the subsequent fall. If TMT stocks are taken out of the equation, the rest of the market (sometimes called the "old economy") was much less buoyant in early 2000; until spring 2001, it seemed to be partly recovering, confirming its inverse relationship with TMT (see chart 2). Yet bear markets can always be defined away by excluding those sectors that have fallen farthest: that does not make them any less real. Besides, shares have declined right across the board.

Alongside the cyclical market rise, and now fall, there has been a structural factor at work in the 1980s and 1990s. This factor, which might be called the equitisation of world finance, forms the main theme of this survey, which will seek to answer one of the big questions of the moment: can the new "equity culture" around the world survive a bear market?

Equitisation is only part of a veritable revolution in finance that has taken place over the past 20 years. In most countries, including America, capital markets at the start of the 1980s played a much smaller role than they do today. Banks, once the staid but trusty handmaidens of industry, have been subject as never before to competition and to an erosion of their traditional functions. New financial instruments, from derivatives to high-yield ("junk") bonds, and from swaps to sophisticated options, have been invented and popularised. Securitisation has turned almost any income-producing asset into a tradable instrument. And technology has changed finance perhaps more than any other industry outside computing itself.

Under the buttonwood tree

It may seem surprising, against such a background of febrile change, that something as old-fashioned as equity should have come so strongly to the fore. Stock exchanges have, after all, been around for centuries. The New York Stock Exchange (NYSE) dates back to 1792, when traders met under a fabled buttonwood tree close to where the Big Board's floor still stands. The London Stock Exchange began trading in its present form in 1801. Amsterdam's bourse is older than either. Yet for most of their history, stock exchanges traded government bonds far more than equities. Until relatively recently interest in shares was limited, confined largely to wealthy individuals and a few institutions. But over the past two decades four related trends have changed that.

The first is rising issuance of equity on the public markets, not least shares in companies that had been either state-owned or privately held. Dick Grasso, the combative chairman of the NYSE, likes to cite his two conservative heroes of the 1980s, Margaret Thatcher and Ronald Reagan, as chief inspirations for both privatisation and the spread of share ownership. Mr Grasso now declares that "equity is the crude oil of the global economy". Ironically, the net supply of new equity in America has actually shrunk recently, thanks mainly to share buybacks by companies.

Elsewhere equity supply has steadily increased. Privatisation, a term coined only in the early 1980s, has given a huge boost to stockmarkets and equity ownership in Europe. The fashion for private or mutually owned firms to list on public stockmarkets, not least to raise capital more cheaply, has spread. The bear market will slow things down: global equity issuance in the first quarter of 2001 fell by 63% compared with a year earlier, to $48 billion. But it seems sure to pick up again.

Second, there has been a growing appreciation of the huge demographic challenge that faces most countries' pension systems. The old ways of relying on state pensions and pay-as-you-go financing both look increasingly unsatisfactory. Whatever soothing noises governments may make, few prospective beneficiaries now believe that they can depend on these systems in their old age. Instead, the trend is towards greater emphasis on privately funded pensions.

Within the private pension business itself, another significant change has been taking place: a steady shift from "defined benefit" to "defined contribution" schemes. In the first (also known as "final salary"), the employer guarantees the level of the pension and assumes the risk; in the second (often called "money purchase") the risk is shifted to the employee. Individual pension-fund investors, for instance those with 401(k) plans in America, are likely to be especially interested in equity investment. If demographic change is the biggest problem in the provision of pensions, equity has to be the biggest part of the solution.

Third, almost all investors, almost everywhere, have come to understand that, in the long run, only shares hold out the promise of sufficiently large returns to pay for people's pensions. Over the past two decades the notion that there are better returns to be had from equities, with less risk, than from almost any other financial asset has become entrenched in investors' minds – perhaps too much so, as they became used in that period to above-average annual returns in double figures. The result has been a proliferation of equity investing, and especially of equity mutual funds, first in America and Britain, but more recently even in such previously unpromising countries as Germany and France.

Today's bear market, if it endures, will certainly test the enthusiasm for this new-found equity culture. Indeed, one apparently perverse reason for welcoming the arrival of a bear market is that it will remind investors of the main reason why equities have offered better returns: because they are riskier. As the hackneyed phrase from the brochures, usually in small print, has it: "Shares can go down as well as up." If shares only ever went up, the long-run returns from investing in them would inevitably fall to match their lower risk.

It is because of the riskiness of equities that, over time, they outperform other investments, as repeated studies over many decades, including periods of previous bear markets, have confirmed. Table 3, drawn from a long-running annual equity-gilt study undertaken by Barclays Capital, shows comparisons for America of equity, bond and cash returns for as much of the past century as there are reliable records. Equities can underperform significantly in any one year – 2000, for example, was one of the worst in living memory, and 2001 could well prove worse still. But over most longer periods (barring such an exceptionally gloomy decade as the 1930s) returns have been substantially higher for equities than for either bonds or cash. Jeremy

Shares on top

3

US real investment returns
annual average, %

	Equities	Bonds	Cash
1931–40	3.6	6.4	1.6
1941–50	7.5	-3.1	-5.1
1951–60	13.8	-0.4	-0.2
1961–70	5.3	-1.5	1.3
1971–80	1.4	-3.6	-1.1
1981–90	7.9	8.8	3.9
1991–2000	14.1	7.1	1.9

Source: Barclays Capital

Siegel, a professor at Wharton Business School and author of "Stocks for the Long Run", showed similar results going as far back as 1802 when he compared the returns on shares, long-term bonds, short-term bills, gold and cash.

These three structural trends pushing the process of equitisation have, however, become conflated and confused with the fourth (and perhaps biggest) factor of all, which is the two-decade-long bull market itself. In retrospect, even the crash of 1987 now looks like a mere blip. It is thanks largely to the bull market that stockmarket capitalisation as a share of GDP had everywhere risen to record levels by the end of 2000. Against the background of such big share gains over such a long period, it is hardly surprising that so many new investors have been lured into the stockmarkets.

In America, for instance, nearly half of all households now own shares, either directly or through mutual funds, 401(k) plans or directly managed pension plans. In Australia, the level of share ownership is even higher. In Britain, the proportion is a little over one-quarter. Germany and France still lag, with less than a fifth of the population owning shares – but, thanks not least to privatisations, they have made tremendous strides from a far lower base. The number of shareholders in Germany now exceeds that of trade union members. Even in Japan, despite its long bear market, the stock exchange claims that around 30m individuals now own shares directly or indirectly.

The impact of equitisation stretches wider than the number of people investing in the stockmarkets. It reflects the broader triumph of capitalism in the post-cold-war era. There are few better symbols of capitalism's success than the spread of share ownership. It is also part of a shift in favour of what is often tagged as the Anglo-American model of capitalism, in which markets, not banks (and still less governments), become the key allocators of capital.

The rise of equities is also affecting the management of companies. Now that larger numbers of investors pay closer attention to the daily movement of their companies' share prices, bosses' main concern has become the promotion of "shareholder value" – all the more so when their own rewards are linked, as they increasingly are, to share perform-ance. In many companies, employees have got in on the act as well. Stock options for staff and employee share-ownership plans have pro-liferated everywhere, becoming particularly important in America's technology industry.

In Europe, this has pushed company managers into paying far more attention to short-term profit and share-price performance. In America, it has also led to the fad for share buybacks by firms, which have become so popular as to shrink the net supply of publicly traded equity. Everywhere, people now pay far more attention to what is happening in the stockmarkets. One sign is the mushrooming of personal-finance journalism in many countries.

There are broader economic effects too. The spread of share owner-ship means that a growing proportion of people's savings is tied to the equity markets. This creates a potentially far bigger direct "wealth effect", with consumers adjusting their spending with an eye on the rise and fall of the stockmarkets, regardless of whether they realise their own capital gains or losses. Even more important, stockmarkets are having a growing effect on consumer confidence, and therefore on the economy itself. One of the reasons that consumer confidence fell off a cliff in America at the end of 2000 was the poor performance of the equity markets. Now a vicious cycle may be at work: falls in equity mar-kets contribute to a slowing of the economy, which leads to further falls in the markets.

Equitisation has microeconomic effects as well. Avinash Persaud, an economist at State Street Bank, talks about the equitisation of innovation in the 1990s, by which he means that venture (or private equity) capital was freely provided to innovators, especially in the technology busi-ness, in the knowledge that there was an early and profitable exit route through an initial public offering (IPO). Mr Persaud has also shown, on the basis of information in State Street's custodial database, that equity flows across borders account for a growing share of all capital flows, so they are helping to determine the course of exchange rates and the bal-ance of trade.

The effects of equitisation on the world's economies are thus huge. But the biggest question now is how a bear market will influence things. Might it encourage investors to cast around for safer havens, putting an end to the incipient equity culture? And that invites another question: what determines the value of an equity – and a stockmarket?

Exchange places

America's leading stock exchanges need modernisation

IF YOU ARE looking for a totem of the long bull market, and indeed of the world's new equity culture, you will find one on your television screen, which daily relays the drama of the opening bell being rung on the New York Stock Exchange. On the packed floor below, traders mill about, brokers shout and paper is thrown in all directions, most of it ending up on the ground. It makes a splendid picture. Yet it also prompts a question. Is this not the new age of disembodied, computerised trading? If so, why is there still a trading floor at all?

That question is one of many that make some observers despair of the Big Board's future. But before joining the NYSE's critics, it is worth pausing to ponder the exchange's spectacular success – testimony to the strength of America's equity culture. Fifteen years ago, the NYSE traded 107m shares a day; now it trades 1.2 billion. In the mid-1980s, fewer than 100 foreign companies were listed; now over 400 are, albeit mostly in the form of American Depositary Receipts (ADRs), with the underlying shares held overseas. Most of the archaic rules that protected the exchange from competition have gone. Fixed commissions went in 1975, and more recently rule 390 (which sought to ban trading in a NYSE-listed stock on other exchanges) and rule 500 (which made it hard for a company to delist) were both repealed.

Nor has the NYSE shunned new technology. The Big Board's chairman, Dick Grasso, claims to have invested more in computers than any other exchange has. Indeed, in a reference to his upstart new rivals, he calls his own exchange the biggest "electronic communications network" (ECN) in the world. Over 90% of NYSE trades, he says, are now handled electronically. Three-quarters of all trades directly match buyers and sellers, with no spread for an intermediary. Only for the biggest trades does the exchange's system of "specialists", who have an exchange-sanctioned monopoly on market-making for each stock, come into play.

As for the floor, the NYSE not only plans to keep it: it wants to build an even bigger one at 30 Broad Street, for which it is seeking support from the city council. Mr Grasso jokes that he keeps all the paper around the place mainly to amuse his critics. He likes to tell the story of

Seymour Cray, who was present when his eponymous computer maker was listed, and advised the exchange to cover up its floor to pretend that the trading was all high-tech. The real battle between exchanges, says Mr Grasso, is no longer about electronics, still less about floors against screens: it is about liquidity and price.

If he is right, the NYSE, as the world's biggest exchange, should enjoy all the natural advantages of any incumbent. Studies of trading costs at different exchanges conducted by Elkins McSherry, a research firm, suggest that the Big Board is one of the cheapest marketplaces in which to do business. Its overheads may be larger than those of rivals; but it more than makes up for this through "price improvement" (getting investors a better deal by exposing their orders to the floor) and greater liquidity. Another study of execution costs in different markets, conducted in 2000 by the Securities and Exchange Commission (SEC), confirmed that, for most shares, the NYSE had lower costs than its arch-rival, Nasdaq – and, often, than the newer ECNs.

Nasdaq blues

The Nasdaq has had more than its share of troubles in the past few years. It was set up in the 1970s when the NYSE allowed no IPOs; that is why Nasdaq became the market of choice for new-technology companies such as Microsoft and Intel. Unlike the NYSE, which is essentially an auction or order-driven market, the Nasdaq is mainly a dealer- or quote-driven market, meaning that dealers quote prices at which they are prepared to buy or sell. That makes Nasdaq unique among the world's biggest exchanges; London, which in 1986 adopted the Nasdaq approach as the closest to its old jobber/broker model, has since abandoned the quote-driven market in favour of a continuous electronic auction.

Although dealer markets are said to be better at handling large trades, the evidence of the marketplace now suggests that continuous auctions with an open order book do a superior job at lower cost. ECNs have won business from the Nasdaq by offering just such an electronic order-driven system. A dealer system is better for intermediaries, who can maximise spreads, than for investors, who in an order-driven system have the chance of cutting out the spread altogether. Worse, in a dealer system there is a risk of collusion among market-makers to keep spreads wide.

The SEC has successfully pursued cases against Nasdaq dealers for collusion, partly on the basis of questionable academic evidence that

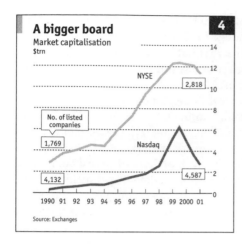

A bigger board `4`

Market capitalisation
$trn

NYSE

2,818

No. of listed
companies

1,769

Nasdaq

4,132

4,587

1990 91 92 93 94 95 96 97 98 99 2000 01

Source: Exchanges

purported to show that prices moved suspiciously more often in eighths than sixteenths. The NYSE went fully decimal (ie, its prices are now quoted to the nearest cent, instead of the nearest sixteenth) in January 2001, a feat the Nasdaq managed only in April, just ahead of a deadline set for the change by the SEC.

It is also notable that the competition from low-cost ECNs, such as Instinet (owned by Reuters), Island and Archipelago, has been more serious against the Nasdaq than against the NYSE. Some 30% of trading in Nasdaq stocks now takes place outside its organised market, against less than 5% for the NYSE. The Nasdaq is fighting back with the introduction of its "SuperMontage" system, which will pull together all quotes to ensure that investors get the best price, but it will find it hard to beat the ECNs on cost.

As if to cap all these troubles, the great Nasdaq/TMT bubble has deflated. In the 1990s, the Nasdaq became almost synonymous with the great bull market. Remember those stories of frenzied online day-traders? Most had no knowledge at all about their chosen companies (sometimes to the point of not even knowing what they did) and relied on Internet chat rooms for stock tips and news. Not surprisingly, most have disappeared as the Nasdaq has deflated, pulling down the broader bull market and also raising questions about the equity culture itself. And although exchanges insist that bear markets can be as busy (and profitable) as bull markets, they tend to translate into fewer trades and less money for exchanges.

Yet Frank Zarb, Nasdaq's chairman, remains ebullient. Like Mr Grasso, he believes that the secular forces driving America's (and the world's) conversion to an equity culture will outlive a bear market: indeed a correction has its uses, because it reminds investors of the link between risk and return. On the SEC study of relative trading costs, he notes that, in the few cases where there is head-to-head competition between his exchange and the NYSE (ie, for large-capital stocks), Nasdaq actually came out cheaper. As for the ECNs and other "alternative trading systems", he welcomes competition – so long as the playing-field is level, and so long as it does not lead to damaging fragmentation.

Can competition between exchanges be harmful? This is one of the theological questions that most divides practitioners around the world. Mr Grasso, like most bosses of established exchanges, talks sourly of trading systems that are parasitical free-riders on the NYSE's price information, which is available free of charge. He is increasingly unwilling to subsidise the inter-market trading system that, in effect, keeps America's remaining regional exchanges alive by allowing them to trade freely using NYSE data. Plenty of exchanges also sound warnings about the danger of a fragmentation of liquidity that could damage the process of price formation. This, they say, is why they are more like public utilities than private markets, and why they were, until recently, permitted to maintain so many restrictive practices. Such practices were, you see, for the good of investors, not for the exchanges.

Yet a combination of new technology and deregulation has blown such protectionist twaddle out of the water. Stock exchanges, it has become clear, are not public utilities at all: they are money-making enterprises. Moreover, market forces are also proving good at dispelling any fears of fragmentation. In principle, there is no reason why competition should diminish liquidity; the great virtue of computer technology is that it makes it simple to link together different pools of liquidity to avoid this. Besides, liquidity in a market will tend naturally to collect in one location (which is what should give incumbents their strongest advantage). Meanwhile, now that most, if not all, restrictive practices at exchanges are on the way out, market forces can surely be relied on to drive trading costs down.

That may well, in the end, be bad for both the NYSE and the Nasdaq. As Benn Steil, an analyst at the Council on Foreign Relations, puts it, "The economics of the exchanges are being unravelled." Once an electronic trading network has been put in place, the marginal cost of additional transactions is, in effect, zero. The arrival of e-brokers that can automatically search out the lowest-cost market for their clients adds to the pressure. How can a high-cost marketplace ever hope to compete in these circumstances?

There are three answers. The first is to rely on inertia. All the established exchanges benefit from the reluctance of many investors and brokers to change their trading places. The second, and more important, is high liquidity. Once a market has captured most of the trading volume in equities, it can reap economies of scale that enable it to see off even a potentially low-cost rival, and its grip on liquidity then becomes self-reinforcing. This is clearly the NYSE's secret: its apparently low trading costs reflect the fact that its high cost base is spread over enormous volumes.

But the third answer is more brutal: to rig the market in some way. In practice, few investors, even among institutions, are fully aware of the true costs of trading, since they are bundled up in their overall charges. The SEC study on execution costs concluded that as many as 85% of equity transactions were not carried out at "best prices". Yet that may be because investors prefer immediacy of execution to marginal price improvement. Kenny Pasternak, boss of Knight Securities, which is the biggest market-maker on the Nasdaq, says his deals are done in seconds, as opposed to several minutes on the NYSE.

However, there are other, less respectable factors at work. One is the practice of payment for order flow, under which ECNs pay brokers a kick-back of a few cents for every order sent their way. Knight does this too. Not surprisingly, the established exchanges would like to ban payment for order flow, or at least make sure the customers know what is going on. But they themselves often benefit from "soft commissions", a term that embraces the provision of research, computer terminals and other goodies by investment-banking intermediaries to institutions, in exchange for their business – which is then normally carried out on the NYSE or Nasdaq.

Then there is the value of the information contained in customer orders. Nothing so crude as "front-running" (putting through your own orders before your customers', so that you benefit from any price effect), to be sure; but knowing about the direction and magnitude of orders can be crucially important to any firm's proprietary trading. Mr Steil is harsh about the length of time it takes to put through an order at the NYSE: "Price improvement is just another name for front-running," he says. NYSE specialists' enviable profitability seems to be linked largely to their knowledge of order flow.

The great levellers

What can be done to prevent market abuses and ensure that the playing-field is indeed level? The answer is mainly in the hands of the regulators, and particularly the SEC. Arthur Levitt, who was chairman of the SEC throughout the Clinton presidency, devoted much time to improving standards of disclosure and transparency in the equity markets.

From the start of 2001, the SEC has required brokers to tell investors on which markets their orders have been executed and whether any payment was made for them. Yet regulators may not be enough, on their own, to ensure fair competition. And there are plenty of suspicions that ultimately the SEC is not willing to jeopardise the NYSE's and the Nasdaq's position; it is keen to keep out foreign competitors' trading screens, for example, and has not yet licensed any ECN to operate as a full exchange.

The most important players in the game are not, however, the regulators, the investing institutions, the exchanges or even the ECNs. They are the big investment banks such as Merrill Lynch, Morgan Stanley and Goldman Sachs, which act as intermediaries between investors and exchanges, and so handle most of the order flow. They employ most of the well-known equity researchers. They are powerful members of the exchanges. They derive huge fees from underwriting IPOs and other new equity issues, as well as from arranging mergers. And they run large proprietary trading operations.

The investment banks had some fantastic years during the bull market – reflected in fantastic salaries and bonuses for their traders. But, perhaps because the staff have proved so adept at creaming off profits that might otherwise have gone to shareholders, they are now under pressure. Consolidation has become the fashion: in 2000, CSFB bought Donaldson Lufkin Jenrette, UBS Warburg acquired Paine Webber and Chase Manhattan took over J.P. Morgan. Rumour has predators circling Merrill Lynch or Lehman Brothers. The bear market has also started a round of lay-offs in the industry.

Investment banks are also suffering from a reputation for being "conflicted". This is clearest in such areas as trading on their own account while also acting on behalf of investors – two activities that, at one time, were separated into stockjobbing and stockbroking precisely in order to avoid conflicts. There is the much-publicised conflict between independent equity research and the handling of IPOs or mergers for client companies. Bankers insist that they maintain strict Chinese walls to avoid conflicts of interest. But Robert Pozen, head of Fidelity, one of America's biggest institutional investors, is not alone when he complains that less than 1% of investment-bank equity research comes with a "sell" recommendation. Now that a bear market has arrived, plenty of sell-side analysts look foolish.

Live and let live

The conflicts extend also to the banks' love-hate relationship with the exchanges, and particularly with the NYSE. Goldman Sachs, for instance, has long been a critic of the exchange for its hidebound practices, and has been careful to invest in several rival ECNs to keep its options open. But more recently Goldman seems to have tacked back, by buying two firms of NYSE specialists, including one of the biggest, Spear, Leeds & Kellog. This is more a case of "if you can't beat 'em, join 'em". In the past, Goldman has been critical of the monopoly privileges of specialists. Even fans of the Big Board find their role hard to justify. But with the exchange keeping such a firm grip on its market share, the specialist firms have been highly profitable – and they hold unrivalled information about order flow.

Not that Goldman, or anybody else, would dream of exploiting any such information. Yet Goldman's interest in Spear, Leeds & Kellog is not simply about profits or even technology. It also says something else about the big investment banks: that they see themselves as the biggest potential rivals to the exchanges. They are, for instance, keen to internalise orders, by offsetting one transaction against another – a practice that is of obvious benefit to an intermediary, if not to its clients. Charles Schwab, a big discount broker, also likes to internalise orders.

The NYSE and the Nasdaq are, in short, not without competition, even from among their own members. They insist that they are responding to that competition as any business would – by cost-cutting, better marketing, fighting hard to preserve market share and so on. Yet they are handicapped in one further way: whatever they pretend, they are not in fact structured like businesses at all. They are, rather, mutually owned members' clubs. That means they are beholden to special interests – the NYSE to the floor traders and specialists that its critics would like to get rid of, the Nasdaq to its broker-dealer firms.

Both exchanges, it is true, have talked vaguely of demutualising and becoming proper publicly traded companies (just as they have also talked, even more vaguely, about a possible merger between themselves, so that they can jointly fend off the ECNs). But for the NYSE, at least, such plans are, as Mr Grasso puts it, "on the back burner" – ie, unlikely to proceed. The Nasdaq recently sold a chunk of convertible debt to a private buyout firm; but even so it still has some way to go before it becomes a separate public company. This makes the American exchanges quite unlike another potential set of rivals: the European stock exchanges, which have been falling over themselves to become public limited-liability companies. As the equity culture goes global, so, increasingly, will the equity business. The Europeans could then become the biggest threat of all to the American leaders – if only they could sort out their act in Europe first.

The battle of the bourses

Europe has been slow to rationalise its stock exchanges

HOW MANY EXCHANGES does the European Union, with its much-ballyhooed single financial market, actually need? Nobody knows the answer, but it must be fewer than the 30 or so that it has today (counting derivatives as well as stock exchanges). So much has, however, been clear for a long time. Some 15 years ago, Europe's bourses first talked of setting up joint ventures, such as Pipe and Euroquote, which might have been forerunners of a single European equity market. But such attempts have come to nothing. Rüdiger von Rosen, now boss of the German shareholders' institute but at the time head of the Frankfurt exchange, sadly recalls a meeting in Copenhagen in mid-1991 at which the last rites for Euroquote were read, over many beers.

Yet the pressure to tidy up Europe's patchwork of exchanges has, if anything, increased, for three reasons. The biggest is the rapid spread of an equity culture across the continent. Britain has long had such a culture: indeed, it was its own George Ross Goobey, as head of Imperial Tobacco's pension fund in the 1950s, who first pioneered the "cult of the equity". But even in Britain, investor interest was stimulated by the Tories' privatisations in the 1980s and 1990s. Efforts to foster share ownership through tax relief, and by encouraging people to take out private pensions, have also had an impact.

More striking still, over the past decade, has been the development of an equity culture in Germany, France and across much of the rest of the continent. In Germany, for instance, investors used to put almost all their savings into banks or bonds. The seminal moment in converting them to equity, says Mr von Rosen, was the first privatisation of Deutsche Telekom in November 1996. In the four-and-a-half years since then, there have been more IPOs than in the previous 50 years put together. Germany now boasts 10,000 investment clubs and a host of investment magazines. Bosses of DWS, the country's biggest fund manager, say that in the 1980s they put 10% of their assets into equities; now the proportion is more like 50-55%, and rising.

In France, similarly, big fund managers such as Axa are putting far more of their money into shares. There are even the beginnings of a

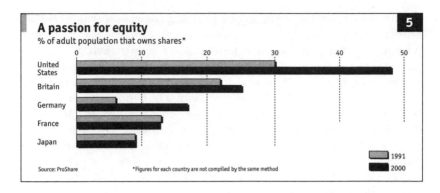

A passion for equity

5

% of adult population that owns shares*

Source: ProShare   *Figures for each country are not compiled by the same method

1991
2000

thriving private-equity (venture-capital) business. French bankers date the origins of new French interest in shares to the *Loi Monory* of 1978, which offered tax reliefs for equity investment. President Mitterrand's nationalisations of the early 1980s interrupted things, but when they were reversed in the 1990s, the upward trend in share ownership in France resumed. As in Germany, private pension funds are also growing fast, even if the phrase remains taboo in France because it sounds too Anglo-Saxon.

Now nearly a fifth of the adult population in Germany own shares (see chart 5). A similar upsurge has taken place in other European countries, with Scandinavia and the Netherlands somewhat ahead and France and the southern European countries still behind. Patterns of saving have changed. Mutual funds, in particular, have boomed since the mid-1990s. And they are increasingly turning to equities: in 2000, according to Morgan Stanley, the equity weighting of European mutual funds rose from 36% to 49%. There is scope for more: bonds still represent nearly a quarter of European mutual fund assets, compared with only 11% in America.

This new European equity culture is now likely to be severely tested by the first bear market that new investors have ever encountered. The decline in the shares of privatised Deutsche Telekom and France Telecom will have been particularly distressing. So has the experience of the Neuer Markt, Germany's high-tech second market, which has been replicated in other secondary markets across Europe, slowing down these countries' nascent venture-capital industries. Yet so far few German or French investors seem to be ready to give up on equities altogether and return to bonds. This means that demand for more efficient stockmarkets, and especially for cheaper and better cross-border trading, will grow.

The second source of renewed pressure for consolidation among Europe's stock exchanges has been the arrival of the euro. Even before the single currency was born in January 1999, a single European financial market was supposed to be in place, but it has always been more of a myth than a reality. Now that investors and companies in the euro area face no currency risk, however, sticking to national stockmarkets, either for saving or for raising capital, seems increasingly anachronistic. Paul Roy, of Merrill Lynch, reckons that in 1997 only 22% of his clients made equity investment decisions in Europe on a sectoral rather than a national basis; in 2000 the sectoral approach accounted for 67%.

The potential gains from a fully integrated European capital market are mouthwatering. The European Commission's first estimates for the benefits from its 1992 single-market programme suggested that Europe-wide GDP might rise by as much as 0.5%. A sizeable chunk of that increase was expected to come from financial services. A unified capital market remains a key source of the potential benefits from monetary union. Over the past 15 years, American pension funds, free of all investment restrictions, made average annual returns of 10.5%, compared with only 6.7% for European pension funds, which are subject to tight regulations over asset classes and local-currency exposure. To catch up with the Americans may require not just abolition of such regulations, but also a closer integration of equity markets across Europe.

The third thing that is pushing Europe's stock exchanges together, inevitably, is competition. In contrast to America, ECNs and alternative trading systems have so far pinched little business from the established stock exchanges, mainly because the incumbents too have developed order-driven electronic trading. But the threat is growing. And meanwhile the battle for business among the exchanges themselves is intensifying. The prize they are all going for is a single European marketplace for blue-chip stocks, rather along the lines of the New York Stock Exchange. Everybody agrees that investors and companies alike want such a market. But nobody can agree on how it should be created.

There have been several solo attempts to build a Europe-wide market. After Big Bang in 1986, the London Stock Exchange renamed itself the International Stock Exchange and created a special market, SEAQ (International), which grabbed big chunks of trading in European blue chips from sleepy continental bourses. But nationalism and protection play as big a part in the equity business as in airlines. Europe's governments were not content to sit idly by as London hoovered up "their" business, so they belatedly reformed their bourses to make them more competi-

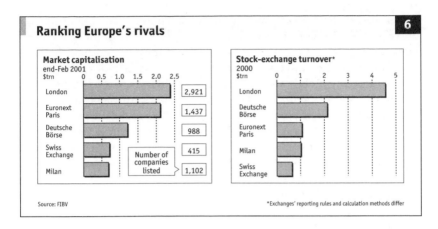

Ranking Europe's rivals — 6

Market capitalisation, end–Feb 2001, $trn

- London: 2,921
- Euronext Paris: 1,437
- Deutsche Börse: 988
- Swiss Exchange: 415
- Milan

Number of companies listed: 1,102

Stock–exchange turnover*, 2000, $trn

- London
- Deutsche Börse
- Euronext Paris
- Milan
- Swiss Exchange

Source: FIBV

*Exchanges' reporting rules and calculation methods differ

tive. As a result, exchanges all round Europe became more efficient, and trading in most domestic equities was repatriated from London.

The next obvious ploy to try was for the exchanges to construct a joint platform for trading the biggest European securities. The pioneers were the derivatives exchanges: France's Matif forged a somewhat tenuous link with Germany's Deutsche Terminbörse, and later the DTB itself merged with its Swiss counterpart to form Eurex. Eurex, a screen-based exchange, did so well that it became the world's biggest derivatives exchange, taking over from the floor-based Chicago Board of Trade. Along the way Eurex unceremoniously demolished the European leadership of London's floor-based Liffe, which lost its near-monopoly in the German bund futures contract in a matter of months. Europe's stock exchanges noted that episode carefully.

Even so, most attempts to forge cross-border links among stock exchanges have failed. The French and Germans tried half-heartedly to join forces in the mid-1990s. In 1998 the two biggest exchanges, London and the Deutsche Börse, announced an alliance. The Paris bourse was furious at being left out. After much politicking, it and five other exchanges joined the British and the Germans in an eight-way link-up. Yet this alliance too fell apart. In the spring of 2000, the London Stock Exchange and Deutsche Börse announced a full-blown merger to form a new exchange, to be called iX. They even signed up America's Nasdaq in a planned venture to form a joint high-tech market. In response to this new competitive threat, Paris swiftly signed up Brussels and Amsterdam into a joint grouping to be called Euronext.

But the story of iX was to be even unhappier than previous episodes.

On each side there were claims that one exchange had sold out to the other. London brokers who had invested a lot to adopt the exchange's SETS trading system were furious to be told they would now have to switch to Frankfurt's Xetra system. The plan was also beset by regulatory uncertainty. Politicians and small shareholders were dissatisfied. A lot thought (correctly) that iX had been dreamt up by the big investment banks, many of them American, largely for their own benefit.

The next chapter was the most extraordinary of the whole tale: the Swedish-based OM Group, operator of the much smaller Stockholm stock exchange, launched a hostile bid for the London Stock Exchange. After some debate, shareholders in the exchange decided to reject both that bid and the iX merger, the exchange shed its chief executive, Gavin Casey, and everything went back to square one. Ironically, Euronext, which was conceived in large part as a reaction to iX, has now taken shape, even though it has so far operated essentially as three exchanges under a single umbrella, rather than one.

Meanwhile the ECNs have not been standing still. Instinet is already active around Europe. Tradepoint, which was set up as a rival to the London Stock Exchange in 1992, struggled for years but then attracted some powerful bank shareholders and is now a recognised exchange. In 2001 it embarked on a joint venture with the Swiss Stock Exchange, called virt-X. Antoinette Hunziker-Ebneter, virt-X's chief executive, is confident that the new exchange, with its existing base of big Swiss companies, will do far better than previous ECNs. Virt-X planned to launch a Europe-wide market for blue-chip equities in June 2001. One of its selling-points over London will be avoidance of stamp duty, which remains in place for British share trades despite frenzied lobbying against it by the London exchange.

Other plans are on the drawing board. Morgan Stanley and OM have launched Jiway, a new exchange through which retail investors can invest in European blue chips. America's Nasdaq, which wanted a piece of the iX action, is prowling around afresh now that iX has failed. It has taken a large stake in Easdaq, a sort of European equivalent to Nasdaq that was largely moribund until Knight Securities took an interest in it. Ironically, Knight now occupies the old trading floor in the London Stock Exchange's building – which the exchange plans soon to vacate entirely.

Exchanges plc, GmbH and sa

All these manoeuvrings have brought about two key changes in Europe. First, competition has pushed all the exchanges into modernising and investing in technology, so that their trading systems are now electronic, order-driven and efficient. Indeed, the exchanges are so proud of their technology that they are touting for other business: the Deutsche Börse's Xetra system handles trading for exchanges in Austria, Ireland and Finland, and London's SETS is about to do the same for Johannesburg. Indeed, rivalry among Europe's stock exchanges is now more about trading technology than anything else. The efficiency of the big European exchanges' trading platforms is a big reason why the ECNs have found it hard to break into the market.

Second, and perhaps more significant, the exchanges have recognised that, faced with the need to respond commercially to competitors, they needed to become traded companies themselves. The Swedes led the way with the flotation of their stock exchange, which is now part of OM. Deutsche Börse is now listed and traded (Werner Seifert, Deutsche Börse's chief executive, is proud that his is the only exchange that, albeit briefly, went to a premium above its issue price). London has demutualised and limited trading in its shares takes place: it planned a full public listing later in 2001. Euronext also planned an IPO in summer 2001.

There are three arguments in favour of publicly traded stock exchanges. One is that flotation resolves the problem of the exchanges' governance: instead of being cumbersome bodies answerable to the vested interests of their members, the exchanges' managers, like bosses of other companies, have to deliver results to shareholders. Second, flotation removes the presumption that exchanges occupy some special national position that merits protection against competition from new upstarts, whether through political or regulatory support or via their membership. And third, it increases the chance that one exchange can take over another (although the failure of OM's hostile bid for London suggests that takeovers will seldom be easy).

America in the dark

Where does this leave the two big American exchanges, which seem in no hurry to follow suit? "In the dark," opines Deutsche Börse's Mr Seifert. Don Cruickshank, chairman of the London Stock Exchange, echoes this view. He says he is prepared to talk to anybody about the future, but only so long as they too have to face the discipline that comes from being traded on the capital market. Yet London and Frankfurt no longer seem to be talking to each other, partly because the Germans are seeking to enforce a contractual clause that would make London compensate them for the failed merger. With Euronext bedding down its merger, the two biggest exchanges in Europe seem both to have lost their way – though the arrival of a new chief executive in London, Clara Furse, may soon change that.

As for the Americans, they may be in the dark, but they still matter. They are the model for other countries' burgeoning equity cultures. They control the biggest capital market in the world, which is why so many European companies have chosen to list in America. And a bigger dream still is emerging on the horizon, once Europe sorts out its own internal structure: of a global equity market, to serve a global equity culture. In any such market, both the NYSE and the Nasdaq would play a key role.

The third leg to such a global equity market would have to be the Japanese stockmarket, and later perhaps some of the biggest emerging markets. Japan is worth some study, for one big reason: it has had long experience of a grim bear market. This has clearly impeded the growth of an equity culture in Japan. Yet in the long term Masaaki Tsuchida, the Tokyo Stock Exchange's chairman, remains optimistic. The demographic and pension pressures facing Japan are even worse than those in prospect in Europe. Alternatives to equity investment are unattractive because yields are so low. It is notable that even in the 1990s bear market the number of individuals owning shares in Japan has risen. And on some measures the Tokyo market now looks cheap.

The Tokyo Stock Exchange has also modernised considerably. Fixed commissions went in 1999, the same year that the trading floor was closed. Trading is now by continuous electronic auction. ECNs have yet to make inroads in Japan, but the Tokyo exchange is ready to battle against them. It is even in the throes of considering demutualising and becoming a listed company. Mr Tsuchida is keen that Tokyo should play a big role in any global equity market. His ambition now is to attract mainland Asian companies, making Tokyo the regional market of choice. But he will have to compete not just against other developed markets such as Hong Kong and Singapore, but also against Shanghai, which after unifying its share structure will soon be the biggest Asian equity market.

The rise of China is sure to have a big effect on plans to create a global equity market. But before considering them further, a closer look is needed at one other aspect of equity trading. All those discussions in Europe have led to the discovery, pretty late in the day, that the main obstacle to increased cross-border equity trading (and so to a putative global market) does not lie in the trading platforms of the exchanges at all, but in the usually boring business of clearing and settlement of trades. In Europe, this can cost ten times as much as it does in America. Now, belatedly, European financiers are seeking to do something about it – but they are running into big obstacles.

Paper tigers

Why the back office often costs more than the front

AMID ALL THE enthusiasm for the rise of equity markets and for a new global equity culture, it is easy to overlook the infrastructure of share trading; yet the ease and the cost of buying and selling shares are crucial factors in how far and how fast such a culture takes root. As we have seen, stock exchanges in both America and Europe could do with some reforms on both these scores. But the biggest obstacles in Europe are stored up in the back office.

In equity trading, especially the international sort, it is the back office that often accounts for a surprisingly large chunk of the costs. When an investor buys a share, he may believe that the only thing to worry about is the cost of commission and the spread he pays to his stockbroker. But the trade has to be confirmed. It has to be cleared, a cumbersome business given that equities constitute a stake in a company, so any change of ownership has to be registered. And the whole deal must be settled, with money changing hands.

In Europe, three huge problems loom over this whole process. The first is that clearing and settlement, like so much of the rest of the equity business, are havens of vested interests and restrictive practices. The second is that the systems have been designed for national, not international use. And the third is that, because clearing and settlement seem so boring, the business has been largely neglected not only by investors but also by traders, bankers and regulators. They have tended to focus instead on the wrong part of the picture: the stock exchanges' trading platforms, which are in fact quite efficient in Europe.

In this respect, at least, it is the Americans who have shown the way. Their exchanges may still be stuck in the dark ages (or at least that is what the Europeans say); but their clearing and settlement systems are state of the art. In the late 1970s, America had as many as seven separate clearing and settlement organisations. New York was notorious for its "paper blockages", and from time to time the markets would have to close in order to allow everybody to catch up on the paperwork. To resolve these problems, the various groups were cobbled together into one body, which has since become the Depository Trust and Clearing Corporation.

The DTCC, which is mutually owned by its member banks, now handles the clearing and settlement of almost all American security trades. It acts as the central counterparty (CCP) for all shares traded on both the NYSE and the Nasdaq, and registers changes of ownership. Thanks to the DTCC, share certificates in America no longer physically change hands and registrars are out of a job. And its costs are low, at five cents for an average equity trade, whereas the European average is nearly ten times as much.

Even so, the DTCC will have to run hard merely to keep up with volumes. It has to be able to cope with the peaks in business, and those peaks are getting ever more vertiginous. On its busiest day in 1998, it handled some 6.3m securities trades; only three years later, trading on the peak day had risen to over 18m, worth a gross total of $722 billion. The volume of actual settlements is kept down by "netting": of that $722 billion, for example, only $22 billion had to be settled, after offsetting debits and credits. Yet Jill Considine, the DTCC's boss, says it is no longer fanciful to talk of capacity constraints.

Of silos and hourglasses

Japan has sensibly adopted a model similar to America's, with a single clearing and settlement organisation, albeit one that is owned by the Tokyo Stock Exchange. But the capacity constraints in Europe are far more obvious. The continent has as many as 30 clearing and settlement organisations. Links between them are poor or non-existent. Settlement dates are not compatible: some settle one or two days after trades (known as T+1 or T+2), others take much longer. Worse still, attempts to improve the system and its cross-border co ordination have so far failed to do much good.

The London Stock Exchange, for example, decided soon after Big Bang to embark on the task of speeding up settlement (then done on a rolling fortnightly basis). It devised a scheme called Taurus that was to dematerialise share certificates and bring in wholly paperless settlement. But the project's cost ran out of control, and there was resistance to change from bank registrars, who were making a comfortable living out of the existing system. As so often when there is trouble in Throgmorton Street, the exchange parted company with its chief executive, Peter Rawlins. Soon afterwards it lost responsibility for settlement altogether, to a new organisation called Crest.

That loss turned out to be no bad thing. In continental Europe, the bourses retained ownership of their domestic clearing and settlement organisations, while the banks owned the two international bodies that handled cross-border business, Euroclear and Clearstream (formerly Cedel). Yet this ownership structure is now one of the biggest impediments to change.

What needs to be done? The most urgent requirement is to have a Europe-wide CCP. The London Stock Exchange and Euronext now have CCPs of their own. Since February 2001, the former has been using the London Clearing House, which works closely with (and may one day merge with) Crest, and the three Euronext members use Clearnet, a joint venture between Euroclear and the French clearing and settlement agency, Sicovam. The Deutsche Börse has plans to use Clearstream, in which it has half-ownership. The trouble is that none of these three clearing and settlement groups relates all that easily to any of the others.

The European Securities Forum, a body set up by the big banks to campaign for a European CCP that would maximise the scope for netting, looks to the DTCC as a model of what Europe needs. It cannot be replicated exactly, if only because Europe has neither a single legal system nor a single regulator. But, at least in theory, it should be possible to push together Clearnet, Clearstream, Crest and the LCH, either through a formal merger or by making them "interoperable" (the buzzword of the moment).

The trouble is that those vested interests get in the way. Now that Europe's stock exchanges are becoming publicly traded companies, they relish the revenue streams that are brought in by their clearing and settlement arms. After all, the higher cost of clearing and settlement in Europe compared with America translates into higher income for those that operate the system. The upshot is that Europe's exchanges are now more reluctant than they were to shed their clearing and settlement arms.

The DTCC's Ms Considine comments mildly that she does not like the notion of an exchange owning its clearing organisation. Pen Kent of the European Securities Forum shares that view. He deplores the building of such vertical "silos", and suspects that there is scope for cross-subsidy between the clearing and settlement arms (which have a national monopoly) and the trading systems (which do not). Setting up a Europe-wide CCP does not sit well with the silo model, says Mr Kent, because it has all the characteristics of a public utility, and perhaps even of a regulated monopoly.

It would be better to have a single public body in Europe to act as a CCP and deal with trade clearing, even if there were more than one settlement organisation. This is known as the "hourglass" model, in contrast to the continent's silos. It would have competing trading platforms at the top, a single CCP in the middle to maximise the scope for netting, and maybe two or three settlement bodies at the bottom. But, partly because Europe's exchanges are becoming publicly quoted companies, the transition from silo to hourglass will be hard.

Don Cruickshank, chairman of the London Stock Exchange, hopes that the European competition authorities might look into the subject to ensure not just interoperability but fully equal access. As a former telecoms regulator, he likens the system to one in which a regulator may have to ensure that an incumbent telephone monopoly offers its competitors fair and correctly priced access to its wires. The recent Lamfalussy report on the regulation of Europe's securities markets agrees, and hints that, unless the markets resolve the situation satisfactorily, governments may have to act to cure Europe's clearing and settlement ills. They might even have to impose a ban on exchanges owning clearing and settlement organisations. Since the German and French exchanges disagree with the entire diagnosis, there may well be a need for some intervention.

Globalism rules?

What about the global market? If there is a case for one CCP in Europe, or at the very least for a system of interoperability, there is one on a world level too. As if to demonstrate the strength of interest in this subject, the first-ever world conference on CCPs was held early in 2001 under the auspices of the DTCC, in London. It was sold out within days.

Right on cue, the Group of 30, a high-level industry think-tank, has set up a committee under Sir Andrew Large, a former securities regulator who is now at Barclays Bank, to look into clearing and settlement on a global level. Sir Andrew does not tout a single global clearing and settlement organisation: that might be a monopoly too far. Nor does Ms Considine, who is also on his committee. Instead, both talk of using the three natural time-zones to spread the volumes, and thereby provide, if not competition, then at least some scope for benchmarking. The committee may also delve into such matters as speeding up trades, to T+1 everywhere, and even ultimately to delivery-versus-payment (DVP), the model that the foreign-exchange market is moving towards.

Does the world want a global equity market? Plenty of bankers and traders think it is moving in that direction. The favoured idea is a single trading platform (or two or three linked platforms) on which all of the world's blue-chip equities can be traded, with a similarly consolidated back office. After all, the foreign-exchange and American Treasury-bond markets trade more or less continuously round the clock. Why not shares in, say, GM, Volkswagen and Toyota as well?

It is a seductive idea, and one that stock exchanges are working towards. In 2000 the New York Stock Exchange, Euronext and the Tokyo Stock Exchange announced the formation of a global equity market (GEM). Other exchanges, including Australia's, Hong Kong's, Mexico's and Brazil's, were quick to sign up. Mr Grasso, who uses the analogy of airline code-sharing for the GEM, recently announced plans for a pilot programme trading its stocks on its partners' exchanges, starting with Asia.

The then planned iX touted a similar global marketplace via its linkage to Nasdaq, which also operates in Japan and has just relaunched Easdaq as Nasdaq (Europe). Nasdaq remains interested in links with the London and Frankfurt exchanges, if only to rival the NYSE's GEM. There are precedents for global marketplaces in the securities business, notably Globex, which tried to hook up derivatives exchanges around the world to allow trading books to be passed around with the sun.

Yet for now, at least, a true global equity market is, as one banker puts it, "pie in the sky". Most equity investing remains stubbornly local: even in America, for example, there is a geographical bias towards local companies. As much as 95% of American equity investment is domestic, although the burgeoning ADR market is introducing more investors to foreign companies. The figures are similar in other countries. The bear market is unlikely to encourage more foreign venturing. And if Europe cannot rationalise its own nationalist-minded exchanges, what chance is there of doing anything meaningful at a global level?

Even so, the demand for something worldwide in scope is likely to grow. Investing institutions, investment banks and companies are increasingly global. The spreading world equity culture is oblivious to national boundaries. Companies that sell in many markets are waking up to the virtues of having shareholders spread across those markets; a few are even looking for foreigners to sit on their boards. And technology is pushing in the same direction: if stock exchanges do not provide a global service, plenty of ECNs would love to try. After all, access to an e-broker trading on the Internet is global by definition: screens can be anywhere.

There is, however, another possible problem lurking in the wings: regulation. Already regulatory differences are complicating the task of creating a single European equity market. These difficulties are bound to multiply in any effort to construct some form of global market. And although regulators (and governments) are doing their best to keep up with capital markets that nowadays stretch across borders, the suspicion must be that they will tend to lag behind. The next article looks more closely at the regulation of the equity markets and the way it affects the world equity culture.

Regulators' arbitrage

Markets are evolving faster than regulators

CAPITAL MARKETS, INCLUDING equity markets, are much like other markets, save perhaps for two characteristics: their speed and their regulation. They react all but instantaneously to changes in supply and demand, which is one reason why they can be so volatile. And both they and those who operate in them are overseen by a complicated mishmash of government rules and regulations, designed (at least purportedly) to protect investors. As the number of investors grows, this job assumes increasing significance.

As ever, America was the pioneer. The Securities and Exchange Commission was set up as long ago as 1934, with the legal remit of supervising and policing not just stock exchanges but all the public capital markets. Like all regulators, it operated with and through the established exchanges, especially the NYSE, which retained a large self-regulatory role. The SEC has formidable investigatory powers and can levy substantial fines for infringements of its rules. Indeed, the amounts it collects in fines typically far exceed its (relatively high) operating costs.

Yet although the SEC remains the model to which other countries aspire, it has not always found that the course of regulation runs smooth. Not the least of the problems in America has been the hotchpotch of different regulators for different bits of the financial-services industry, mainly for reasons of history rather than deliberate strategy. For instance, banks may be supervised by the Federal Reserve or the Office of the Comptroller of the Currency (part of the Treasury) as well as state bank regulators. Deposit insurance is handled by a separate agency. Anybody involved in the equity business also has the SEC breathing down their necks. The derivatives markets are mostly regulated by the Commodities and Futures Trading Commission (CFTC). As for insurance, it remains regulated almost entirely at state level.

This higgledy-piggledy structure may have suited a time when, thanks partly to such laws as the Glass-Steagall act, financial institutions generally engaged in only one activity. But the scrapping of Glass-Steagall and the arrival of universal banks on the European model have blown it apart. Many of America's big banks now have to deal with several different regulators, which significantly increases their compliance costs. Citigroup, the biggest financial institution in America, has to satisfy not just several but hundreds of different regulators, because it is active right across the country in banking, securities, derivatives and insurance.

The SEC's long-standing chairman during the Clinton administration, Arthur Levitt, eschewed battles over the structure of American regulation, although his organisation has long wanted to take over the CFTC. Instead, Mr Levitt focused his attention on a basic question: what is regulation for? His answer was to put protection of individual investors at the top of the SEC's priorities so as to encourage the country's equity culture. His weapons were tough enforcement, greater transparency, full disclosure and spirited attacks on conflicts of interest. That did not always make him popular with the professionals. Despite his own background in the equity business, for instance, Mr Levitt was no friend of the NYSE, which he saw as hogtied by its own special interests. He would much prefer it to demutualise and become a public company, perhaps shedding its regulatory responsibilities along the way.

Elsewhere, Mr Levitt did not always get what he wanted either. His struggle to stop the accounting firms from offering consulting services to audit clients, for example, ended rather limply in a requirement for disclosure rather than a ban. He similarly failed to push through accounting changes that would have required companies to take the full cost of stock options into their income statements. And one of his last acts, known as Regulation FD, which requires companies to disclose market-sensitive information to everybody in the market, preventing them from discreetly briefing analysts, remains highly unpopular on Wall Street. Mr Levitt had made it clear that he was worried about conflicts of interest within investment banks – and especially about the compromising of analysts' research by pressure from banks' mergers-and-acquisitions teams.

It is a pity that Mr Levitt made no attempt to sort out America's regulatory muddle, even so. True, he might not have been able to achieve much, if only because changes would require congressional approval, but at least he could have put the issue on the agenda. However, Phil Gramm, the Republican senator who chairs the Senate Banking Committee, and who had frequent clashes with Mr Levitt, rejects suggestions that America should adopt a single financial regulator. His principle, he says, is "first, do no harm". He sees no reason to change a system that does a good job supporting the country's equity culture. But the problem is not so much that the American regulatory system has not worked; it is that it costs too much and that it may not be well-suited to international regulatory co-operation, at a time when capital markets are going global.

In other countries, the regulatory picture remains mixed. For many years, most of them relied largely on their stock exchanges to regulate their markets, which were anyway relatively small. The message for the individual investor, who was often regarded as more trouble than he was worth, was *caveat emptor*. Until recently, for instance, insider trading was not illegal in much of continental Europe. Accounting standards, provisions for disclosure, transparency requirements, takeover rules, the permissible treatment of minority shareholders: all these varied hugely between markets. And the agencies in charge varied a lot, too: they might be the exchanges themselves, or government ministries, or sometimes central banks.

More recently, countries have been learning a good deal from each other, not least because a growing equity culture has brought so many new investors into the marketplace. In 1997, Britain scrapped the cumbersome regulatory structure set up after the 1986 Big Bang. This had involved a string of self-regulatory bodies placed beneath a Securities and Investments Board that was, in essence, a weakish version of the SEC. It was replaced by an independent Financial Services Authority designed to regulate not only the securities business but banks and insurance as well. The FSA's chairman, Sir Howard Davies, has become a keen advocate of the case for a single financial regulator – though he has also, generously, conceded that the British approach is only one among many.

Still, there is now a discernible trend in financial regulation towards the British model. Most countries are coming round to the view that central banks should not be the regulators of commercial banks, partly because it might distract them from their main function of setting monetary policy and partly because a banking scandal might damage their reputation. Sweden, Australia, Ireland and the Netherlands, among others, have recently gone down the British route of setting up an autonomous single regulator for the entire financial-services industry. Japan too has its own FSA, though since its boss is a member of the cabinet, doubts must linger about its true independence. Early in 2001, the German federal government announced its own plans to set up a single financial regulator, although the Bundesbank and the German states are stoutly resisting any efforts to reduce their role.

Twin peaks

Besides America, only France and Italy, among rich countries, still insist on a separate regulator for banks and for the securities business. Michel Prada, head of France's stockmarket regulator, the COB, believes strongly in a "twin peaks" approach, the banking commission of the Bank of France being the other peak. He says the two regulators have different, and sometimes conflicting, objectives: his concern is protection of the investor, whereas the Bank's concern is with prudential regulation. He suggests that a single regulator would be blamed for every trivial financial scandal, making it less effective. He also argues that a large agency might be formidably difficult to manage. Whereas the COB employs just over 200 people, Britain's FSA has over 2,000.

These differences of style might be mere curiosities but for one thing: the globalisation of both the capital markets and the equity investor. Because both investors and intermediaries (and, as we have seen, stock exchanges themselves) increasingly operate across borders, regulators must do so too. That throws differences in regulatory structure into much sharper relief.

The regulators have responded in several different ways, most directly by drawing up the Basle rules on minimum standards of capital adequacy. The idea was to set common rules for how much capital internationally active banks should set against their risk-adjusted assets. The rules were first introduced in 1988 and have been updated several times since, for example to add capital charges for market risks to those for credit risks. A revision has been sent out for final consultation, and is due to come into force in 2004.

The trouble with the Basle rules is that the weightings are crude, even misleading (for example, South Korea and Mexico are ranked with all other OECD countries for credit riskiness), which sometimes produces perverse effects. One beneficial effect, however, has been to encourage the growth of capital markets at the expense of bank financing. For firms operating in the securities business, there are no internationally agreed minimum capital standards, although most national regulators impose rules of their own (as does the EU, through its capital-adequacy directive). Efforts to negotiate Basle-like standards through IOSCO, the international body for securities regulators, have come to nothing.

Banks and securities firms have tended to trespass heavily on each others' territory, and most countries are now heading for a single financial regulator, so the differences in the treatment of banks and securities houses have become somewhat moot. But the Basle process also confers benefits in the shape of the constant exchange of information between bank regulators, which the capital markets miss out on, and for which they have tried to find substitutes. The past decade has seen a mushrooming of memoranda of understanding (MOUs) between regulators. But even MOUs may not be enough to cope with globalisation. How can the world manage, in the absence of a single, omniscient global regulator?

A Euro-SEC?

The problem is, inevitably, most acute inside the European Union, which is seeking to construct a single financial market even while retaining national regulators. So far, the results have been disappointing. Plenty of obstacles remain in the way of a true single financial market, especially at the retail level. For instance, several EU countries require their pension funds to invest largely in domestic government securities. In France, a recent tax break for equity investment was, extraordinarily, restricted to investment in French companies.

Early in 2001 a committee of "wise men" under the chairmanship of Baron Alexandre Lamfalussy, a former head of the European Monetary Institute (the forerunner of the European Central Bank), issued a report on the regulation of European securities markets. The Lamfalussy report drew attention to the failure of the investment-services directive, passed in 1996, which was supposed to create a single securities market in the EU. It suggested a new streamlined legislative process that would revolve around the creation of a European regulators' committee and an EU securities committee, staffed by senior finance ministry officials. The Stockholm EU summit in March broadly endorsed the report.

Does this herald an EU-wide SEC? Mr Lamfalussy, an arch-federalist, says it might. But for the time being the appetite for any such body remains small. Although some continental bankers say that an EU-wide regulator would be a help, most fear that it would simply impose an additional layer of regulation, on top of the national ones. So long as legal systems and enforcement remain national and not supranational – which means, in effect, so long as there is no single EU government – the regulatory structure seems likely to remain largely national too.

A second reason for thinking that a Euro-SEC may be some way off is that, predictably, even the relatively mild Lamfalussy proposals are caught up in a typical power struggle between the European Commission, the Council of Ministers and the European Parliament. One senior regulator argues that the process of creating a single securities market in

Europe would be smoother if the European institutions were kept out of it altogether.

And what about that bear market? It may well make regulators and governments busier, because more scandals and abuses tend to be uncovered when equity prices fall. A rising market, in contrast, disguises a variety of sins. Yet apart from that, there is no reason why regulators – or governments, for that matter – should have much of a stake in a bull as opposed to a bear market. Indeed, there is a strong argument against any such bias. One reason why the American bull market defied earlier efforts to talk it down was that investors persuaded themselves that the Fed would support equity prices by cutting interest rates as much as was necessary. Despite the markets' recent rally, the "Greenspan put", as it was once christened, now seems to have been over-optimistic. In the long run, that can only be good for the world's equity culture.

Governing the modern corporation

The spread of share ownership will affect company management too

EQUITIES ARE NOT, of course, mere financial assets, to be compared only with such other assets as bonds or bank deposits. They are, as we have seen, much riskier than these. This is because equities represent the ownership of the company itself, rather than merely some claim to a company's cashflow, which is what most assets are. So the spread around the globe of share ownership, and of an equity culture, are bound to have implications for the running of those companies: in the jargon, for countries' systems of "corporate governance".

The awkward relationship between many dispersed shareholders on one hand and a single manager or group of managers on the other has been the subject of a vast economic literature, going back at least as far back as 1932, when Berle and Means published their classic book on the modern corporation. Since then there have been many attempts to deal with the "agency problem" (ie, the difficulty of ensuring that company managers will act in the interests of the shareholder owners for whom they are, in theory, supposed to be mere agents). And, as with the structure and regulation of equity markets, different countries have adopted different solutions.

Once again America, with both a much wider distribution of share ownership and the strong regulatory arm of the SEC, leads the way. It imposes legal constraints on companies' ability to override the interests of minority shareholders. It allows shareholders to join together to launch proxy battles (enabling groups of small shareholders to exercise substantial voting power at company meetings), and to bring class action suits against a company's management.

The government officially encourages investing institutions that are significant shareholders, such as pension funds and insurance companies, to vote on company resolutions at annual general meetings. Many of them also use their voting power to exert leverage over a company's management at other times. Boards of directors are under constant pressure to assert their independence vis-à-vis chief executives. And bosses are increasingly remunerated in either shares or stock options, in the hope that this will align their own incentives with the interests of their shareholders.

Above all, America more or less invented the use of the public equity markets to gain corporate control via takeover bids. It does not matter that takeover bids, especially hostile ones, are rarely mounted. Still less does it matter that they are rarely successful. What counts is that the managers of a publicly quoted company, and its board of directors, know that the company can become the subject of a takeover bid if they fail to perform.

Yet there are plenty of complaints about the American system of corporate governance – and not just from well-known shareholder activists such as Robert Monks. Institutional shareholders are more likely to sell their shares – taking the "Wall Street walk" – than to invest time and money in trying to improve a company's management. The takeover threat has often been likened to the nuclear option: it is so disruptive that it can be used only as a last resort, if a company's managers have gone way off course over a long period. Worse still, it can easily rebound on shareholders. Repeated studies have shown that, in most mergers, the shareholders of the acquiring company suffer, and that their loss is often greater than the gain for the shareholders of the acquired company. Indeed, many empire-building managers now indulge in takeovers in spite of, rather than because of, pressure from shareholders.

The boss is right

Meanwhile bosses have tilted the playing-field to benefit them in a variety of ways. They have made proxy fights more difficult to stage by putting obstacles in the way of shareholders communicating with each other. They have persuaded Congress to legislate to limit "frivolous" shareholder suits. Ironically, strict insider-dealing laws, meant to protect the interests of investors, have also made it more difficult for those investors to intervene with management: if, in doing so, they acquire inside information, they are no longer legally able to trade.

As for the takeover threat, managers increasingly register their companies in the state of Delaware, which is notoriously manager-friendly. Many companies have put in place "poison pills" that make it hard or even impossible to take them over. As a result, there have been few successful hostile bids in the past few years. Worst of all has been the abuse of stock options. Company bosses have manipulated these to reward themselves for mediocre performance or worse, which has

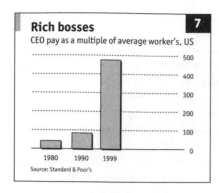

Rich bosses 7

CEO pay as a multiple of average worker's, US

Source: Standard & Poor's

allowed them hugely to increase their remuneration (see chart 7). The cult of the chief executive, which has grown up alongside both the long bull market and the equity cult, has encouraged bosses to ignore many of the norms of accountability.

What are shareholders doing to fight back? Quite a lot, as it happens. Institutional shareholders, especially large ones such as Fidelity or TIAA-CREF (an educational pension fund that is now the biggest pension manager in America), are taking corporate governance more seriously. They are so big that they find it hard to sell their shares without depressing prices; anyway, many track broad share indices, so may not want to sell. Instead, they take trouble to exercise their votes, and are ready to tackle company bosses direct. Robert Pozen, the head of Fidelity, describes himself as a "reluctant interventionist" – but intervene he does, all the same. TIAA-CREF has campaigned long and hard against the abuse of stock options. CalPERS, the pension fund for Californian public employees, has made a career out of intervening to shake up poorly performing managers.

Life on the edge

Perhaps most significant has been the newly acquired habit of sacking the boss. Turnover of chief executives in America is at an all-time high. Boards of directors are more assertive than they were. Institutionalising job insecurity for companies' chief executives may yet prove the most effective of all systems of corporate governance. And, like the rest of the American system – indeed, like the equity culture itself – it is seeping into other countries.

More vigorous corporate governance is certainly needed outside America. Even in Britain, the country whose system most resembles the American one, shareholders do not always seem forceful enough in calling managers to account. For every activist fund manager who is careful to exercise all his votes, such as Alastair Ross Goobey of Hermes, there are a dozen inactive ones. Companies such as BT have managed to get away with strategic mis-steps and underperformance over a number of years without their managers being punished or sacked – although BT's managers have come under increasing pressure (ironically enough, Hermes started life as BT's pension fund).

But the system in other countries is less vigorous still. For many years, this was seen to be a virtue. Academics extolled the German-Japanese model (as against the Anglo-American one), in which companies relied largely on banks for finance and one or two shareholders (often also the banks) dominated. This was deemed to deliver splendidly "patient" capital, as opposed to the unhelpful "short-termist" Anglo-American variety. Two-tier boards in Germany, with a supervisory and an executive level, enforced accountability and allowed companies to take into account the interests of all their "stakeholders", not just their capital providers. In Japan, the *keiretsu* system of cross-shareholdings within a family of companies, centred on a "main bank", worked in a similar fashion. Both systems put the shareholder much lower down the pecking order than did America and Britain.

One of the most striking features of the past decade is that most of the arguments in favour of the German or the Japanese models of corporate governance seem to have vanished. An obvious explanation is that, whereas in the 1980s the German and the Japanese economies seemed to be doing better than the American one, in the 1990s the balance of economic performance was reversed. But the model is itself quietly being dismantled. For as an equity culture has spread in Germany, France and even in Japan and Italy, these countries have been inexorably evolving in the American direction. Bank and cross-shareholdings have been unwound (in Germany, Allianz's recent takeover of Dresdner Bank was a big step in this direction). Institutional shareholders are now courted and individual shareholders encouraged. And companies now pay more attention to their share prices than they did.

It is true that there is still some way to go. Ask Ekkehard Wenger, an economics professor at Würzburg University and the best-known shareholder activist in Germany, about the arrival of new institutional shareholders, and he responds tartly: "You do not solve the agency problem by creating more agencies." He points to DaimlerChrysler, Germany's biggest company, whose boss, Jürgen Schrempp, remains at the helm despite the company's lamentable performance. When Mr Wenger sought to question the company's strategy at one of its recent annual meetings, his microphone was switched off.

Minorities lose out

The abuse of minority shareholders remains endemic in many European countries. Some companies use the Netherlands' extraordinarily management-friendly corporate law to protect themselves from takeover. In 1999 Gucci, a luxury-goods firm, exploited the Dutch rules to avoid putting a takeover bid from LVMH, a bigger French rival, to its shareholders. Italian companies routinely ignore shareholders' interests, as Olivetti did in 2000 when it sought to move the mobile-telephone assets of the newly acquired Telecom Italia into a vehicle that it controlled. In France, Vivendi, often seen as the pioneer of American-style corporate governance, got into trouble at about the same time, for unilaterally altering voting weights to suit its management. In Japan, some cross-shareholdings, so far from being unwound, are actually being increased – and most companies still hold their annual meetings on the same day in June.

Yet the broad thrust of change in the direction of the Anglo-American system is clear, even to Mr Wenger and fellow activists such as Switzerland's Martin Ebner. Two strong forces are behind it. The first is Europe's and Japan's desire to learn from the American economy's success over the past decade. Rightly or wrongly, a part of that success is now attributed to the superiority of the Anglo-American model of corporate governance. Europe's and Japan's patient capital may have virtues, but it also has the vice of not being quick enough, or tough enough to insist on better corporate performance.

Foreigners rule

The second force is even harder to resist: the growing influence of foreign shareholders and, particularly, of the American investing institutions. CalPERS, Fidelity and TIAA-CREF are typical of the new breed. As big European and Japanese companies eagerly list on the American stockmarkets, they have to comply with American rules on accounting standards, disclosure and transparency – and inevitably, they find, with the norms of American corporate governance too. But even when companies do not choose to list in New York, their shareholder register is increasingly dominated by foreigners. As much as half of the shares traded on the Paris bourse, for example, are now in foreign hands; in some other countries the proportions are similar.

When Britain's Vodafone, a mobile-phone operator, hit the headlines with its hostile bid for Germany's Mannesmann in December 1999, there were suggestions that the Mannesmann team might resort to various "barbed-wire" defences permissible under German corporate rules, or that the German government might intervene. In fact neither happened, and commentators applauded the Germans for their restraint. But in truth Mannesmann had little choice, because most of its shareholders were foreign already, and they wanted the takeover battle fought out on its own merits. It was one more sign of the triumph of Anglo-American capital markets and of the new equity culture. Yet it did not answer perhaps the biggest question of all: will that triumph be good or bad for the world's economies?

When capital markets rule

The growth of equity will be good for economies

THE RIVALRY BETWEEN different models of corporate governance partly reflects a broader battle over the best way of financing a modern economy. In this battle, the world's growing equity culture plays a crucial role, for it turns on one big question: is it better for economies if their companies rely mainly on capital markets for equity and debt, or on banks? It is a question that is pertinent not just to the debate about the respective merits of the Japanese/German model and the American/British one, but also to the choices that emerging economies should make about their future.

At first sight capital markets might seem a pretty dubious proposition to rely upon, especially in today's bearish climate. Capital markets are naturally short-termist and volatile. They attract huge inflows that can just as quickly turn into huge outflows. Investors' crowd behaviour can move prices out of line and lead to speculative bubbles. When such bubbles burst, the capital tap can be turned off just as quickly as it was turned on. Contrast the dotcom boom, when finance for even the most bizarre business proposition was to all intents and purposes free, with the bust, when even sound business plans could not attract capital at any price.

The consequence of all this is surely a damaging misallocation of capital that, so far from fostering growth, might actually discourage it. Even in America, in the early part of 2000 there were howls that the new economy and the Internet were gobbling up all the money available for investment, starving "old-economy" companies (which, unlike "new-economy" ones, actually made profits) of capital. Within months the position was reversed, and a lot of investors, many of them first-timers, had lost their shirts. No wonder that some countries (and some investors) mistrust capital markets, and especially stockmarkets; they seem so often to resemble Keynes's notorious casino.

Yet there are also substantial virtues in relying on capital markets. Because they react continuously and almost instantaneously, equity and debt markets immediately capture any changes in perception about the future course of economies, or about confidence, or about risk. This process of "marking-to-market" means that assets are quickly repriced to reflect new circumstances, including new ideas, new techniques and new technology, to all of which capital markets respond more quickly than banks. One example is the development of the junk-bond market in the late 1980s. Because they cut out a layer of intermediation, capital markets are also generally cheaper than banks.

Banks, on the other hand, have several virtues of their own. They are excellent instruments for gathering together small deposits into large pools of capital that can be made available for bigger borrowers. They can employ skilled loan officers to judge different credit risks, and they offer helpful advice to small entrepreneurs. Their intermediation miraculously transforms short-term, highly liquid cash (deposits) into long-term, largely illiquid assets (loans). They can redirect capital from low-return or poor-risk activities to high-return or lower-risk ones. And they can be more "long-termist" than markets.

And yet the downside to relying on banks can be huge. The tumble taken by most of the world's stockmarkets in 2001 may have grabbed the headlines, but to nothing like the extent that a big bank bust would have done. The 1930s depression was a consequence of America's bank meltdown (made worse by foolish monetary and trade policy), not of the 1929 stockmarket crash. Banks, it turns out, are even more influenced by popular delusions and the madness of crowds than markets, as repeated bubbles in many different countries have shown. Bank lending can be subject to political interference. But above all, banks do not mark all their assets to market. In bad times they find themselves sitting on assets for which there is no market.

This has a number of adverse consequences. It aggravates bad-lending sprees: because asset prices do not adjust speedily, price signals are jammed and loans continue to go into the wrong activities. Hence the building of so many pointless office blocks during the savings-and-loans crisis in America, or the massive bursts of overinvestment in Japan and South-East Asia. Worse, the failure to mark to market means that getting out of a bust can be slow and tortuous – as Japan showed in the 1990s. Even today, the true price of Japanese banks' property collateral is unknown, because regulators do not allow it to be traded in the marketplace. The big difference between capital markets and banks, then, is not that one is prone to bubbles and crashes and the other is not; it is that capital markets bring home the pain immediately, making recovery quicker and easier.

Indeed, the Japanese and East Asian crises of the 1990s, rather like the depression of the 1930s, can best be understood as only the latest in a series of bank-created disasters. Governments everywhere have compounded the problem by devising schemes to underwrite deposits to protect depositors (who have presented banks with all those highly liquid liabilities) from such disasters. Because that exposes the exchequer to bank losses, governments then have to regulate banks more heavily, and depositors lack any incentive to monitor the health of their banks – a pernicious moral hazard.

Banks, in short, are what the late Professor Merton Miller once called a 19th-century technology that is also highly disaster-prone. Which is not to say, as some enthusiasts have suggested, that they can be got rid of altogether. The best-functioning economies are those that diversify their sources of finance, relying on markets when things go well but able to fall back on banks when risk appetites change. The classic recent example unfolded in the autumn of 1998, when debt and equity markets in America both seized up. President Clinton spoke of the worst crisis in 50 years; the Fed cut interest rates three times. But banks were able to step into the breach until markets recovered their nerve.

The evolution of finance

The evidence of the benefits of capital markets, and in particular stockmarkets, is not just theoretical. One study in 1998 of 47 countries found a strongly positive correlation between the size and liquidity of stock exchanges and economic growth. Similarly, investigations of development have found strong links between the growth of non-bank financial intermediaries and the growth of economies. For this reason, the IFC, the private-sector arm of the World Bank, is especially keen to promote stockmarkets in emerging economies.

Indeed, an evolution of finance seems to be at work. In the early stages of development, local banks (eg, country banks in Britain's industrial revolution) are needed to gather local savings together in order to provide enough capital for growth. Later, big clearing banks that can operate at national level start to emerge. At that early stage companies rely largely on internal financing and bank loans. Banks are useful mainly because capital is so scarce. The problem is not so much a matter of allocating plentiful capital to the best use as of finding enough capital in the first place.

In the next stage of growth, capital is relatively more abundant, so markets are better placed to take over the task of capital allocation from banks. The initial capital markets, for bonds and equities, are soon complemented by others, such as commercial-paper markets. Once these are in place, the scene is set for the arrival of ever more sophisticated instruments for slicing and dicing credit risk to suit different investors. Convertibles, derivatives, high-yield bonds and the rest join the panoply, blurring the distinction between debt and equity. After all, most debt has what might be called an equity element embedded in it.

Consider the story of venture capital in Silicon Valley in the late 1990s. As the Internet revolution spread, the preferred mode of finance for its pioneers became venture capital, usually committed by risk-taking funds that had gathered together savings from rich individuals and institutions. Traditionally, venture capitalists have had to wait for many years, until their companies could point to a solid record of achievement and profit, before they could cash out. However, the Netscape IPO of August 1995 changed all that: the public equity markets seemed willing to invest in risky businesses that had never made profits and might never do so. The consequence was an explosion of venture capital, a rash of new Internet businesses, the dotcom mania – and the speculative bubble that gripped the Nasdaq stockmarket up to March 2000, after which the market crashed and venture capital dried up again.

What are the lessons from all this? Some maintain that the whole episode was a disaster, in which capital was thrown away on lousy business propositions, reputable investment banks ripped off gullible investors by sponsoring dubious IPOs supported by questionable research analysts – and lots of individuals got burnt. There is some truth in this picture, but it is nevertheless the wrong lesson to draw. The real significance was that, in a period of less than five years, capital markets were able to finance cheaply an entirely new industry; and when parts of the industry turned sour, promptly to reallocate the capital elsewhere.

The contrast is not just with the Japanese and East Asian experience of bank-financed overinvestment; in America, it is with the Texan oil bust of the mid-1980s and the New England property bust of the early 1990s. The pain from these was more widespread and longer-lasting than today's pain in Silicon Valley. And excessive as the TMT/Nasdaq bubble may have become, it has helped to finance a whole infrastructure that has boosted the American economy – and it has done it faster than a bank-led economy might have managed.

Equity culture vultures

America's greater reliance on capital markets than on banks is, according to the widely experienced Baron Lamfalussy, one of the reasons

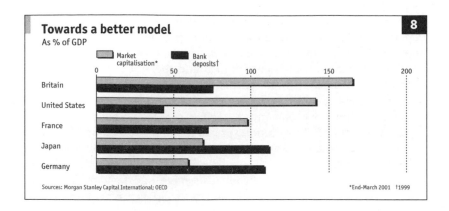

Towards a better model   **8**
As % of GDP

Market capitalisation*   Bank deposits†

| | 0 | 50 | 100 | 150 | 200 |

Britain

United States

France

Japan

Germany

Sources: Morgan Stanley Capital International; OECD   *End-March 2001 †1999

why, despite the excesses of its bubble, its economy has outperformed Europe's and Japan's over the past decade. Chart 8 illustrates the difference. Now the arrival of better-developed capital markets, and a stronger equity culture, first in Europe but increasingly elsewhere as well, should help the rest of the world to catch up. Banks will, of course, have to change a lot in a market-led system. Investment banking will become more important than normal commercial lending. Deposit-taking will shrink in relative terms; asset management will grow. These trends can already be seen at work in the rash of recent mergers to create financial-services giants. More mergers are likely.

The question remains: could nascent equity cultures be marred by the markets' current troubles? In the short term, the answer is clearly yes. Even in America, the vogue for equities is fading, after so many investors have been punished so heavily. Early in 2001, the equity mutual-fund industry saw outflows for the first month in over a decade. Investors in other rich countries are also showing signs of aversion to shares. As for the developing world, equity markets have recently been something of a disappointment. The share of emerging economies in global stockmarket capitalisation fell from about 11% in 1996 to 6.5% in mid-2001, far below their near-40% share of world output.

And yet most of this constitutes a blip, rather than a reversal, in a long-term trend. Even after the setbacks, global stockmarket capitalisation has tripled since 1990. Equity has grown in value faster than debt, and a lot faster than bank deposits. Most countries are seeing a slow but steady increase in the number of shareholders.

This change is unambiguously positive. A bigger role for capital markets should mean fewer and less persistent economic crises. The spread of share ownership will help to secure better pensions for today's baby-boomers. Above all, equitisation will underpin the system of market capitalism itself, by giving more people a bigger and more direct stake in the success of their companies. It is a far cry from the scene in Ivan Goncharov's 19th-century Russian novel *Oblomov*, when the crook Tarantsyev explains the concept of shares to a colleague in crime:

> *It's a German invention! ... Some swindler undertakes to build a town of fireproof houses, for instance. He needs money, of course, so he starts selling papers at 500 roubles each and a crowd of blockheads buy them and sell them to each other. If the business is reported to be doing well, the bits of paper rise in price; if it's doing badly, the whole thing goes bust. All you've got left is worthless bits of paper. Where is the town? you ask. Oh, they say, it's burnt down, or there wasn't enough capital to finish building it – and the inventor has meanwhile run off with your money. That's what shares are!*

In countries with primitive financial systems – not least Russia – such things still happen. But these days shares are more familiar, the regulation and operation of stockmarkets are better, and even corporate-governance systems are improving. The new century is set fair to be the age of the equity.

Sources

This survey has drawn on many published sources and interviews. Among the books used are *Stocks For The Long Run* by Jeremy Siegel (McGraw Hill, second edition); *Irrational Exuberance* by Robert Shiller (Princeton University Press); *Valuing Wall Street* by Andrew Smithers and Stephen Wright (McGraw Hill); *A Random Walk Down Wall Street* by Burton Malkiel (Norton, seventh edition); and *What Is An Exchange?* by Ruben Lee (Oxford University Press). Several articles in the *Journal of Applied Corporate Finance* were also useful, especially "Financial Markets and Economic Growth" by Merton Miller, in the Fall 1998 issue. The author is grateful to all those who helped with the survey's preparation.

The material on pages 105–51 first appeared in a survey written by John Peet in *The Economist* in May 2001.

4

Goodbye to taxpayers?

*It was Benjamin Franklin who said that death and taxes are
life's only certainties. Largely owing to globalisation,
governments today are fearful that soon only death will
remain. This chapter considers the effect of globalisation – and
the Internet in particular – on the taxman. It examines the
fabled "race to the bottom", the merits of taxing individuals
versus taxing companies, and the challenges posed by e-
commerce. It argues that governments, confronted with
potentially more mobile taxpayers and businesses, must
become savvier in their tax-collection methods.*

*Since this chapter, written by Matthew Bishop, appeared as a
survey in* The Economist *in January 2000, governments have
become no less fearful, and no more competent. The European
Union, for example, still toys unwisely with the notion of tax
harmonisation. But nor have people, or even capital, become as
mobile as governments feared. "Is government disappearing"
(September 2001) in chapter one (pages 27–38), offers
additional thoughts.*

The mystery of the vanishing taxpayer

Globalisation, accelerated by the Internet, is exposing serious flaws in the world's tax systems. So will we all be paying less tax in future?

IT WAS NOT a pretty sight. In 1839, the roads of Wales were crowded with men wearing women's clothes, in an obscure reference to a story from the Bible. By the time they were back in their usual attire, several turnpikes (tax collection points) had been demolished. During the following five years, these "Rebecca rioters", as they became known, donned their frocks and smashed turnpikes many times, doing what most taxpayers before and since could only dream about. But now some governments are starting to worry that globalisation, spurred by the Internet, will do to their tax systems what those transvestite Taffies did to the turnpikes.

Like the boy who cried "wolf", governments have raised the alarm about globalisation so often that their credibility is in doubt. For all the talk of footloose capital heading for low-tax countries, starting a "race to the bottom" in which governments slash taxes and services to lure global business, the taxman's cut of world income is larger today than it has ever been. Yet in the story the wolf eventually did attack the sheep, and the boy's shouts for help went unheeded. Is the same thing about to happen to the world's governments?

It does not help that globalisation can mean many things to many people, but a minimum definition would probably include a diminishing role for national borders and the gradual fusing of separate national markets into a single global marketplace. The term "globalisation" was probably first coined in the 1980s, but the idea has been around for a long time. Indeed, by some measures the world was more globalised a century ago than it is now: certainly people were far likelier to emigrate to find work. After an anti-trade backlash in the 1920s and 1930s, globalisation has been accelerating during the past three decades. And thanks to innovations in communications and transport that let people and capital travel at great speed, it is now moving into a different gear altogether.

As globalisation ebbed and flowed, the taxman's share of economic output went relentlessly up, despite warnings from politicians that

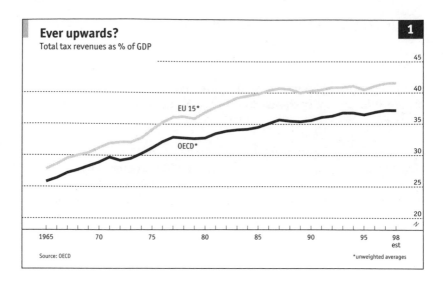

Ever upwards? `1`
Total tax revenues as % of GDP

EU 15*

OECD*

45
40
35
30
25
20

1965   70   75   80   85   90   95   98
est

Source: OECD   *unweighted averages

globalisation would make it harder for governments to collect taxes and thus to provide public services. But now a new factor has entered the equation: the Internet. It epitomises borderlessness, and the irrelevance of being in a particular physical location. By being everywhere and nowhere at once, it seems certain to speed up globalisation. And in doing so, according to the Organisation for Economic Co-operation and Development, it might damage tax systems so badly that it could "lead to governments being unable to meet the legitimate demands of their citizens for public services".

Shopping around

The Internet age has dawned just as tax collectors are getting worried about another aspect of globalisation: tax competition. Both the European Union and the OECD have declared war on "harmful" low-tax policies used by some countries to attract international businesses and capital. The OECD says that tax competition is often a "beggar-thy-neighbour policy" which is already reducing government tax revenues, and will start to be reflected in the data. The Internet has the potential to increase tax competition, not least by making it much easier for multinationals to shift their activities to low-tax regimes, such as Caribbean tax havens, that are physically a long way from their customers, but virtually are only a mouse-click away. Many more companies may be able to emulate Rupert Murdoch's News Corporation, which has earned

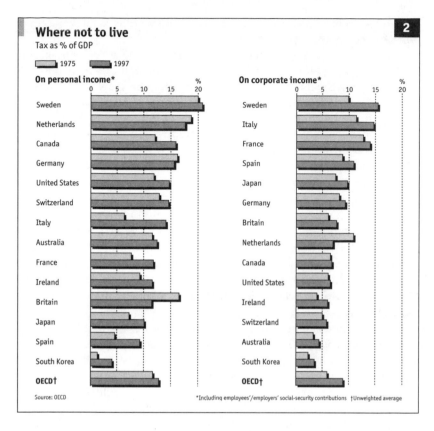

Where not to live   **2**
Tax as % of GDP

☐ 1975   ▩ 1997

On personal income*   %
0   5   10   15   20

Sweden
Netherlands
Canada
Germany
United States
Switzerland
Italy
Australia
France
Ireland
Britain
Japan
Spain
South Korea
OECD†

On corporate income*   %
0   5   10   15   20

Sweden
Italy
France
Spain
Japan
Germany
Britain
Netherlands
Canada
United States
Ireland
Switzerland
Australia
South Korea
OECD†

Source: OECD   *Including employees'/employers' social-security contributions †Unweighted average

profits of £1.4 billion ($2.3 billion) in Britain since 1987 but paid no corporation tax there.

This survey will seek to discover whether all this poses a real threat to tax revenues. Inevitably, this will involve a good deal of speculation. The Internet is still young, and nobody can know how big it will grow. For the taxman, its increasing use raises two main challenges. The first is unique to the Internet. The World Wide Web is an entirely new channel for moving goods and services from producers to customers, and taxing virtual goods and retailers is much more difficult than taxing physical ones. Music can now be downloaded via the Internet, from a retailer located who knows where, without a need for discs or tapes. Other products may similarly dematerialise, making it hard for the taxman to pinpoint them. New Internet taxes, such as the proposed "bit tax", levied on the volume of electronic transmissions, make little sense, and would face huge political opposition from those who want to keep the taxman out of cyberspace.

Taxpayers, too, may dematerialise. In a famous *New Yorker* magazine cartoon showing two dogs sitting in front of a computer screen, one tells the other: "On the Internet, nobody knows that you are a dog." The ability to collect tax is contingent on knowing who is liable to pay it, but taxpayers may become increasingly hard to identify as anonymous electronic money and uncrackable encryption technology are developed.

As almost everybody knows, there are two ways of cutting your tax bill. Tax avoidance is doing what you can within the law. As a great American judge, Learned Hand, put it, "There is nothing sinister in so arranging one's affairs as to keep taxes as low as possible. Everybody does so, rich and poor; and all do right, for nobody owes any public duty to pay more than the law demands." Tax evasion is what happens outside the law. There may be a thin line between the two, but in one sense it is a solid one: as Denis Healey, a former British chancellor, once put it, "The difference between tax avoidance and tax evasion is the thickness of a prison wall." The Internet is likely to make it easier to break the law.

The second challenge the Internet raises for the taxman is its potential for intensifying tax competition between governments. Tax collection around the world is built on the belief that every nation-state has the right to decide for itself how much tax to collect from the people and businesses within its borders. Governments may be willing to pool their sovereignty by joining international bodies such as the UN, the IMF or the EU, but they cling to their right to set their own taxes. Even in what some see as the nascent EU superstate, member countries refuse to give up their control of direct taxation.

Competing visions

Many countries have bilateral tax treaties with other countries, mainly to avoid double taxation. But again the rules of such treaties assume that the nation-state is what counts: they merely determine which nation-state has priority where more than one country has a claim. Multinational companies complain that nationally based taxation inhibits them from operating as truly global businesses. But for governments, it makes sense to design tax systems that attract footloose wealth.

Tax competition raises three big questions which this survey will try to answer. First, is there really such a thing? Some pundits doubt that tax-cutting governments are indeed motivated by hopes of poaching economic activity from other countries. Yet, as we shall see, there is enough evidence to suggest that tax competition should be taken seriously, and that without intervention it will only get fiercer.

Second, can it be stopped? It will not be easy. Not many people will defend tax havens. But although they make fine whipping boys, tax havens simply do in a more extreme form what many "respectable" governments themselves increasingly indulge in. Ireland opposes harmonising corporate tax rates in the EU because its low rates give it a competitive edge. Britain blocks an EU savings-tax directive because it might hurt the City of London. Luxembourg and Switzerland will not agree to share information with foreign tax authorities because people who want to cut their tax bills come to them looking for discretion. And America may well ask for a worldwide ban on new Internet taxes because as a net exporter of e-commerce it would be the biggest beneficiary.

Some policymakers think that a World Tax Organisation should take its place alongside institutions such as the UN, NATO, IMF, World Bank and World Trade Organisation (WTO). But tax nationalism is likely to ensure that this will not happen. The OECD lacks sufficient clout, especially over non-members. The EU has a better chance of curbing tax competition among its own members, both through its directives and through the European Court of Justice, which is steadily, if slowly, enforcing tax harmony in the name of the single European market. But any success the EU achieves internally may simply make it more vulnerable to tax competition from non-EU countries.

Third, is tax competition really so bad? The OECD thinks it could undermine democracy by stopping countries from pursuing the tax policies their voters want. Footloose capital is free-riding on less mobile taxpayers, getting the benefit of services provided by governments in higher-taxing countries while paying taxes in low-tax jurisdictions, if at all. The EU objects mainly to special tax treatment offered to some taxpayers but not others, on the ground that it interferes with the single market. Some EU governments also argue that tax competition makes it ever harder to tax mobile factors of production such as capital. Instead, they complain, they have to increase taxes on less mobile factors, notably labour, which may drive jobs away.

Charles Tiebout, an American economist, argued back in the 1950s that competition between governments can be as good for everybody concerned as competition in any other marketplace. Like companies, governments can compete by offering different combinations of public services and taxes; if people want bigger government and are happy to pay for it, they are free to choose it, just as some people choose a snazzier car, or fly business class. Tax competition will put pressure on governments to provide their services efficiently, but that need not mean they have to be minimal. There are limitations to this theory, notably Tiebout's assumption that every taxpayer is mobile, and can vote with his feet. In reality, richer taxpayers tend to be more mobile than poorer ones. If tax competition becomes stronger, using the tax system to redistribute money from rich, mobile taxpayers to poor, less mobile ones may become worryingly hard. The Internet will make more people mobile, rendering the rest even more wretched.

A brief history of tax

"No taxation without representation."

THE SLOGAN OF the American revolution has long been a rallying cry for taxpayers and tax evaders alike – though not always with such dramatic consequences. Arguably, the struggle to tax people in ways they find acceptable has been the main force shaping the modern nation-state. But are tax policies designed when the nation-state was all-powerful still appropriate now that globalisation, spurred on by the Internet, is rapidly eroding national borders?

Prostitution may be the oldest profession, but tax collection was surely not far behind. The Bible records that Jesus offered his views on a tax matter, and converted a prominent taxman. In its early days taxation did not always involve handing over money. The ancient Chinese paid with pressed tea, and Jivaro tribesmen in the Amazon region stumped up shrunken heads. As the price of their citizenship, ancient Greeks and Romans could be called on to serve as soldiers, and had to supply their own weapons – a practice that was still going strong in feudal Europe. As Ferdinand Grapperhaus recounts in *Tax Tales* (International Bureau of Fiscal Documentation, Amsterdam, 1998), the origins of modern taxation can be traced to wealthy subjects paying money to their king in lieu of military service.

The other early source of tax revenue was trade, with tolls and customs duties being collected from travelling merchants. The big advantage of these taxes was that they fell mostly on visitors rather than residents. One of the earliest taxes imposed by England's Parliament, in the 13th century, was "tonnage and poundage" on wine, wool and leather, targeted at Italian merchants. Sometimes rulers went a little over the top. Excessive taxation was one reason why King Charles I of England lost his head. Many of those guillotined during the French Revolution of 1789 were much-resented private tax collectors. And the Boston Tea Party was a protest by American patriots against the tea tax imposed by their British rulers.

Income tax, the biggest source of government funds today, is a relatively recent invention, probably because the notion of annual income is itself a modern concept. Governments preferred to tax things that were easy to measure and therefore to calculate liability on. That is why early taxes concentrated on tangible items such as land and property, physical goods, commodities and ships, or the number of windows or fireplaces in a building. The first income tax was levied in 1797 by the Dutch Batavian Republic. Britain followed suit in 1799, and Prussia in 1808. Like most new taxes, these imposts were first introduced as temporary measures to finance war efforts. After the European powers had made peace in Vienna in 1815, Henry Addington, the British prime minister of the day, swore that an income tax would never be imposed again. But in 1842 the British government revived the tax.

What stands out about the 20th century – and particularly its second half – is that governments around the world took a growing share of their countries' national income in tax, mainly to pay for ever more expensive defence efforts and for a modern welfare state. Taxes on consumption, such as the sales tax that is a big source of revenue for America's state and local governments, and the value-added tax on goods and services in Europe, have become increasingly important.

Big differences between countries remain in the overall level of tax. America's tax revenues amount to around one-third of its GDP, whereas Sweden's are closer to half. There are also big differences in the preferred methods of collecting it, the rates at which it is levied and the definition of the "tax base" to which those rates are applied, as well as the division of responsibility for taxation between levels of government.

Global economy, national taxes

The increasing globalisation of economies in the 20th century was accompanied by a rare outbreak of internationalism by the tax authorities. Many countries chose to tax their citizens – individual or corporate – on their global income, whether or not they had already paid their due on some of it abroad. The League of Nations, the forerunner to the United Nations, in 1921 commissioned a report by financial experts who concluded that this practice of "double taxation" interfered with "economic intercourse and ... the free flow of capital". It suggested rules for determining when tax should be paid to the country in which the income is generated, and when to the taxpayer's country of residence. It drafted a model treaty (now updated by the OECD) that spawned many bilateral agreements. Initially intended to stop income being taxed twice, these bilateral treaties opened the way for multinational companies to avoid tax on their profits altogether by setting up in business where taxes were lowest. Combined with greater mobility of capital, this new flexibility encouraged tax competition between countries.

Net losses

Why the taxman fears the Internet

LIKE A NEWBORN baby, the Internet is still young enough for people to predict all manner of things for it without anybody being able to prove them wrong. Some people say that e-commerce will never really take off. Others insist that it is the most important development since the invention of the printing press. Whoever is right, taxmen the world over would be wise to prepare for the worst.

Whereas most people worry that the Internet will reduce personal privacy, some tax experts reckon that it will allow unwilling taxpayers to hide more easily. According to Jeffrey Owens, head of fiscal affairs at the OECD, the Internet may make it hard to pinpoint the identity or location of people who are carrying out potentially taxable activities. A domain name used on the web may give no clue to the location of its originator. Even websites of well-known international businesses may not reveal the location of the offices that maintain them. The tax authorities still rely on paper-based records, yet the Internet will encourage the keeping of electronic records – which may well be stored in some foreign jurisdiction, safe from the taxman's dawn raids.

When gathering information, tax collectors also rely heavily on independent third parties such as retailers, who have little to gain by helping others to evade taxes and can therefore be a valuable source of impartial data. However, e-commerce may well cut out many of these middlemen. Over the Internet, customers can buy direct from producers. One area of e-commerce that is expected to grow rapidly is online business-to-business auctions which allow, say, widget producers and widget users to make direct deals. These sites could make traditional brokers and dealers redundant, removing a useful information source for the taxman. The sites may also establish themselves in a country whose rules make data hard for tax authorities to get hold of. On the other hand, the Internet may make it easier for different countries' tax authorities to communicate with each other, privacy rules and national interests permitting.

The Internet may also make it possible for secret transactions to take place through the use of anonymous e-money and highly secure encryption. Tax authorities, as well as the police, fear that this kind of

163

technology will foster a culture of evasion and lead to an increase in money-laundering – moving money obtained by criminal activity into legitimate bank accounts.

How justified such fears are is difficult to judge. E-money has yet to catch on with e-commerce consumers, who seem to have come to terms with using their credit cards online. Thanks to government pressure, most of the different versions of e-money now being developed deny their users the anonymity needed to evade the taxman, and certainly the anonymity provided by old-fashioned cash.

Oakington, a firm developing a digital-cash system called eBits, is trying to persuade the American government to throw its weight behind its not-wholly-anonymous product so that fully anonymous alternatives never get established. However, the American government's attempts to stop encryption technology being exported to places that might put it to nefarious uses have merely caused much of the development of the technology to be carried out in other countries.

Even if they can pinpoint their elusive taxpayers, the tax authorities may find it harder than ever to collect the money. Some of the third-party information gatherers that are now being cut out by technology have also played an important role as tax collectors. Retailers, for example, often collect taxes on the sale of goods, and companies collect income tax on behalf of their workers. In an effort to replace those middlemen, some tax authorities are now casting an eye in the direction of shipping companies such as FedEx, as well as credit-card companies, but are getting an unenthusiastic response.

Governments worry that the wired world may make it easier for many more people to take advantage of tax havens, hitherto the preserve of a wealthy few. Mr Owens of the OECD sums up the argument: "Internet banking will offer simple access, low transaction costs, a degree of anonymity and instant ability to move money around the world, to an extent not widely available now. If this is combined with well-run, well-regulated offshore institutions, a much wider clientele is likely to be attracted to these services than are using them today."

Everywhere and nowhere

But it is the potential of the Internet to revolutionise the nature of work that may create the biggest challenge to the tax authorities. Today's tax system relies on knowing where a particular economic activity is located. But the Internet may enable individual workers to operate in many different countries while sitting at the same desk.

Multinational companies may increasingly operate as seamless global organisations, with teams of workers based all over the world, passing projects backwards and forwards via the Internet or the companies' private in-house intranets. This will make it more difficult for the tax authorities to demand that economic activity and value creation be attributed to a particular physical location. In the past, a company was deemed to have a taxable presence in a country if it had a "permanent establishment" there. But at the moment it is not clear whether the existence of a server or a website qualifies as such a presence. Tax authorities have shown considerable enthusiasm for a proposal by Luc Hinnekens, a lawyer at the University of Antwerp, for servers to be designated as "virtual permanent establishments". The old trick of finding out where a company's board meets to establish its place of residence may no longer work, because such meetings are increasingly conducted via satellite or the Internet.

Tax choices may play a much bigger role in deciding whether the Internet is a success than for previous technologies. "The costs of illuminating manuscripts were so much greater than those of printing them that the taxation of printed matter would probably have had little impact on the choice of technology," says Charles McLure, an economist at the Hoover Institution. E-commerce, by contrast, is one of several different ways of delivering essentially the same product. These delivery channels are quite close substitutes for each other, so if one of them has a tax advantage, that may well give it the edge, he says.

Moreover, Mr McLure points out, "The taxation of electronic commerce faces technological constraints." The Internet is so new that the direction of technological change is fiendishly hard to predict. By contrast, tax rules are precise and inflexible, and take a long time to change. As one frustrated taxman puts it, "They can move millions of dollars at the click of a mouse, and five years later, when we've changed the rules, they've come up with another scheme." Mr Owens concludes: "Tax authorities cannot remain passive in the face of such developments." But what should they do? The first place to look for an answer is online shopping.

The happy e-shopper

How feasible is it to tax Internet spending?

"**R**OAD-KILL ON THE information superhighway." According to one sage, that is the likely fate of America's sales tax. It is possible. Buy a novel from your local Manhattan bookstore, and you will pay a combined state and city sales tax of 8.25%. Purchase the same book over the Internet from Amazon.com, and there will be no tax to pay. This advantage is doing wonders for e-retailers in their battle against traditional high-street stores. If e-commerce grows as big as some predict, this could blow a large hole in tax revenues. In America, sales tax is levied at the state and local rather than the national level, and many state governors are getting nervous about the potential loss of yield from a tax that currently supplies around half of state and local-government revenues. Most other countries have different arrangements, but face many of the same issues.

Some American states decided on pre-emptive strikes, such as slamming taxes on Internet access, which upset the don't-tax-the-net lobby. Now the two sides have been brought together in the Advisory Commission on Electronic Commerce, set up by Congress under the 1998 Internet Tax Freedom Act. The very name of the act gives a strong hint of what the tax collectors are up against: the idea that the Internet is the true land of the free, in a way that offline America no longer is. The act also included a three-year ban on "new Internet taxes" while a permanent arrangement is debated. The inclusion of the word "new", however, may be a piece of political weaselry: it leaves open the possibility that the "old" sales tax might simply be extended to currently untaxed e-commerce.

Besides, purchases from an online retailer are not, in fact, tax-free, whatever Americans may have come to believe. Rather, the online retailer may simply have no legal duty to collect it, thanks to two Supreme Court rulings on tax disputes involving mail-order companies shipping goods to other states. In 1967, the Court said that states could not require an out-of-state company to collect a sales tax on goods coming into the state unless the company had a physical presence or "nexus" within that state. This decision was reaffirmed by the Court in 1992, in a case involving Quill, a big catalogue seller. Many lawyers had

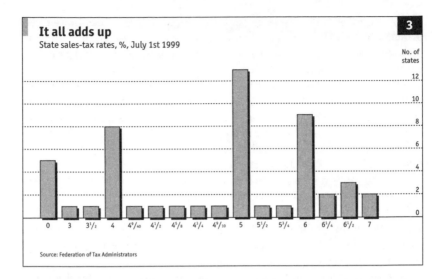

It all adds up

State sales-tax rates, %, July 1st 1999

Source: Federation of Tax Administrators

thought that improved technology would undermine the argument used in the 1967 case that it was too burdensome for the out-of-state seller to discover what tax the customer should pay.

Legally, most consumers buying goods from outside their state are supposed to pay a "use tax" equal to what the sales tax would have been, but hardly anybody does. America's so-called "tax-free e-commerce" really amounts to mass tax evasion. Online-only retailers such as Amazon, unencumbered with a high-street nexus, have neglected to remind consumers that they may have a legal duty to pay a use tax. Many online retailers have added to their advantage by basing what physical presence they do have (eg, warehouses and offices) in the five American states – Alaska, Delaware, Montana, New Hampshire and Oregon – that do not levy a sales tax.

This strategy is not entirely risk-free. Except in states that have explicitly ruled it out, such as California and New York, it is conceivable that the tax authorities will challenge online-only retailers on the ground that using a server or being contacted at a website located within their borders constitutes "nexus", obliging them to collect taxes.

All the same, the "tax break", however doubtful, and however unfair to the (mainly less-well-off) people who do not have access to the Internet, has given the online-only retailers a big boost. According to a study by Austan Goolsbee, an economist at the University of Chicago, 1998 Internet sales would have been 25–30% lower if state taxes had been charged on them, if only because (often high) delivery fees have to be added on top. The overseas sales of American-based online retailers probably benefited as well, because they are trading from what is currently an e-commerce tax haven.

Offline retailers who want to sell online are facing serious dilemmas. If they collect tax, they concede a price advantage to their online-only rivals. If they break the law, they risk being taken to court and having to pay back taxes. One short-term way out is to pay the tax on behalf of the consumer, but this is feasible only as long as e-commerce makes up just a small part of the firm's sales.

Another option is to restructure the business so that for tax purposes the online retail operation becomes a separate legal entity from the offline one. This is what Barnes & Noble, a chain of bookshops, has attempted with its bn.com site. There are some legal precedents; for example, Saks Fifth Avenue Folio is a legal non-tax-collecting direct-mail operation run separately from its high-street sibling.

But many of America's biggest traditional retailers consider this strategy too risky. According to Walter Hellerstein, a lawyer at the University of Georgia, courts in up to 20 states may not be prepared to accept the legal separateness of what is essentially the same brand online and offline. Having dithered for ages, high-street retailers are beginning to throw their considerable lobbying weight behind taxing online sales (and, for that matter, mail order) to create a level playing field with traditional shops.

The Advisory Commission considered several dozen proposals at its meeting in December 1999. At one extreme, Congressman John Kasich advocated no taxation of anything sold online. Some lawyers reckon that this would prompt every high-street store in America to convert itself into an Internet retailer by turning its checkouts into Internet terminals over which customers could "order" and pay for the goods they have just taken off the shelf. Hal Varian, of the University of California at Berkeley, one of the few economists who know a lot about both e-commerce and tax, proposes scrapping the sales tax and raising state income taxes, or levying a new consumption tax based on an individual's annual income minus savings.

Mr McLure, of the Hoover Institution, favours a European-style value-added tax, to be levied on household consumption of all goods and services, whether sold online or offline, in or out of a state. He would reduce the burden on firms of collecting these taxes by adopting a common nationwide definition of the base to which they are applied, and by greatly reducing the number of different tax rates. For the states, Michael Leavitt, the governor of Utah, proposed a voluntary scheme that would both simplify the system and pass responsibility for tax collection to a "trusted third party", such as a credit-card firm.

Some software firms say they have products that allow retailers to charge the right rate of tax even under the current system, so there is no need to simplify the system. However, this kind of software depends on knowledge of the consumer's location, which may be different from the billing address. Credit-card companies often have that information, but supplying it would probably breach confidentiality rules. Besides, consumers may be using e-money rather than a credit card. At least nobody revived the old idea of a "bit tax" based on the amount of digital information transmitted electronically – although if taxing the Internet proves harder than expected, it may well be dusted down.

Even if agreement on the best tax can be reached, it will still have to be implemented. One way would be for all of America's state and local governments to reach agreement on a solution, but that is highly unlikely because some of them benefit from leaving things as they are. Another would be for Congress to pass a law overriding the Supreme Court's Quill verdict, but Congress has no appetite for a federal-versus-state-government turf war, particularly if it might end up being blamed for "taxing the Internet to death".

Many policymakers feel they have time on their side. At present most state governments are running a budget surplus. E-commerce, worth an estimated $20 billion in 1999, or less than 1% of American retail sales, is not yet hurting tax revenues much: as a recent report by Ernst & Young, an accountancy firm, put it, "The Sky Is Not Falling". Yet e-commerce is proceeding in Internet time; blink, and it has doubled. If consumers get used to buying online without paying tax, politicians may face strong opposition to changing that happy state of affairs. "We may have only two more Christmas shopping seasons before it is too late," says Mr Leavitt.

Meanwhile, elsewhere

Most rich countries tax consumption quite differently from the way America does: usually at national level, and generally raising far more revenue from it (see chart 4). Yet some of the problems they face are similar.

Within the EU, online retailers are supposed to collect value-added tax (VAT), a tax levied on purchases made by individuals but not businesses. Although VAT rates in different EU countries vary widely, the

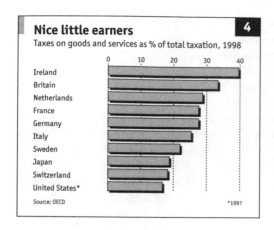

Nice little earners 4
Taxes on goods and services as % of total taxation, 1998

Ireland
Britain
Netherlands
France
Germany
Italy
Sweden
Japan
Switzerland
United States*

Source: OECD *1997

EU has ruled that cross-border retailers should collect the tax at the rate applying in the member state where the purchase is consumed. In theory, that should stop online firms setting up in whichever EU country has the lowest VAT rate on its product, and exporting to countries with higher rates. However, enforcing this policy may prove harder than EU officials suppose. As one British customs official explains: "If we visit a company in Britain and find that it is not charging VAT on goods it is shipping to, say, Germany, we will certainly tell them they are supposed to be charging German VAT. But it is not our job to enforce the collection of German taxes or to tell the German government that it is missing out." Nor is it clear who will ensure that firms deliver any tax they collect to the appropriate government. Retailers selling from outside the EU are even harder to keep in line.

With physical goods, the taxman can at least check that items entering the country have had the appropriate duties paid on them. But if online customers find they have to pay extra when their package arrives, they may get irritated enough to pressure retailers into complying with tax rules. According to Charlie Gilreath, chief executive of Globalfulfillment.com, a firm that helps online businesses with their customers' orders, extra taxes or duties that were not included in the purchase price are among the main reasons why goods ordered online are returned.

The EU has decided that intangibles delivered online should be taxed as services. But collecting tax on services is tricky, and e-commerce can only make it harder. If a supplier sets up in a country that does not require it to collect taxes on the intangible goods it sells, and delivers the product online, the taxman in the consumer's country may never know.

Many products that are currently tangible, and thus fairly easy to tax, may become virtual. Already, music can be sent to customers via the Internet rather than in physical form. Books may soon follow. The dematerialisation of products could accelerate as Internet bandwidth increases. Clearly there are limits: nobody has yet devised a way of downloading a Big Mac. However, even with physical goods it may be possible to "unbundle" the price of a good into a tangible component and intangible ones − such as design, advice or customisation − that could be located in a low-tax regime.

Taxing digital goods where they are consumed may prove almost impossible. Collecting a sales tax from the supplier may be easier, and in America a shift towards such origin-based taxation has been suggested for intangibles. Since the country is a net e-commerce exporter, this is hardly surprising. But imposing such taxes might reduce the competitiveness of American firms if competitors set up in countries that do not impose the origin tax. And even American entrepreneurs may well decide to form new companies in a tax-friendlier place. There are plenty of countries competing to attract them.

Gimme shelter

Is tax competition among countries a good or a bad thing?

"**B**ILL GATES WOULD be fabulously more wealthy if he had started Microsoft in Bermuda," says William Woods, chief executive of the Bermuda Stock Exchange. "He may have known a lot about computer programming when he started the company, but his ignorance about tax cost him a fortune." Mr Gates has not done badly even so, but he knows better now. Teledesic, a company co-founded by the Seattle-based billionaire that plans to offer broadband Internet access by satellite, is incorporated in Bermuda.

Any firm that expects to earn profits from more than one country, and to have shareholders from more than one country, should set up in Bermuda, says Mr Woods – and not just because the British island dependency levies no corporate income tax, but also because it is "tax-neutral" in its treatment of holding companies. A holding company incorporated in America that receives cash dividends from overseas subsidiaries, which have probably been taxed already in their country of origin, would also have to pay some American tax before any money is distributed to shareholders. A Bermudian holding company could pass those dividends, gross, direct to shareholders. The tax savings could easily have been 10–15% for Microsoft, which earns around half its profits outside America, says Mr Woods. This would have meant higher profits and presumably a higher share price – and thus an even wealthier Mr Gates.

Alas, once a holding company is incorporated in a country such as America, the cost of moving to Bermuda can be prohibitive. The taxman is likely to take the view that a firm transferring its citizenship is, in effect, selling off its assets, and hit it with a hefty capital-gains tax bill. Going offshore makes most sense for truly global firms, says Mr Woods. If you are writing software over the Internet, with teams of workers spread across Seattle, Bangalore and Israel, it would be hard for any one country to claim the right to tax you as a holding company – and this is increasingly how companies work, particularly in Internet-related business. That is why Bermuda is busy marketing itself to entrepreneurs as an e-commerce centre.

Ireland wants to be the e-commerce centre for Europe, so, like

Bermuda, it has passed a state-of-the-art e-commerce law. It has identified 100 global technology companies it wants to attract. Like their counterparts in Bermuda, politicians in Dublin are being bashful about what many would consider Ireland's main attraction: low taxes. Instead, they like to emphasise their high-quality regulation, the advantage of being able to do business in English, Ireland's entrepreneurial spirit, and its highly educated yet relatively low-cost workers.

Pssst ... know a good tax regime?

Boasting about attractive tax policies is unwise just now because of international efforts to crack down on "harmful tax competition". This is not, at least not explicitly, an attempt to harmonise taxes. The EU, for example, has been campaigning against the singling out of particular taxpayers for preferential tax treatment, which is how many EU countries now try to attract investment by multinational companies. The main target of this campaign was initially Ireland, which has long annoyed some of its bigger European partners by offering a modest 10% tax rate on profits earned by foreign manufacturing companies that move there, and latterly to foreign financial companies operating there. But in a brilliant (if expensive) pre-emptive move, the government in Dublin agreed to stop giving preferential treatment to some companies and offer the same 12.5% tax rate on profits to Irish as well as to foreign firms by 2010.

This has left other EU countries with more time to accuse each other of offering preferential tax treatment. A report to the EU's Helsinki summit in December 1999 identified 66 different varieties, ranging from the Netherlands' willingness to negotiate secret advance agreements with foreign firms on how much tax they will pay, to Gibraltar's tax exemptions for branches of non-resident companies operating there. The report found that all EU members except Sweden engaged in some "harmful" tax practices.

The OECD is mostly after the more familiar sort of sun-drenched tax haven. In particular, it makes a distinction between tax rates designed to attract "real" economic investment and those aimed at merely "financial" capital flows, which are its main targets. It is particularly hostile to countries that attract "brass plate" or "booking" operations, with no real work or employment attached to them. It gets suspicious when a location offers low or no taxes but is unwilling to exchange information with foreign tax authorities, or if companies setting up there do not appear to have "substantial activities".

173

What constitutes substantial activities is debatable. Gone are the days when finding out what a firm does and where it makes its money simply meant visiting its factories. An increasing share of companies' profits comes from financial and other services, which are much more elusive than manufacturing plants. It can be hard to tell exactly what constitutes substantial activities, and will get even harder as the Internet allows, say, servers and databases to be based in low-tax countries.

The OECD has been preparing a list of countries that it thinks are indulging in harmful tax competition [published in June 2000]. Countries worried about being labelled "tax havens" have mounted a furious lobbying effort. Most of them insist that companies within their borders do many worthwhile and substantial things, and no doubt they often do. Bermuda points out that it hosts a thriving, innovative insurance industry, and that its government takes a full 22% of the country's GDP in taxes, though these are levied on consumption and employment rather than on profits or other income. The Cayman Islands claims that it is the world's fifth-largest financial centre, and is home to 45 of the world's biggest banks.

All this regulatory activity seems to reflect a belief that tax competition does indeed exist, that it is intensifying, and that it can be harmful (although both the EU and the OECD quietly concede that it can sometimes be beneficial by penalising inefficient governments). But is any of this true?

Tax-competition sceptics point out that in most developed countries tax revenues as a proportion of GDP have in fact risen over the past 30 years, and that the share of taxes on corporate profits in overall tax revenues has remained much the same. On the other hand, there is plenty of evidence that lower tax rates have pulling power, and as economies become more open, the pulling power is getting stronger. A 1998 OECD report on harmful tax competition noted that total direct investment by G7 countries in tax havens in the Caribbean and South Pacific grew more than fivefold between 1985 and 1994, to over $200 billion.

So-called tax havens accounted for 1.2% of world population and 3% of world GDP, but 26% of the assets and 31% of the net profits of American multinationals (though only 4.3% of their workers), according to a 1994 study[1]. A more recent analysis[2], by James Hines of the University of Michigan, found that "taxation significantly influences the location of foreign direct investment, corporate borrowing, transfer pricing, dividend and royalty payments." Another study[3] asked, "Has US investment abroad become more sensitive to tax rates?" It analysed corporate tax-return data for 1984–92 (the latest then available), and found that by the end of this period the typical American multinational had become twice as likely to locate its operations where taxation was lowest as it had been at the beginning.

Falling corporate tax rates around the world also provide strong circumstantial evidence that governments are trying harder to cater for international firms' and investors' appetite for lower taxes. Yet such rate cuts have often been accompanied by a widening of the tax base – for instance, by scrapping corporate-tax exemptions – which has reduced the impact of rate cuts on the bottom line.

Are governments wise to engage in tax competition? Ireland's example suggests they may be. The country's recent economic boom owed much to low taxes on foreign firms moving there. Its GDP per head, which as recently as 1990 was 70% of the EU average, now exceeds Britain's, and is expected to exceed the EU average by around 2005. But within the EU, no other country has tried to compete head-to-head with Ireland on tax. By contrast, some developing countries have found that their attempts to attract firms by offering low taxes have been trumped by similar countries taxing even less.

In some countries, the tax authorities have responded to tax competition by getting tough with multinational firms that operate within their borders but try to take advantage of lower taxes elsewhere. When filing tax returns in a high-tax country, multinationals typically claim that they have earned as little of their profits there as they can get away with. Instead, they try to attribute as much profit as possible to their operations in low-tax countries. They do this by arranging "transactions" between their subsidiaries in the two countries, and setting the "transfer price" of those transactions so that it has the desired effect on profits.

In theory the transfer price is supposed to be the same as the market price between two independent firms, but often there is no market, so nobody knows what the market price might be. This is particularly true of firms supplying services or intangible goods. So multinationals spend a fortune on economists and accountants to justify the transfer prices that suit their tax needs. Increasingly, firms try to restructure their operations to get their tax bill down as far as possible. There are plenty of opportunities: according to the OECD, around 60% of international trade involves transactions between two related parts of multinationals. But tax authorities are increasingly looking out for such wheezes. In America, in particular, the taxman has been putting the squeeze on companies, which have responded by allowing more of their taxable profits to arise there to keep him happy. This is prompting other countries to get tougher, too.

America is also trying to get a grip on American-based multinationals' tax behaviour in other countries, using an instrument known as controlled-foreign-company legislation. The main way American multinationals take advantage of low-tax regimes is by "deferral", which means sitting on profits earned in those countries instead of sending them back to the parent. If the tax authorities think that a foreign subsidiary is used only for avoiding tax, the subsidiary can be deemed a controlled foreign company and obliged to repatriate its profits to the holding company, where it is subject to full American taxation.

This kind of tightening up does not necessarily produce a lot more revenue for the tax authorities in question, but it does mean companies are spending ever more money on tax advice and wasting ever more time filling in forms. "Transfer pricing is increasingly complex, and divorced from economic reality," says Huub Haemaekers, of the International Bureau for Fiscal Documentation in Amsterdam, who helped design the transfer-pricing system in the 1970s. The "arm's length principle" on which transfer pricing is based – in essence, that a multinational's businesses in different countries are taxed as if they were independent firms operating at arm's length from each other – makes it ever harder to run multinationals as global businesses.

Philip Gillett, group tax controller at ICI, explains:

> Commercially, transfer pricing makes no sense. It forces us to spend a lot of time doing things that are pointless from a business point of view. We have to waste time trying to price unfinished goods being "sold" from one plant to another. It is like asking Ford to value a camshaft half-way along the production line: a nonsense. Businesses want to organise as if there were a single global or regional product market. Instead, tax is determining how they organise themselves. It makes local managers think more territorially, to start looking after their own particular country issues. The tax system promotes parochial thinking.

National tax systems also put a huge price on reorganising national businesses into single, seamless global operations. For instance, consider a multinational with a buying and selling operation in France that it wants to scale back to the status of a sales agent, transferring most customers to a marketing operation in, say, Germany. The tax authorities in France would say that the multinational had transferred the goodwill in the French operation to another country, incurring a huge tax liability. This is such a big problem in the EU, says Mr Gillett, that "it can be easier for a multinational to come from the US or Japan and set up on a pan-European basis than for an existing European firm to make that transition."

A better way?

Mr Gillett would prefer to scrap transfer pricing and replace it with a system better suited to the needs of global firms. There is no ideal solution, but one option would be a "unitary tax", which involves taking a firm's total profits and allocating different slices of that total to individual countries on the basis of a formula that reflects the firm's relative economic presence in that country. The country can then tax that slice of profit at whatever rate it sees fit. This would still allow tax competition, but without the inefficient corporate structures. "Businesses still want tax competition," says Mr Gillett. "If government faces no downward pressure on tax rates, they tend to rise."

The prospects for the EU and the OECD "harmful taxation" initiatives look distinctly unpromising. Neither carries a big stick, and both are relying on drawing up blacklists and "naming and shaming". Yet it is doubtful whether many countries blacklisted by the OECD will feel shamed. After all, two wealthy member countries – Switzerland and Luxembourg – have said they will not be bound by the OECD's recommendations. Indeed, some of the wilder tax havens regard the whole exercise as a welcome bit of free advertising.

OECD officials speculate that it might be possible to do some sort of deal with tax havens to buy their good behaviour. As one of them puts it, "The amount of tax revenue being lost to the world to give only a very small nick to the tax havens is very large. It would make sense for the bigger countries to buy them off." Or perhaps OECD governments could bring co-ordinated pressure to bear on multinationals not to use tax havens – after all, 85% of multinationals are incorporated in OECD countries. But there is so much tax competition among OECD and EU countries that hopes of such co-ordinated action seem forlorn. As Mason Gaffney, an economist at the University of California, Riverside, trumpeted in a recent speech in the Bahamas in favour of tax competition: "Freedom anywhere foils tyranny everywhere. Tax tyranny is a balloon: seal every leak, or it collapses."

Certainly, if the EU were to put a stop to the "harmful" tax practices within its borders, many of the businesses now taking advantage of them might simply move to, say, Switzerland. All the same, the EU's initiative has a slightly better chance of succeeding than the OECD's. It is possible that the European Commission, the nearest thing the EU has to an executive government, will add muscle to its code of conduct by taking action against miscreants in the European Court of Justice, on the argument that preferential taxes are essentially the same as state aid. The commission has been waging war on such state aids for years on the ground that they distort competition in the EU's single market. It has taken disputes to the European Court, and usually won, so it believes it can do the same with taxes. The trouble is that such cases usually take years to work their way through the court, so the commission would prefer countries to fall into line voluntarily.

Some experts think that the European Court may even cause corporate tax rates within the EU to be harmonised – long a dream of politicians in Germany and France, and a nightmare for their counterparts in lower-taxing Britain and Ireland. According to Albert Rädler, a tax lawyer at Oppenhoff & Rädler in Munich, the court sees its mandate as completing a single market in Europe, and its verdicts on tax have been moving steadily in the direction of harmonised corporate taxation, even though the member states' governments think they have a veto over EU tax policy. If the European Court makes a decision, the member states have to accept it.

In 1999 the European Court found that denying benefits under the German-American bilateral tax treaty to the German permanent establishment of Saint-Gobain, a French firm, amounted to a denial of fundamental EU rights. "This was a revolution in taxes, extending bilateral-treaty benefits to non-residents," says Frans Vanistendal of the University of Louvain. In future, EU member governments may become much keener to co-ordinate tax policies, if only to stop the European Court eroding their political control of taxation, says Pasquale Pistone, a lawyer at the European Tax College in Louvain, who has been working on proposals for an EU model tax convention.

A contradiction in terms

Some officials at the OECD now regret ever using the phrase "harmful tax competition". As one of them puts it, "As an economist, how can you ever say anything bad about competition?" The OECD's main objection to some forms of tax competition is that they reduce another country's tax base, or force it to change its mix of taxes, or stop it taxing in the way it would like. But that seems a bit one-sided: what about the democratic rights of people in poor countries to enjoy a higher standard of living by pursuing tax policies that attract overseas investment? Indeed, says Edward Troup, a lawyer at Simmons & Simmons in London, it would be possible to argue that the OECD initiative is "an attempt to create a cartel among certain developed countries who have an unsustainable activity – raising revenue by taxing capital – that they want to protect".

Economists favouring tax competition often point to an article by Charles Tiebout entitled "A Pure Theory of Local Expenditures", published in 1956. In that article he argued that, faced with a choice of different combinations of tax and government services, taxpayers will choose to be where they get closest to the mixture they want. Variations in tax rates across different countries are a good thing, because they give taxpayers more choice, and thus more chance of being satisfied. They also create pressure on governments to be efficient. That makes harmonising taxes a bad idea.

A fascinating paper[4] by Reuven Avi-Yonah, of Harvard Law School, questions that optimistic conclusion. Certainly, tax competition can make governments deliver services more efficiently. Even so, argues Mr Avi-Yonah, tax competition may reduce redistribution and thus weaken the social safety net that in a global economy is needed more than ever. This could start a backlash against globalisation of the sort that pushed the world into depression 70 years ago.

Tiebout assumed that taxpayers are highly mobile, but many taxpayers, including the great majority of workers, have not so far shown much sign of getting on their bikes. Perhaps they are happy with their lot. Perhaps, though, they are simply unable to move. Will globalisation, supercharged by the Internet, change that?

Notes

1. "Fiscal Paradise: Foreign Tax Havens and American Business", by James Hines and Eric Rice. *Quarterly Journal of Economics*, 1994.
2. "Lessons from Behavioural Responses to International Taxation", by James Hines. *National Tax Journal*, June 1999.
3. "Has US Investment Abroad Become More Sensitive to Tax Rates?", by Rosanne Altshuler, Harry Grubert and T. Scott Newlon. National Bureau of Economic Research working paper, January 1998.
4. "Globalisation, Tax Competition and the Fiscal Crisis of the Welfare State". Harvard Law School working paper, July 1999.

Getting personal

Taxing people is becoming harder, too

LUCIANO PAVAROTTI MAY be a proud patriot, yet the famous Italian singer has gone to court to prove that he does not live in the land of his birth. The Italian government claimed that Mr Pavarotti was resident in Modena, and therefore owed over $2m in taxes. The tenor argued that he lived in Monte Carlo and spent only a few days in Italy during the years in question, not the 183 days a year that usually constitute residency. He also disputed the government's claims that his companies in Italy represented his vital economic interests, another criterion for residency. He said they were mainly vehicles for his hobbies and charitable activities.

After a court ruled against Mr Pavarotti in 1999, he launched an appeal. There has [as of January 2000 when this survey was originally published] been no settlement, but he has complied with a law requiring him to pay some of the money as a deposit. Francesco Tesauro, his lawyer, is up in arms. As somebody who does not spend 183 days a year in any one country, he says, his client has merely been exercising his right to choose a place of residence – which happens to be with other tax-avoiding millionaires in Monaco. He owns houses in Italy, "but so does the queen of the Netherlands, and nobody is claiming that she is resident in Italy". The real issue, says Mr Tesauro, is that the Italian government has launched a campaign against the rapidly growing number of Italians who have shifted their residence abroad to avoid taxes, "and they wanted a person to spotlight; a symbol".

Even so, what differentiates the present period of globalisation from past bursts is not that so many people are moving abroad, but so few. Within the EU, where citizens of member countries have freedom of movement, only 5.5m people, or around 1.5% of the total population, live in a member country different from their own. Even in America, which welcomes foreigners more than most rich countries, new immigrants in 1997 added only 0.3% to the population. Contrast that with the long wave of globalisation in which some 60m Europeans crossed the Atlantic, and which ended in the 1920s. Back in 1900, 15% of the American population were foreign-born, compared with 8% now.

In those days, many migrants were fleeing poverty or persecution. Today's disaffected find it harder to move in search of a new life. Most developed countries grant entry only to a carefully controlled few, usually because they have family ties in the new country rather than because of the economic contribution they might make. Even those who are allowed in may find that pension and welfare rights do not travel easily to another country. But most people stay where they are because they like it there, which suggests that there is more to life than a smaller tax bill.

On the face of it, this lack of mobility looks like good

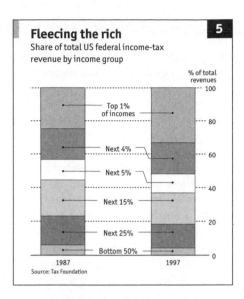

Fleecing the rich 5

Share of total US federal income-tax revenue by income group

news for the taxman. Even if companies become more footloose, and corporate-tax revenue declines, personal income tax can always be relied upon to supply the lion's share of government revenue. Yet income-tax revenue may not be as invulnerable as it appears. Incomes are becoming more unequal everywhere, which means that a growing share of the total income-tax take is being paid by a shrinking group of the population. In America, for example, over 30% of income tax is collected from the top 1% of earners, and over 60% comes from the highest-earning 10% (see chart 5). The highest earners are much the most mobile.

Even within the EU, there is evidence of tax competition being used as a way of attracting wealthy individuals. The French press has run many stories about some of the country's leading entrepreneurs moving to London for its lower taxes. And the Dutch government, according to Carlo Romano, a tax lawyer at the International Bureau of Fiscal Documentation, will "agree tax reductions with highly skilled foreigners to attract them, just as it does with companies".

Moving targets

Globalisation increases the mobility of high earners. As the influence and importance of multinational companies grows, so do the opportunities for their workers to move from country to country. Increasingly, multinationals operate in developing economies which have low taxes, or are willing to negotiate a favourable tax regime to attract the business. While abroad, workers from developed countries can squirrel away large amounts of capital that their home tax authority need never discover. The Internet will increasingly let people work anywhere, or appear to the taxman to be working abroad even if they are not. Companies increasingly contract out work to self-employed consultants, shifting responsibility for collecting personal income tax from usually law-abiding companies to those consultants, who can be hard to pin down.

Even if people themselves do not move abroad in search of lower taxes, their money can, and increasingly does. In most countries the share of direct personal tax revenue arising from taxes on income and capital gains from savings and investments has fallen steadily over the past 20 years. But this may be only the beginning.

Tax havens are starting to market their services much more vigorously to new groups of potential customers. For instance, British Airways mailed details of its own-brand "offshore deposit account", based in Jersey, to members of its frequent-flier club. Among other things, the literature promised the "notable advantages" of gross interest, although the small print did contain all the usual warnings about disclosure and tax liability. The OECD expects the Internet to lead to a rapid increase in offshore banking, but perhaps only in "reputable" tax havens, such as Jersey, because of customers' fears of being ripped off.

According to Joanna Wheeler, of the International Bureau of Fiscal Documentation, in recent years a growing number of continental Europeans have put their assets into offshore trusts – a tax-avoidance device long employed by wealthy people in Britain and America, but not previously much used on the continent. The tax authorities have "not found an answer to this".

Individuals investing money in tax havens are often illegally evading tax, rather than legally avoiding it. Germany has a 30% withholding tax on interest paid on bank deposits that has prompted vast numbers of Germans to put their savings in bank accounts elsewhere, notably Luxembourg and Switzerland, both of which have strong bank-secrecy laws. It is estimated that German tax is being paid on less than one-fifth of all the income earned abroad by German investors. Germany has been a champion of an EU savings directive requiring member governments to collect a 20% withholding tax on interest payments made to foreign residents.

One reason why much of the world has stopped levying withholding taxes on interest is strong tax competition from America, which unilaterally scrapped its withholding tax in 1984. The likely effect of an EU-wide withholding tax would be to drive savings away to more tax-competitive destinations. It is hard to get a grip on tax competition, particularly for financial capital, unless the whole world agrees to co-operate. "I do not think it possible to carry out the taxation-of-savings proposal if we do not have at least Jersey, Guernsey, Switzerland, Liechtenstein and Monaco on board," says Frits Bolkestein, the EU commissioner responsible for the savings directive. As none of these countries is a member of the EU, it seems unlikely that any of them will get on board.

The difficulty of getting co-operation was underscored by Britain's blocking of the savings directive in December 1999. The EU is now pondering what to do next. Britain had argued that investors in bonds traded in the City of London would be driven away to countries outside the EU, such as Switzerland. As an alternative, Britain said it would accept mandatory disclosure of interest payments made by financial firms in EU countries to foreign residents. But Luxembourg, which attracts international capital largely because it is so secretive, would have none of that. It is now hard to see how the EU can come up with anything that would not be unacceptable to, and vetoed by, either Britain or Luxembourg.

Tax havens are widely used not just for tax evasion, but also for another undesirable activity: money laundering. Some officials involved in tackling money laundering fear that international pressure on secretive tax havens to become more open on tax matters will actually make them less co-operative on other crimes. And new technology, such as encryption and anonymous electronic money, may make it even easier to keep financial transactions secret, and hence evade tax.

Rather than try to find out how much investment income their taxpayers have earned abroad, governments may want to copy the Netherlands, which from 2001 will levy a tax on "deemed income", based on the assumption that the taxpayer earns a rate of return of 4% a year on his assets. However, some tax experts fear that this will simply drive wealthy Dutchmen abroad.

The American way

America's approach to personal taxation is at odds with that of most other countries. Instead of taxing its citizens only if they are resident for at least 183 days in the year, it assesses them on their total global income, whether or not they are resident in America; but it allows them to offset income tax paid in their country of residence against their American tax liability. This does not work quite as well as it might because it requires a good deal of transparency and information-sharing, which not all countries are willing to engage in just to oblige the American taxman. Still, other countries might do well to adopt similar systems, if only to give everyone an incentive for more information-sharing.

Greater transparency might reduce tax competition, but this could be dealt with by setting a fair price for changing citizenship. A few years ago stories in *Forbes* magazine about "taxpatriates" – wealthy Americans who had renounced their citizenship to avoid large tax bills – caused a political furore and prompted a series of measures that penalised people for giving up citizenship (eg, by imposing strict limits on being able to visit America). Certainly there is something in the idea of connecting citizenship, and the right to vote, with tax liability. It could be marketed under the heading, "No representation without taxation."

You pluck, we hiss

**To cope with globalisation and the Internet, governments will
need to reform taxes in ways that will make them more unpopular
than ever**

THE TAXMAN HAS never been a popular fellow, and probably never
will be – but he can alleviate his unpopularity by following the
famous advice of Jean-Baptiste Colbert, Louis XIV's treasurer: "The art of
taxation consists in so plucking the goose as to obtain the largest possible amount of feathers with the smallest possible amount of hissing."
Over the next few years globalisation, accelerated by the Internet, is
likely to test the taxman's plucking skills.

The Internet will make the goose harder to catch, and noisier in
defence of its plumage. Tax competition is likely to go on. Although the
EU, urged on by the European Court of Justice, may move towards tax
harmonisation, this will be a slow process, and the only effect it may
have on tax competition in the wider world is to increase the incentive
for countries to offer lower taxes to lure firms and investors out of the
EU. It is hard to imagine any government agreeing to join a World Tax
Organisation, although the existing WTO (World Trade Organisation)
may get more involved with tax matters.

Even so, tax competition is unlikely to result in a "race to the bottom".
As Tiebout argued in the 1950s, governments offering competitive packages of high-quality services and high taxes may well attract mobile taxpayers, perhaps more successfully than governments offering minimal
services and low taxes. But using taxes to redistribute wealth from
mobile firms and people to the less mobile, and less well-off, may
become harder. And even though death and taxes will remain
inevitable, coping with globalisation is likely to require considerable
changes in the tax system over the next few years. Such changes almost
always generate a good deal of political strife.

The present system of taxing multinationals is a source of growing
inefficiency. With each passing day, the transfer-pricing process bears
less relation to the way that global companies operate now – and less
still to how they would like to operate if they had a free hand. A unitary
tax, which allocates slices of a multinational's total profits to different
countries for tax purposes, is not flawless, but it would at least free firms

to organise themselves in whatever way they think will let them use their global resources most efficiently. For such a tax to be introduced, however, several large countries would have to agree on it at the same time. That might be possible within the EU, but probably not elsewhere.

A tax reformer's dream

What would be even better, though even less likely, would be to put an end to company taxation altogether. This would let firms concentrate on doing what they do best, and to establish themselves wherever they can operate most efficiently without wasting time and resources on playing games with the tax authorities. A government of a big country, such as America or Britain, could bring this about by unilaterally scrapping corporation tax and letting tax competition do the rest. But whoever did such a thing would doubtless be accused of giving handouts to the rich. That charge might not be justified: the most sensible way of looking at corporate tax is simply as a pre-payment of tax that would otherwise be collected from a firm's shareholders, employees or customers. But the perception would probably be enough to warn off any politician contemplating such a move.

Governments may also need to make changes to accommodate e-commerce. For instance, in America revenues from sales taxes could plunge if nothing is done to stop the Internet from undermining them. What needs doing is fairly plain; the difficulty is getting politicians to do it, given that "taxing the Internet" is likely to prove a massive vote-loser.

If redistribution through the tax system becomes more difficult, the less mobile, poorer people will have to choose between fewer government services or bigger tax bills. In many countries, this choice will be complicated further by demographic changes which by themselves will require taxes to rise sharply to keep retirement-benefit and health-care promises made to future pensioners. And the harder it gets to tax mobile people and businesses, the bigger the burden that will have to be borne by the immobile. Land taxes, which used to be one of the most important revenue-earners, may regain their former pre-eminence. Consumption taxes on purchases of physical goods and services which the taxman can track may have to rise. In future, local environmental taxes – say pollution taxes, or road pricing – may well come to look attractive to tax-starved governments.

Many economists would welcome greater emphasis on consumption and environmental taxes because they cause fewer economic distortions and inefficiencies than income taxes. But this would not make them popular with those contemporary Welshmen, and their kindred spirits, who are unable to vote with their feet. They may no longer don women's dresses or vandalise the local tax office, but they will certainly complain bitterly. As Colbert might have put it, if they can't run, they can still hiss.

The material on pages 155–187 first appeared in a survey written by Matthew Bishop in *The Economist* in January 2000.

5

How industries go global:
from law to wine-making

To globalise, or not to globalise? And if to globalise, how? On these thorny questions, this chapter examines four industries: law, oil, retailing and wine-making. The differences in approach, and in outcome, are startling. Bigger may be better for oil companies, but it is not necessarily so for law firms. Australian wines may have worked their way profitably to London, but that does not mean that Wal-Mart will as easily be able to play the British market. One lesson rings clear: there is no universal best-practice template for globalisation. Companies and industries are by nature fast-moving, so there have been changes since these articles appeared in The Economist. *(The date of publication is given at the end of each article.) Since our article on retailing was published, for example, Marks and Spencer's has retrenched from overseas, Boots has withdrawn from Japan and Wal-Mart has yet to prove that its international business works well enough to drive the group's future growth. Such developments shore up the article's view that while global tastes certainly exist (look at the success of specialist retailers like Zara or Ikea), cultural differences still matter – especially in food shopping. Developments in other industries, too, have for the most part remained consistent with the arguments presented here.*

The battle of the Atlantic

The world's leading law firms, based in New York and London, disagree about the best way to respond to globalisation

THEY USED TO be the bag-carriers of the business world, a breed of quibblers who tidied up the paperwork after the real work of wheeling and dealing was done. But today few bosses would do any kind of deal, from a takeover to a product launch, without involving their lawyers early on. As regulations and lawsuits have proliferated, so have lawyers, and law firms have acquired a new status. In the biggest deals, top lawyers now help formulate much of the strategy.

The "suits" are now facing similar strategic dilemmas to their clients. Should they expand abroad or stay at home? Should they merge or grow organically? Should they diversify, or stick to their knitting? Confronted with the same globalisation that is reshaping so many industries, law firms are having to think about their long-term future. "In the past, lawyers have not had to be very good businessmen," says Reena SenGupta, editor of *Chambers Global*, a guide to the legal profession worldwide. "Now these firms have to be managed and led like any other company."

Lawyers are a disputatious bunch by inclination. So it is not surprising that the world's top firms disagree fiercely about the best way to thrive in an expanding international marketplace. A spate of cross-border mergers and alliances in Europe was greeted with indifference by most New York firms, who view such moves as too risky and, in any case, unnecessary.

The boldest of these deals was the three-way merger of London's Clifford Chance with New York's Rogers & Wells and Germany's Pünder, Volhard, Weber & Axster, which has created the world's largest law firm. "We're leading the way, others will have to follow," declares Keith Clarke, Clifford Chance's senior partner. Rivals in London are already doing so. Soon after the deal was announced in 1999, Freshfields turned its alliance with Germany's Deringer Tessin Herrmann & Sedemund into a merger. Linklaters hopes to do the same with its alliance with five European firms.

As they watch each other warily and debate what to do next, law firms are being stalked by challengers who are already global businesses: the five biggest accounting firms. Attracted by the high fees

191

lawyers earn and the growth in cross-border business, the big five have expanded their legal arms rapidly in recent years. "We are clearly aiming to be one of the top global players in legal services in the next five to ten years," says Alberto Terol, managing partner of Andersen Worldwide's tax and legal practice. Andersen's network of law firms employs almost as many lawyers as Clifford Chance, although it earns less than half of Clifford Chance's revenues.

Just another tale of service firms scrambling to become global giants? Not quite. As Mr Clarke and Mr Terol know, the peculiar characteristics of the legal profession make this battle for dominance more compli- cated than most. In every country, laws are different. Lawyers are also heavily regulated, with various statutory and professional restrictions on who can practise law where, again differing from country to coun- try. Despite a wave of domestic mergers in many countries, the legal market remains highly fragmented, ranging from one-man operations to businesses employing thousands of people. Top-earning commercial lawyers in New York take home a few million dollars apiece each year, but most lawyers earn far less.

Almost all law firms are run as partnerships, with partners usually taking decisions together, either by voting or through consensus. Heads of law firms cannot indulge in the daring tactics their clients so enjoy. Instead, they have always to carry their partners with them. If they don't, even the best firms can quickly disintegrate, with partners jump- ing ship or setting up in business on their own.

Cross-border profits

For all these reasons, most law firms still do most of their business within their own domestic market. But for the biggest and richest law firms the growth of world capital markets, and the globalisation in most other industries, means that advising on cross-border deals is becoming the fastest-growing and most lucrative aspect of their business. Being big at home is no longer good enough.

If global law giants are ever to emerge, they are likely to grow out of the top-tier New York and London firms. These are the firms that already advise the world's biggest companies and banks. They cream off the best business in two of the world's three biggest capital markets, which generate the most lucrative legal work. They work in English, the lan- guage of international business. More significantly, for historical reasons and because companies everywhere want to tap the London and New York capital markets, a growing proportion of international business is conducted under English or American law, even when the firms involved are continental European or Asian.

But there are also big differences between the New York and London firms. New York firms are in the world's biggest legal market, which has been booming in recent years, and they have close ties to the three largest investment banks – Morgan Stanley, Goldman Sachs and Merrill Lynch. This gives them a prime advantage in winning an advisory role in big deals, even when they do not employ many, or sometimes any, lawyers locally. London firms, by contrast, have a far smaller domestic market and looser ties to the investment banks – and thus feel a greater need to expand abroad.

These differences partly explain what looks like a curious stand-off. A merger between a top London and a top New York firm sounds like an unbeatable combination. Four of the five so-called "magic circle" firms that dominate the legal market in London make no secret of their desire for such a merger. But almost all the top New York firms are adamant that they have no interest at all in merging with a London firm. Clifford Chance claims to have broken this impasse through its merger with Rogers & Wells. Critics point out that, except in antitrust cases, Rogers & Wells is not a member of New York's top tier. Nevertheless, competitors are watching to see whether the combined firm does, in fact, win a lot more international business.

There are other obstacles to big New York–London mergers. Lawyers are prickly, and merger partners often fall out on the way to the altar. In 1999 a merger between White & Case and Brown & Wood, two big New York firms, fell apart after being announced. Even in successful mergers, keeping all the partners happy is often impossible. Rogers & Wells's entire Paris office defected to another firm rather than join the merger with Clifford Chance.

Pay is another stumbling block. Since the top-tier firms in New York are more profitable than London's big firms (see table 1), a merger may end up constraining the pay of their partners. In addition, most top-tier New York firms also share profits among partners based on how much business each brings in. This is known in the trade as "eat what you kill", which gives some idea of the kind of aggressiveness it encourages. All five of London's top firms, by contrast, share profits among partners according to seniority, a system appropriately known as "lockstep", which they believe encourages teamwork and minimises internal squabbling. To persuade Rogers & Wells to merge, Clifford Chance had to agree to a "modified" lockstep, letting the New York firm's biggest

The biggest and the best `1`

Firm	City	Profits per partner, $m	Revenue $m	Number of partners	Number of lawyers
Wachtell, Lipton, Rosen & Katz	New York	3.11	269	65	143
Cravath, Swaine & Moore	New York	2.05	334	77	334
Sullivan & Cromwell	New York	1.65	427	119	454
Cahill Gordon & Reindel	New York	1.60	–	55	204
Davis Polk & Wardwell	New York	1.53	435	124	464
Simpson Thacher & Bartlett	New York	1.50	386	123	490
Skadden, Arps	New York	1.38	890	285	1,187
Debevoise & Plimpton	New York	1.20	255	90	379
Slaughter and May	London	1.16	268	102	590
Milbank, Tweed, Hadley & McCloy	New York	1.11	243	81	372
Cleary, Gottlieb	New York	1.08	366	136	492
Shearman & Sterling	New York	1.05	426	140	683
Willkie Farr & Gallagher	New York	0.96	237	108	376
Freshfields	London	0.93*	463*	275†	1,448†
Allen & Overy	London	0.93	413	175	1,136
Weil, Gotshal & Manges	New York	0.89	400	160	640
Clifford Chance	London	0.84‡	1,000‡	570†	3,100†
Linklaters	London	0.81	479	207	1,210
White & Case	New York	0.67	352	172	742
Baker & McKenzie	Chicago	0.56	785	535	2,330

*Pre-merger †Post-merger estimates ‡Based on 1998–99 results for Clifford Chance and 1998 results for Rogers & Wells and Pünder
Sources: *American Lawyer; Legal Business;* International Centre for Commercial Law; *The Economist*

rainmakers keep their higher earnings until 2002, when lockstep is supposed to be reimposed.

A transatlantic divide

Everyone agrees that the volume of cross-border deals will grow, and that big corporate clients will increasingly need cross-border legal expertise. But there is no agreement on how firms can provide this. At one extreme is Clifford Chance, which is firmly committed to a "one-stop shop" model of a global law firm with offices in many countries around the world, able to practise local as well as American and English law, and capable of handling a wide variety of legal work for big companies and financial institutions. "The clients are demanding it," claims Mr Clarke. He says that the sheer complexity of international transactions means that only a single, unified law firm can deliver a "seamless" global service, and adds that world firms will also be able to attract the best new young lawyers.

Most New York firms scoff at these arguments. For example, Cravath, Swaine & Moore, one of the most profitable firms in the United States, has small offices in London and Hong Kong but no branches in America – and no plan to open any new offices. It is convinced that this will not hamper its ability to win work on the biggest transactions. In January 2000 it was lead counsel to Time Warner, a long-established client, on its merger with AOL.

Bob Joffe, Cravath's presiding partner, maintains that the most demanding and lucrative international assignments will always go to firms with the highest-quality lawyers, not those with the most lawyers in the most places. If a client needs a lawyer in another country, Cravath uses the traditional method of sharing the work with a local firm. "We'll go find the best person we can and we'll tell the client that's what we've done," he explains. "We think that's better than telling the client that we're using our partner in Berlin because he just happens to be idle." Big companies are sophisticated consumers of legal services. They do not need a "one-stop shop", insists Mr Joffe.

This also happens to be the attitude of Slaughter & May, London's most profitable firm and the only one of the top London firms not seeking merger partners in Europe or New York. Slaughter and Cravath describe themselves as "best friends", referring work to each other when necessary.

In fact, most New York firms have not been as emphatic as Cravath. Many, such as Shearman & Sterling; Skadden, Arps, Slate, Meagher & Flom; Sullivan & Cromwell; Cleary, Gottlieb, Steen & Hamilton; Davis Polk & Wardwell; and White & Case, have expanded abroad in recent years. But nearly all have done so more warily than the London firms (see table 2). And all except White & Case share a strong distaste for the idea of merging with another big firm. They view it as enormously risky and a threat to the quality of their service. "We train our own talent," says Cravath's Mr Joffe. "It even disturbs me that our firm is spread over 12 floors here in a single building. I would prefer to be able to see all my partners every day." The head of another firm agrees: "There are real diseconomies of scale in this business. We're not making widgets."

The New York firms point to the example of Baker & McKenzie, perhaps the only truly global law firm. Originally based in Chicago, Baker has expanded internationally for the past 50 years and has offices in 35 countries, more than any competitor, including Clifford Chance after its recent mergers. This entitles it to be called a pioneer, but the path it has blazed is not one that any top firm in London or New York wants to go down.

Who's global	2	
Firm	Lawyers outside home country,%	Number of countries
Baker & McKenzie	79.6	35
White & Case	46.8	24
Clifford Chance*	62.0	20
Linklaters	na	17
Allen & Overy	34.5	17
Freshfields*	51.1	15
Skadden, Arps	7.6	11
Shearman & Sterling	25.0	9
Cleary, Gottlieb	32.9	8
Sullivan & Cromwell	12.6	7
Weil, Gotshal & Manges	18.6	6
Slaughter & May	13.2	6
Davis Polk & Wardwell	12.7	6

Sources: *American Lawyer; Legal Business; The Economist*   *Post-merger

Rivals sneer at Baker as a "franchise" operation: one with the same nameplate screwed to the doors of all its offices, but really consisting of a conglomeration of local partnerships that act independently and keep their own profits. "Baker has some good lawyers," says the head of one London firm, "but the quality varies tremendously." Rivals say this locks it out of the biggest and most lucrative deals, and it earns much lower profits per partner than other leading American firms.

Christine Lagarde, the chairman of Baker's executive committee, vehemently disputes these views. "We're a single global partnership," she insists. "We've built the infrastructure and we have a genuinely international culture. That's something that takes years to create." If others want to compete internationally, they will have to do the same. And they, too, will discover that local regulations make a single global profit pool impossible. All Baker's partners share a portion of profits, but national rules in many countries dictate that profits earned locally have to be shared locally. According to Ms Lagarde, this has been no hindrance to internal co-operation.

As for Baker's lower profits per partner, this is a misleading measure. "The cost of living and earning potential varies tremendously around the world," explains Ms Lagarde, lowering the overall figure. Baker's partners in New York or London earn as much as their peers at other top firms. If other firms expand abroad, they too will see profits per partner fall. Ms Lagarde may be right, but this is not an argument any of Baker's rivals want to hear or accept.

Despite disagreement about how to tackle globalisation, there is universal agreement that the big five accounting firms represent little threat, except in the specialist area of tax advice. "I don't want to sound complacent, but they're not even a blip on the horizon," says the head of one

New York firm. "Maybe in five or ten years, but I doubt it." "We just don't meet them in the marketplace," says Clifford Chance's Mr Clarke.

Ironically, the accounting firms, which nowadays prefer to be known as "professional service" firms, are using the same "one-stop shop" argument as Mr Clarke to justify their foray into legal services. But their idea of one-stop shopping involves not just a collection of different legal specialties, but advice on business strategy, financing, management, computer systems and personnel as well. "Clients like teams that are integrated," says Samuel DiPiazza, head of PricewaterhouseCoopers's tax and legal services practice in North America. The accounting firms also have huge international networks of offices, dwarfing those of even the biggest law firms. PricewaterhouseCoopers, for example, has 150,000 employees in 150 countries, compared with Clifford Chance's 6,500 in 20 countries.

The accounting giants must still clear regulatory hurdles in many countries to compete in legal services, especially in America, where bar associations continue to ban lawyers from sharing profits with other professions. But the top law firms are not counting on such barriers to defend their turf. Most believe that, despite opposition from some lawyers, the barriers will soon fall, and they agree with the accountants that conflict-of-interest concerns can be resolved. Yet they believe that the accounting firms will never be able to attract the very best lawyers needed to compete at the top of the market. "The culture's different. None of us would want to work for them," says a senior partner at one New York firm. A similar argument is heard from top strategy consultants, whose turf the accountants have also sought to invade. The accountants' real targets, say lawyers and consultants alike, are hundreds of middle-ranking practitioners working for less money and for smaller companies. Many of these are already starting to lose business.

Being best is what counts

In essence, all the top law firms, including Clifford Chance, the most outspoken champion of globalisation, are using the same argument against the ambitions of the accounting firms that the New York firms use against those of Clifford Chance and other London firms: that market segmentation is the key to legal services, because quality and reputation matter more than size or geographical reach. Being global will be less crucial than being best, even in the competition for international business.

In many other industries, this might sound self-deluding. But in the legal business it could turn out to be true. Market segmentation has been powerful in the past. In the United States, the same New York firms dominate the top of *American Lawyer's* profitability tables as when the magazine first began ranking law firms in 1985, despite huge changes in the American economy over that period.

In addition, the accounting firms are already struggling to hold together their global, multi-disciplinary partnerships. A dispute between the auditing and consulting partners of Andersen Worldwide has been in arbitration for more than two years [a divorce occurred in August 2000]. PricewaterhouseCoopers is currently considering a reorganisation that would split the firm into three separate units.

Globalisation may not be the most competitive model for such a demanding and specialised service as legal advice. Big companies do not want a cross-border deal, especially a large one, to unravel because of an unanticipated legal snag. When billions are at stake, nobody is sacked for hiring the best lawyers. Even the sometimes inflated bills of the top firms are a small fraction of the cost of such deals, and far less than the investment bankers' fees. For these reasons, the world's biggest companies have traditionally played safe and reached for one of the top New York or London firms.

That is why these firms have long dominated the most lucrative end of the legal marketplace in a way only recently achieved by the world's three biggest investment banks. But, unlike the investment banks, they do not need to raise large amounts of capital to stay in business, and so do not need to grow beyond a certain size to maintain their position. Moreover, it is harder to hold together a law firm than an investment bank, whose employees cannot easily walk out and establish a rival firm. That makes extensive global networks riskier to build and more difficult to manage.

London firms such as Clifford Chance are gambling that they can overcome these difficulties and strike it rich by offering a variety of legal services across the globe to the world's biggest companies. But most New York firms are gambling on the opposite proposition: that excelling in a few key areas of the law will continue to win them work on the biggest and most lucrative deals, even if more world-straddling law firms do emerge. "You might be willing to settle for second-best when hiring a podiatrist," says Cravath's Mr Joffe, "but not when you need a brain surgeon."

The material on pages 191–98 first appeared in a Special in *The Economist* in February 2000.

In praise of Big Oil

Why consolidation among big oil firms need not be cause for alarm

BASHING BIG OIL has been a popular sport of late. The soaring oil price and high petrol taxes helped to inspire widespread protests across Europe in September 2000. Though the initial target was government, the oil majors inevitably came under attack from all sides. Oilmen have met with rough treatment in America too. High petrol prices in summer 2000 and the spectre of a heating-oil shortage the following winter made energy a hot issue in the presidential campaign. While the price fixers at the OPEC cartel received some jabs, the lion's share of the populist attacks from [then] Vice-President Al Gore were aimed squarely at big oil companies. Rather than offering a vigorous rebuttal, George W. Bush managed only timid retorts that the real culprit is "big foreign oil" – in other words, not his chums back in Texas.

This seems a poisonous atmosphere in which to announce a big oil takeover. Yet that is precisely what America's Chevron did in October 2000 in revealing plans to gobble up its compatriot Texaco, in a deal worth more than $35 billion. The combination, if approved, would create the world's fifth-biggest oil firm. Consumer-rights advocates cried foul, and the Gore camp responded: "Given the fact that oil companies saw their profits rise by over 300% in the past year, it raises the question whether big oil is getting too big."

Is this deal really so worrying? The answer is no, for three reasons. For a start, the deal is merely part of a broader trend toward consolidation in the oil industry. In the two previous years, a frenzy of mergers and acquisitions has created such "super-majors" as America's Exxon Mobil and Britain's BP (which swallowed two American firms, Amoco and Arco, in rapid succession). Taken in this context, the union of Chevron and Texaco is not worrying: even the combined entity would be but half the size of its recently merged peers.

Another reason not to take alarmists seriously is that the only legitimate question that should concern regulators – are consumers harmed by the deal? – is straightforward to assess and, if necessary, to remedy. That is because the downstream bits of the oil business, be it refining or retail marketing, that most affect consumers are relatively transparent. What is more, the painfully low margins typical of this end of the oil

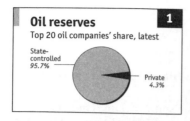

Oil reserves 1

Top 20 oil companies' share, latest

State-controlled 95.7%

Private 4.3%

business are evidence of the intense and increasing competition (including from independent refiners and supermarkets peddling petrol) that keeps abuses in check. Even in markets like California, where Texaco and Chevron both have a strong retail presence, regulators have quick and effective remedies: they can order the firms to sell gas stations and refineries.

The real game

The most compelling reason not to worry is the competition upstream, in the wild world of oil and gas exploration. Petroleum is probably the only global business in which the industry's largest firms and best assets are controlled by governments. Even the likes of Chevron and Texaco are midgets compared with the state-run oil giants like Saudi Arabia's Aramco, which alone produces a fifth of the world's oil exports. What is more, the industry's best, lowest-cost reserves are also controlled by governments. This leaves the private sector to fight ferociously over those oil and gas fields still left to be discovered; even here, they are finding that once-sleepy state firms from Brazil, China and elsewhere are now competing with them for exploration rights. It is this frenzied hunt for the next big bonanza that is really behind the mergers.

Moreover, the emergence of "super-majors" in the private sector may even be good news for consumers. That is because it will help check the power of the true threat to consumer welfare: OPEC. The cartel derives its power to manipulate prices from its control over much of the world's hydrocarbons: two-thirds of the world's proven reserves lie in the Middle East. There is surely more oil in the world, hidden away in Siberia and at the bottom of the deep blue sea. Finding and exploiting it increasingly takes the sort of money, fancy technology and, crucially, the appetite for risk that only the biggest firms can afford.

The discovery of oil in the North Sea played an important role in checking the excesses of OPEC's power. Now, those fields are mature and, in time, will decline in importance. The rise of super-majors increases the odds that other sources of non-OPEC oil will be found, which will help keep the cartel's power in check. Which is surely good news for consumers.

The material on pages 195–200 first appeared in an article in *The Economist* in October 2000.

Shopping all over the world

Retailers are trying to go global. They will struggle to succeed

A T FIRST GLANCE, Wal-Mart's £6.7 billion ($10.7 billion) bid for Asda, announced on June 14th 1999, was a huge threat both to British supermarkets and to the rest of Europe's retailing elite. But the American firm's triumph was marred by a tiff close to home. On the day it swooped on Asda, Bob Martin, Wal-Mart's long-standing international head, resigned unexpectedly. Although Mr Martin was passed over for the top job at Wal-Mart in January 1999, the timing of his departure suggests that, just as the world's most powerful retailer is seeking to double its international sales, it is divided about how far and how fast to push globalisation.

Wal-Mart's British acquisition comes at a time when retailers have caught globalisation fever. They are behind most manufacturers, but the bug was the more virulent for that. In the first half of 1999, Royal Ahold, a Dutch supermarket operator, bought supermarkets in Poland, four rival chains in Spain, one in America and two in Argentina. France's leading hypermarket, Carrefour, which is in 20 markets, opened stores in Chile, Colombia, Indonesia and the Czech Republic; it also announced that it would move into Japan. Tesco, Britain's biggest food retailer, set up shop in South Korea, its sixth overseas market. And Promodès, another French hypermarket group, has become the market leader in Argentina. Meanwhile, fast-growing clothes chains, such as The Gap, Sweden's Hennes & Mauritz (in 12 markets), and Spain's Zara (in 17), are opening a branch in a new country every few weeks.

Despite this enthusiasm, however, retailers seem to be finding it hard to make a success of the transition from national to multinational. Although a few firms, such as IKEA, a Swedish furniture retailer, have done well, established international retailers still make most of their money and their highest returns at home (see table 1). Carrefour's operating margins in France are more than 6% of sales, whereas, after operating internationally for 30 years, it still loses money in much of Asia, Latin America and even some parts of Europe. Meanwhile Wal-Mart, which first went abroad in 1991, makes a return on capital of 5.8% on its international business, far lower than in America. Can today's headlong rush succeed?

Home is where the cart is

Selected global retailers	Home country	Sales 1998, $bn	% of sales overseas	No. of countries	Market capitalisation June 15th, $bn
Wal-Mart*	United States	150.7	17	10	199.7
Royal Ahold	Netherlands	37.1	71	17	22.0
Promodès	France	362	54	12	12.6
Carrefour	France	36.0	44	20	30.5
Home Depot	United States	30.2	neg	4	84.5
Tesco	Britain	28.4	13	9	19.5
Marks and Spencer	Britain	13.3	16	34	16.8
Toys "R" Us	United States	11.2	27	26	5.3
Pinault Printemps	France	10.0	30	23	19.3
Hennes & Mauritz	Sweden	14	82	12	17.9

Sources: PricewaterhouseCoopers; company reports   *Assuming merger with Asda, 1999 sales

One reason for scepticism is that retailers are being driven by slow growth at home as much as by the sight of opportunities abroad, according to Felix Barber of Boston Consulting Group (BCG) in Zurich. The small size of the Swedish market encouraged several of the country's retailers to move overseas as early as the 1970s. A few, such as IKEA and Hennes, have built strong international businesses, although they have taken years to do so. French retailers, such as Carrefour and Auchan, have gone into emerging markets to escape the constraints of planning laws. Even Wal-Mart, which is still producing sales growth in America, is going abroad partly because it already has a dominant share of the country's non-food market.

Shop flaws

As everybody piles in abroad, the opportunities are dwindling. Many local retailers in Latin America have either been bought or are already in joint ventures. The price of those that remain is rising. Multinationals are snapping up partners all over Asia – witness Carrefour's move into Japan.

However, retailers assert that globalisation is about more than simply adding to their turnover. Sir Geoff Mulcahy, boss of Kingfisher, which launched an earlier, lower bid for Asda, argues that the main reason retailers want new sales is to exploit economies of scale and to spread the rising costs of marketing and technology. In Europe, international scope may also help retailers to cope with the single currency, which will make it easier for consumers to compare prices across borders.

In practice, however, international scale economies are hard to achieve. In the excitement of their charge into new markets, many retailers forget that the crucial ingredient of their success at home is their relative size and market share. Without enough sales and profits in a particular market, even the most long-term management will find it difficult to justify the expense of setting up a large distribution network or installing the latest technology – and without these, the international newcomer cannot compete with entrenched locals. In America, Carrefour opened a mere three stores in Pennsylvania, and abandoned its investment before getting anywhere near the scale needed.

The secret may be to arrive in force. Ahold, which has bought itself a concentrated market share on America's east coast, is doing well. So is Carrefour in Spain, where the French firm is now the second-largest retailer. Ahold's frantic recent purchases in Spain are an attempt to catch up, though it still has less than 1% of the market.

Cross-border scale economies are particularly elusive in food retailing – precisely where overseas expansion has been most enthusiastic, notes Keith Wills, a retail analyst at Goldman Sachs in London. BCG's Mr Barber says that almost all retailers overestimate the scope for savings from aggregating lots of local orders for a product into a single worldwide contract. Few deals manage to produce even 1–2% of sales in savings.

The reason is partly that the biggest suppliers have not yet woken up to such "global sourcing". Meredith Prichard, J.P. Morgan's Latin American retailing analyst, argues that Procter & Gamble's priority in, say, Brazil, is not going to be Wal-Mart, but CBD, the country's biggest retailer. "P&G's managers negotiate locally, their goods are made locally and their internal targets are local," she adds.

In time, worldwide contracts will become more widespread – in June 1999 P&G announced plans to reorganise itself along global lines. However, the regional managers of suppliers are unlikely to embrace global sourcing with enthusiasm. Ira Kalish, a retail analyst at PricewaterhouseCoopers, predicted that as suppliers succumb to pressure from retailers, perhaps a third of a supermarket's lines could be sourced globally or regionally by 2005, up from less than 10% in 1999.

Yet global sourcing is no panacea, because it conflicts with the need to cater for local tastes. Stores in different countries stock very different goods, which undermines the point of global sourcing and complicates relations between local and global managers – of both the retailer and its supplier.

Pile 'em high
Global cross-border retail M&As
value $bn

No. of deals

Source: Thomson Financial Securities Data   *Year to June 16th

Local taste crucially affects the way retailers sell their goods too. In 1996 Wal-Mart set up efficient, clean supercentres in Indonesia, only to find that Indonesians preferred Matahari, the shabbier shop next door, which reminded shoppers of a street market where they can haggle and buy the freshest fruit and vegetables. Two years later, Wal-Mart pulled out. Boots, a British pharmacy, found the number of visitors to its Thai shops soared after it started playing pop-music videos at full volume. Customers had found the shops too quiet. And Boots plans that staff at its checkouts in Japan will be standing up – its research has shown that Japanese shoppers find it offensive to pay money to seated staff.

Trouble in store

Even concepts that have global appeal need local tinkering. Jose Castellano, the chief executive of Zara, insists that "as tastes for music and television have gone global, so has fashion". Yet MTV, the epitome of a global media brand, decided to adapt its musical mix to local markets. Equally, Zara has lost sales in Britain, because its sizing is considered too small for the British figure.

If they are to overcome such obstacles, multinational retailers need a fanatical attention to detail, and a willingness to do whatever local whim dictates. Wal-Mart had to abandon its attempt to sell Brazilians (cheaper) Colombian coffee: they insist on drinking their own. IKEA tried to sell Americans its own beds, before discovering that they were the wrong size for their bedlinen; sales of its four-legged desks to Germans also flopped – five legs are preferred.

One way of getting an inside track on local tastes is to join a local partner, something that in many developing countries is required by law. But even that often leads to conflict, since many big western retailers think they know better. In Brazil, Wal-Mart failed to tap the local knowledge of its joint-venture partner, Lojas Americanas. Failing to spot that most families have one car and shop at the weekends, Wal-Mart built car parks and store aisles that were too small to accommodate the weekend rush. Because many joint ventures fail, local firms are reluctant to give up trade secrets or surrender their best sites. After all, they could be competitors again within a few years.

Yet multinational retailers do have some advantages. Know-how is probably the greatest, according to Cees van der Hoeven, the chief executive of Ahold. At its heart, this is a sophisticated understanding of supply chains, beginning with electronic links to suppliers who can tell instantaneously what customers are buying at the checkout. The next, much trickier, stage is to persuade suppliers to share information with both retailers and rivals, so that they can minimise inventory and put more of what customers want on the shelves.

If cultures are similar or the retailer is established, it is relatively easy for suppliers to accept new buying systems and new technology, and this can lead to savings. Following a flurry of acquisitions in America, Ahold USA expected to save around $85m in 1999 and $115m in 2000. Similarly, Wal-Mart should be able to improve Asda's supply-chain management and make better use of its floorspace. Meanwhile, 7-Eleven, a chain of convenience stores that is Japan's most successful retailer, is starting to apply its expertise to stores in Hawaii.

However, even best practice is hindered by cultural differences. Wal-Mart has worked with Grupo Cifra, a Mexican retailer, since 1991 and has had a controlling stake since 1997, but only recently introduced a modern till-information system (years after local rivals had installed one). So far, it has had little effect on margins, as employees are still learning how to use it. Because labour is so cheap, local managers are loth to announce the layoffs that the new technology allows. Similarly, new owners often meet resistance when they try to get their new subsidiary to cut links that were established with suppliers over many years.

Given that globalisation is fraught with such difficulties, which sort of retailers will make a good fist of it?

The leaders so far are "category killers" with a strong focus, products with universal appeal and their own brands. The Gap, with its khakis and white shirts, and the IKEA furniture chain combine large volumes with higher margins and control over their design, distribution and sourcing. Some Internet retailers may turn out to fall into this group too, though maintaining a global brand over the long term could prove cripplingly expensive for what are, after all, loss-making start-ups. And the international failures of Britain's Laura Ashley and Body Shop, and America's Toys "R" Us show what happens if expansion abroad is not carefully managed.

Food and general-merchandise retailers have a harder job. Crucially, they must dominate their home base, as do both Wal-Mart and Ahold – but as Promodès does not. Otherwise they will find it difficult to pay for their expansion. They also need to offer a variety of formats, from convenience stores to supermarkets and hypermarkets, in order to ensure market coverage.

On the shop front

Most important, a general retailer needs a strong brand if consumers are to trust it with their personal details or buy its higher-margin products and services. Tesco and 7-Eleven Japan have successfully used information from loyalty cards to adapt their stores, products and prices to local tastes and to move into services such as banking and bill payments. A recent survey by CLK, a market-research group, shows that trusted retail brands have great power: a third of the 1,000 British adults surveyed said they would buy a house from an estate agent with a supermarket brand; 15% would buy a supermarket-branded car. Boots is trusted by 85% of young people in Britain (only 10% have the same feeling for the royal family).

Yet, a well-known brand takes a great deal of time to create – partly because, unlike manufacturers, whose products are promoted by shops, retailers must do all the promoting themselves. As Marc Berman, an analyst at Euromonitor in London notes: "Most retailers entering new markets are unknowns to suppliers and customers. Building trust takes years."

Despite the time and the investment that will be needed, a small group of rich firms with skilled managers will probably succeed. They may even be able to pay over the odds for "strategic" acquisitions – as Wal-Mart is doing with Asda – if this allows them eventually to dominate markets. British and continental European retailers are, in this sense, right to fear the arrival of Wal-Mart on their shores. But for many other retailers, the hoped-for economies of scale from globalisation will prove elusive. Local tastes will often get in the way; best practice will take frustratingly long to put into action. No doubt managers will persist in trying to go global. But too often they will be motivated less by the chance of creating value than by the fear of being left out and gobbled up themselves.

The material on pages 199–206 first appeared in an article in The Economist in June 1999.

The globe in a glass

European wine makers believe in tradition and regulation. New-world producers are keener on technology, innovation and consumer research. The new-world approach is winning out

"WINE MAKING IS really quite a simple business," Baroness Philippine de Rothschild likes to tell visitors to her *château* near Bordeaux. "Only the first 200 years are difficult." The museum at Château Mouton Rothschild is full of artefacts tracing the story of wine back to Roman times; a special cellar is devoted to vintage bottles going back to the mid-19th century. The whole place reeks of history, as well as wine.

But the baroness's remark is stronger on grandeur than candour. Leave aside the fact that the Rothschilds did not take over the *château* until 1853. More significantly, wine critics and ordinary consumers alike are becoming increasingly aware that you do not need a long history of wine making to produce great wine. New Zealand's wine industry got going properly only in the 1970s, but according to Oz Clarke, a respected British critic, New Zealand sauvignon blanc is now "arguably the best in the world". America's Robert Parker, the most influential wine critic in the world today, is a great lover of Bordeaux wines, but he has written that Grange, Australia's most famous wine (which was first produced in the 1950s), "has replaced Bordeaux's Pétrus as the world's most exotic and concentrated wine".

The notion that the best wines of the new world can match or even surpass the great wines of the old world was first established in 1976, at an event subsequently labelled "the judgment of Paris". Steven Spurrier, a British wine merchant based in Paris, brought together 15 of the most influential French wine critics for a blind tasting of top wines from France and California – for this purpose, whites made from chardonnay grapes and reds made from cabernet sauvignon. The critics were shocked to discover that, without the benefit of labels to guide them, they had awarded the highest marks to Californian wines, both white and red. This caused an outcry in France, and led to accusations that the results had been rigged. But when the tasting was re-staged two years later, it produced similar results.

Since the 1970s, more and more new wine-making areas have come on stream. These days the Californian producers are part of the establishment and sometimes appear disquieted by the success of upstart new producers to their north, in the states of Washington and Oregon. The Australians first began to break into the world market in the 1980s. In the past decade, wines from Chile have become the fastest-growing imports into the United States. Argentina is likely to be next to make a big breakthrough in international markets. Producers in Eastern Europe and South Africa, too, have been handed new opportunities by the collapse of communism and apartheid.

Even so, the globalisation of wine still has a long way to go. One big obstacle is the parochialism of consumers in wine-producing countries. In France, one of the biggest consumers as well as producers of wine, imports command less than 5% of the market. "French people absolutely refuse to drink foreign wines," says Françoise Brugiere, head of research at the Office National Interprofessionel des Vins in Paris, with a certain fierce pride. But a frustrated would-be importer puts it differently: "It's no accident that Chauvin was a Frenchman."

To be fair to the French, they are not alone in their wine chauvinism. For example, around 90% of the wine drunk in Australia is home-grown. At least the Australians can reasonably argue that most potential suppliers are half-way round the globe (although distance has proved no barrier to their own successful export drive), but Italy and Spain have similar figures. Of the major producing countries, only Germany and the United States are also significant importers. In Germany, this is largely because very little red or really dry white wine is produced at home. The Americans are very open to trade, and – as a nation of immigrants – perhaps less prejudiced about foreign wine.

Despite the advent of a horde of new-world producers, some 70% of the world's wines are still made and drunk in Western Europe. Anyone scanning the wine shelves of British supermarkets might well conclude that Australia had joined the ranks of the big producers, but they would be wrong: it accounts for only 2.3% of world production, less than Bordeaux alone.

However, new-world producers are having a much bigger effect on the world wine market than the production statistics would suggest. In the late 1980s around 85% of all the wine exported in the world came from just four West European countries – France, Italy, Portugal and Spain. By 1997 that figure had fallen to 72%, and has almost certainly fallen below 70% since. New-world exports have surged over the past decade; those from Chile are up over 400%, and those from Australia up 350%.

The British market provides a particularly useful gauge of the state of competition, because Britain is the world's biggest importer of wine. It has no serious domestic producers to favour, and has strong historical ties both to the traditional producers and to those of the new world. In this vital market, the traditional European producers are clearly struggling. In 1993, French, German and Italian wines between them accounted for around two-thirds of British consumption by both volume and value; by 1999 the figure had dropped below half, and is still heading down.

New-world producers have well over a third of the British market. In 1999 Australia led the field with a share of over 15%, and Chile and South Africa each leapt from around 1% of the market to about 6% in only six years (see chart 1). What is more, wines from Australia and New Zealand now command higher average prices in Britain than wines from France, Italy or Spain – a considerable achievement in an industry where all producers are struggling to get into the fastest-growing and most profitable niche of "premium" wines.

New world, new ideas

Most important of all, the influence of the new world goes well beyond market share and price. It is being felt most keenly in the techniques for making and marketing wine. Australia may have only a tiny share of the world's wine output, but it produces 20% of the world's scientific papers on viticulture and oenology. "Flying wine makers" from Australia and New Zealand are advising vineyards and winemakers in every corner of the world.

Their impact is being felt even in Bordeaux, the heart of the French wine industry. Vintex, one of Bordeaux's leading *négociants* (middlemen who buy wine from local producers and sell it on to retailers in France and abroad), relies heavily on wine makers from Australia and New Zealand to advise the vineyards it works with. Although some of the most revered wine makers in the world are Bordelais, Bill Blatch, the president of Vintex, thinks that outside the rarefied world of the very top producers, the Australians and New Zealanders have the edge on professionalism and sensitivity to the tastes of foreign consumers.

John Worontschak, an Australian wine maker who works in Bordeaux as well as with producers in places as diverse as Uruguay, Italy, Mexico and Sussex, is blunt about why experts from his part of the world are now in such demand: "It's because we're open to new ideas, and we're not full of pretentious bullshit." Warming to his theme, he

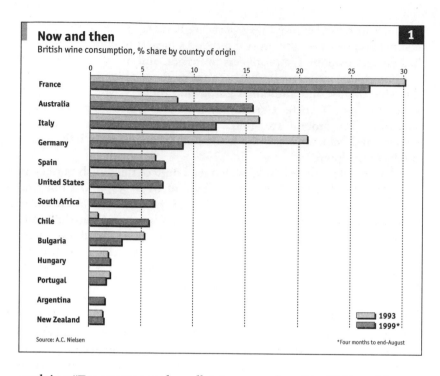

Now and then 1

British wine consumption, % share by country of origin

France
Australia
Italy
Germany
Spain
United States
South Africa
Chile
Bulgaria
Hungary
Portugal
Argentina
New Zealand

1993
1999*

Source: A.C. Nielsen

*Four months to end-August

explains: "Too many people walk into somewhere like Château Mouton Rothschild, swoon at the art collection and get an inferiority complex." Flying wine makers like Mr Worontschak happily acknowledge that the top Bordeaux wines are "pinnacles of the industry". But they also insist that the key to making consistent, high-quality wine lies in the careful application of scientific methods and modern techniques.

Who can argue with that? As it happens, quite a lot of people, and not just French producers worried about market share. Some critics fear that the flying wine makers from the new world, and the spread of large wine companies, will gradually eradicate the diversity and sense of place that is wine's most distinctive selling point. The Jeremiahs fear the rise of a few homogenised styles of "world wines" – generic chardonnays and merlots – that could be produced almost anywhere. In the process, they say, wine will lose its magic, and ultimately its market.

The material on pages 207–10 first appeared as part of a survey in The Economist in December 1999.

III
RICH AND POOR

6

By invitation: on inequality, aid and the environment

This chapter contains essays by three noted thinkers on some of today's most contentious development issues. Robert Wade of the London School of Economics writes on inequality; Jeffrey Sachs of Harvard University discusses American foreign aid; and Bjorn Lomborg, author of "The Sceptical Environmentalist", gives an optimistic – and controversial – account of the health of our planet. All three essays, like the rest of this book, were first published in The Economist, as part of the newspaper's occasional series of signed pieces, By Invitation.

Not all their views are necessarily shared by The Economist. Indeed, a friendly rejoinder to Mr Wade (originally published in The Economist alongside Mr Wade's piece) is reproduced here. Each piece offers a matchless basis for discussion and debate.

Winners and losers

The global distribution of income is becoming ever more unequal. That should be a matter of greater concern than it is, argues Robert Wade

ANYBODY INTERESTED IN the wealth and poverty of nations must be interested in what is happening to the global distribution of income, one would suppose. A lot turns on the question. If the world's income distribution has become more equal in the past few decades, this would be powerful evidence that globalisation works to the benefit of all. It would give developing countries good reason to integrate their economies closely into the world economy, as the IMF and the World Bank – and their mostly rich-country shareholders – urge them to do. It would answer some of the fears of the anti-globalisation protesters. And it would help to settle a crucial and long-standing disagreement in economic theory, between the orthodox view that economic growth naturally delivers "convergence" of rich and poor countries, and alternative theories which, for one reason or another, say the opposite.

Despite its importance, this issue has received rather little attention within the fields of development studies, international relations and (until very recently) international economics. Neither the World Bank nor the IMF has devoted significant resources to studying it. Many analysts apparently take it for granted that global inequality is falling. Others think it sufficient to focus on poverty, and ignore inequality as such. Both these views need to be challenged. New evidence suggests that global inequality is worsening rapidly. There are good reasons to worry about that trend, quite apart from what it implies about the extent of world poverty.

Distributing the spoils

What exactly does "world income distribution" mean? This article is concerned with distribution among the planet's 6.2 billion people, regardless of country or region. World income distribution can be thought of as the combination of (a) the internal income distributions for all the countries and (b) the distribution of average incomes across countries. Most of the inequality in world incomes reflects inequality in country averages rather than inequality within countries.

215

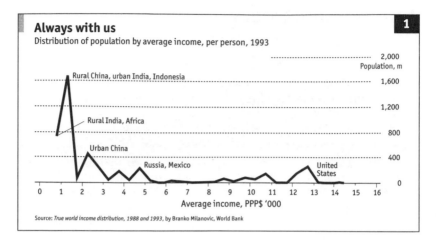

Always with us

1

Distribution of population by average income, per person, 1993

Rural China, urban India, Indonesia

2,000
Population, m

1,600

1,200

Rural India, Africa

800

Urban China

400

Russia, Mexico

United
States

0

Average income, PPP$ '000

Source: *True world income distribution, 1988 and 1993*, by Branko Milanovic, World Bank

Chart 1 shows the distribution of the world's population by average income of each country (using compatible data from 1993). Income is measured in terms of purchasing power over comparable bundles of goods and services, or purchasing-power parity (PPP), rather than in terms of actual exchange rates. China and India, with between them almost 40% of world population, are each divided into urban and rural sectors and treated as four separate countries.

The distribution has two poles. One, at the bottom end, is at an average income of less than $1,500 a year. It contains the populations of most of Africa, India, Indonesia and rural China. At the other pole, with average PPP incomes of more than $11,500, are the United States, Japan, Germany, France, Britain and Italy. Some of the space between $1,500 and $11,500 is occupied by countries such as urban China, Russia and Mexico. But notice the strange "missing middle": relatively few people live in countries with average PPP incomes that fall between $5,000 and $11,500. If incomes were measured using actual exchange rates, the range from poorest to richest would be much larger.

Nobody denies that world income distribution became vastly more unequal after the industrial revolution. On this timescale divergence dominates, big time. But what happened in the past three or four decades?

Having ignored world income distribution for decades, international economics has lately seen a burst of interest. But the statistical difficulties are so formidable that the debate has so far revolved around questions of econometric technique. Standing back from the fray, we can see that much of the controversy concerns how to compare income in different countries.

The answer to what is happening to world income distribution turns out to depend heavily on whether countries are weighted by population, and whether income in different countries is measured in PPP terms or by using actual exchange rates. These two criteria can be set out in a matrix of four cells, with

Worsening			2
World income distribution movement over the past quarter century			
		Income measured in:	
		market exchange rates	PPP exchange rates
Countries weighted by population?	No	Very much more unequal	More unequal
	Yes	Much more unequal	Little change

Source: R. Wade

countries treated equally or weighted by population on one axis, and income measured in current exchange rates or in PPP terms on the other. Table 2 summarises the findings of the existing literature, dividing the studies among the four cells.

If countries are treated equally (not weighted by population) and average income is measured in PPP terms, most studies find that world income distribution has become more unequal in the past few decades. If countries are weighted by their populations (so that China's change in average income counts for many times more than Uganda's), the world's PPP income distribution over recent decades shows little change.

It may seem obvious that one should weight countries by population, giving every individual in the world equal weight. For some purposes, though, it may make sense to weight countries equally. To test the growth theories mentioned earlier, or to assess the effectiveness of policy advice on how to raise growth rates, one can treat each country as a laboratory trial – an observation of a set of policies, institutions and resources – and take the average over all the trials. Likewise in the context of understanding co-operation in multilateral organisations such as the United Nations, where small-population states have more of a voice than their share of world population would warrant, it may make sense to look at world income distribution with countries weighted equally.

What about the second measurement issue: actual exchange rates or PPP? When incomes in different countries are compared using actual exchange rates, the evidence shows that world income distribution has become much more unequal over the past several decades, and that inequality accelerated during the 1980s, whether countries are treated equally or weighted by population. When incomes are compared using PPP calculations, the degree of inequality shrinks, and so does the rate of widening.

Many assume that PPP measures are always superior. Certainly the exchange rate is a flawed measure of purchasing power: it fails to reflect the large amount of non-monetary exchange in developing countries, or money payment for services that are not subject to international competition. Also, exchange rates are much affected by capital flows and by monetary policy.

But PPP measures have their drawbacks as well. Different methods of measuring purchasing-power parity, all plausible in themselves, yield different results. Comprehensive estimates of PPP incomes for developing countries, based on actual data on prices of comparable goods and services, go back only to the 1970s. This makes longer-run analysis difficult. Finally, incomes based on actual exchange rates may be a better measure than PPP of relative national power and national modernity – matters of more interest to sociologists and political scientists, no doubt, than to economists.

In any event, the bulk of the evidence on trends in world income distribution runs against the claim that world income inequality has fallen sharply in the past half-century and still faster in the past quarter-century. None of the four cells in the table supports this idea.

From poorer to richer

So much for the existing research. However, we can now go further. Two studies based on new data challenge the finding in the fourth cell that world PPP-income distribution weighted by countries' population shows little change over the past few decades. The studies show, on the contrary, a rapid rise in inequality.

They differ from others in being based solely on household income and expenditure surveys. Earlier ones either used average GDP, ignoring inequality within each country, or used indirect methods to estimate within-country inequality, including production surveys and revenue surveys, which typically miss important components of household incomes. Branko Milanovic at the World Bank assembled the database, using the Bank's formidable statistical organisation to obtain household survey data from just about all the Bank's members, covering 85% of the world's population, for the years 1988 and 1993. The result is probably the most reliable data set on world income distribution.

Then Mr Milanovic computed the Gini coefficient for world income distribution, combining within-country inequality and between-country inequality, and measuring it in PPP terms. (The Gini coefficient is a commonly used measure of inequality: 0 signifies perfect equality, 100 means that one person holds all the income.) The results are startling.

World inequality increased from a Gini coefficient of 62.5 in 1988 to 66.0 in 1993. This is a faster rate of increase of inequality than that experienced within the United States and Britain during the 1980s. By 1993 an American on the average income of the poorest 10% of the population was better off than two-thirds of the world's people.

The other new study, by Yuri Dikhanov and Michael Ward, uses the same data set with a different methodology. It confirms

More unequal 3

World income distribution

Inequality measure	1988	1993	% change
Gini coefficient, world	63.1	66.9	6.0
Poorest decile's % of world income	0.88	0.64	-27.3
Richest decile's % of world income	48	52	8.3
Median as % of poorest decile	327	359	9.8
Richest decile as % of median	728	898	23.4

Source: R. Wade, based on *Measuring the distribution of global income*, by Yuri Dikhanov and Michael Ward, World Bank

that world income distribution became markedly more unequal between 1988 and 1993. Like the Milanovic study, it finds that the Gini coefficient increased by about 6%. It finds, further, that the share of world income going to the poorest 10% of the world's population fell by over a quarter, whereas the share of the richest 10% rose by 8%. The richest 10% pulled away from the median, while the poorest 10% fell away from the median, falling absolutely by a large amount. In short, we have to revise cell 4. World PPP income distribution with countries weighted by population (and China and India split into urban and rural) became "much more unequal" between 1988 and 1993 (see table 3).

Why has global inequality increased? The answer is in four parts: (1) faster economic growth in developed OECD countries than developing countries as a group; (2) faster population growth in developing countries than in OECD countries; (3) slow growth of output in rural China, rural India, and Africa; and (4) rapidly widening output and income differences between urban China on the one hand, and rural China and rural India on the other. The income of urban China grew very fast during 1988–93, which reduced the gap between China's average income and that of the middle-income and rich countries, and so reduced the world Gini coefficient; but the widening gaps between rural China and urban China and between urban China and rural India increased world inequality by even more.

These trends in turn have deeper causes. Technological change and financial liberalisation result in a disproportionately fast increase in the number of households at the extreme rich end, without shrinking the distribution at the poor end. Population growth, meanwhile, adds disproportionately to numbers at the poor end. These deep causes yield an important intermediate cause that makes things worse: the prices of industrial goods and services exported from high-income countries are increasing faster than the prices of goods and services exported by low-income countries, and much faster than the prices of goods and services produced in low-income countries that do little international trade.

These price trends mean that the majority of the population of poor countries are able to buy fewer and fewer of the goods and services that enter into the consumption patterns of rich-country populations. The poorer countries and the poorer two-thirds of the world's population therefore suffer a double marginalisation: once through incomes, again through prices. Hence the figures in table 3, which show that the gap between the richest 10% of the world's population and the median is widening, and the gap between the median and the poorest 10% is also widening.

Polarised zones

Income divergence helps to explain another kind of polarisation taking place in the world system, between a zone of peace and a zone of turmoil. The regions of the wealthy pole in chart 1 show a strengthening republican order of economic growth and liberal tolerance (except towards immigrants), with technological innovation able to substitute for depleting natural capital. The regions of the lower- and middle-income pole contain many states whose capacity to govern is stagnant or eroding, mainly in Africa, the Middle East, Central Asia, Russia and parts of East Asia. Here, a rising proportion of people find their access to basic necessities restricted at the same time as they see people on television driving Mercedes cars.

The result is a lot of unemployed and angry young people, to whom new information technologies have given the means to threaten the stability of the societies they live in and even to threaten social stability in countries of the wealthy zone. Economic growth in these countries often depletes natural capital and therefore future potential. More and more people see migration to the wealthy zone as their only salvation.

It is remarkable how unconcerned the World Bank, the IMF and other global organisations are about these trends. The Bank's *World Development Report* for 2000 even said that rising income inequality "should not be seen as negative" if the incomes at the bottom do not fall and the number of people in poverty falls. Such lack of attention shows that to call these world organisations is misleading. They may be world bodies in the sense that almost all states are members, but they think in state-centric rather than global ways. They neglect not only matters of world income distribution, but also world inflation, world exchange rates and world interest rates; and, in the case of the World Bank, the global environmental issues of the oceans, the atmosphere and nuclear waste.

It is striking that most of the organised opposition to more globalisation comes from North America, Western Europe and Oceania. Why have elites from developing countries for the most part subscribed to the globalisation agenda that western states, businesses and multilateral organisations have been promoting, if a case can be made that the gains of free markets for goods and capital tend to be concentrated in the top levels of the income distributions of their countries? Why are they doing so little to integrate their economies into the world economy in a strategic way, not open-endedly?

Part of the reason may be that elites in developing countries, like their counterparts in the rich world, are content to believe either that world inequality is falling, or that inequality is good because it is the source of incentives. They, like the multilateral economic organisations (and the reformers of Victorian England), worry about poverty. But they see no link between widening world income distribution and poverty; and they think that poverty can be fixed by providing the poor with welfare and opportunities without changing larger structures like income and asset distributions. Academic analysts have a responsibility to counter the current neglect by analysing the relationship between trends in world income distribution and poverty as a way of getting distribution issues on to the world agenda.

Growing inequality is analogous to global warming. Its effects are diffuse and long-term, and there is always something more pressing to deal with. The question is how much more unequal world income distribution can become before the resulting political instabilities and flows of migrants reach the point of directly harming the well-being of the citizens of the rich world and the stability of their states. Before that point is reached we should mobilise our governments, the multilateral organisations and international NGOs to establish as an overarching priority a more equal world income distribution – and not just, as now, fewer people in poverty.

The author would like to thank Michael Ward and Branko Milanovic for discussions about income distribution.

The material on pages 215–21 first appeared in a By Invitation in *The Economist* in April 2001.

Winners and losers: afterword

THE PICTURE OF world income received by each quintile of the world's population resembles, appropriately enough, an old-fashioned champagne glass – the wide shallow bowl at the top representing the 85 percent of world income received by the richest 20 percent, the slenderest of stems below representing the 15 percent received by the poorest 80 percent. Regardless of whether the distribution is becoming more or less unequal, the sheer magnitude of the inequality should make its reduction an international priority. The terrorist attacks of September 11th and the efforts of migrants to enter rich countries are reminders that the west cannot insulate itself from the results of inequality.

The liberal says that globalisation – fuller integration between developing countries and the world economy – is the answer. There is no question that the people of sub-Saharan Africa, eastern India and western China would be better off with more capital development. The question is whether the remedy should be – as the WTO, the World Bank, the IMF, and the G7 governments assume – mainly an "integrationist" agenda of low barriers to trade and capital, complemented by domestic reforms focused on making full integration viable.

There is another way, too, one suggested by East Asia's experience, and by China and Vietnam today. They show that countries that are highly integrated in the sense of having high volumes of trade and foreign investment while also having high protection and vigorous industrial policies – creating a virtuous cycle of higher growth, and more trade and investment. The rules of the multilateral organisations need to be changed to give countries the scope to pursue this kind of "third way" between liberal globalisers and anti-globalisers.

ROBERT WADE

Of rich and poor

In "Winners and Losers" on pages 215–21, the economist Robert
Wade argues that global inequality is increasing faster than
hitherto suspected, and that governments should respond. Is he
right? *The Economist* responds

IN POLITE POLICYMAKING circles, inequality is like the subject that
dares not speak its name. In recent years, egalitarianism has lost much
of whatever political appeal it ever had, in the rich industrialised countries, in the developing world, (especially) in the ex-communist
economies of the former Soviet Union and Central and Eastern Europe,
and certainly in communist-run China. Governments and development
institutions such as the World Bank and the IMF express their concerns
about poverty, and frame policies intended to reduce it, but do not seem
to regard inequality, as such, as worthy of much attention. *The
Economist*, it must be admitted, has also subscribed to that point of view.

The invited article by Robert Wade, a professor of political economy
at the London School of Economics, draws attention to some important
new findings on global inequality and urges governments to start taking
the matter much more seriously. Inequality matters, in Mr Wade's view,
above and beyond what it implies about poverty. For one thing, it may
be an indicator of global political strain: if the world's poor see the
world's rich getting ever farther ahead of them, they may begin to
object. "The result is a lot of unemployed and angry young people, to
whom new information technologies have given the means to threaten
the stability of the societies they live in and even to threaten social stability in countries of the wealthy zone."

Perhaps governments are neglecting the subject because they think
that growth will reduce both poverty and inequality in due course? If so,
they are wrong – or so Mr Wade argues. Studies cited in his article show
that inequality has been rising, and rapidly.

What is one to make of all this? Mr Wade undoubtedly raises some
interesting and important questions. But one may beg to differ with him
on some things, and especially on the conclusions he draws (or invites
his readers to draw).

First, one must be cautious about the data. Unfortunately, one must
always be cautious about the data. The information feeding into the

new calculations cited by Mr Wade is better, and certainly much more detailed, than the information used in earlier studies. But the adopted time-period is short: 1988–93, just five years. You might say that makes the reported substantial rise in inequality all the more alarming. But without longer runs of data it is hard to know whether this change is part of a well-established trend, as Mr Wade suspects, or a short-term fluctuation.

Still, take the worst case, and assume it is indeed a part of a trend. What might be driving it? Mr Wade cites four proximate causes: faster growth in rich countries than in poor; faster population growth in poor countries; stagnation in Africa, rural China and rural India; and a rapidly widening gap between urban China, on one hand, and rural China and rural India on the other. Behind these factors he conjectures that there are deeper causes, and one above all: "technological change and financial liberalisation result in a disproportionately fast increase in the number of households at the extreme rich end, without shrinking the distribution at the poor end."

But is it not something of a leap from those proximate causes to that primary underlying cause? The interesting new information that Mr Wade draws attention to does not, on the face of it, confirm that inference. At a minimum, the data are consistent with other explanations.

To most people, the really alarming new finding in Mr Wade's article is that the extent of absolute poverty in much of the world has increased. Certainly, this ought to concentrate the minds of policymakers. Most egalitarians, even, ought to find the rise in poverty much more worrying than the fact that incomes at the top have streaked away – even though, so far as inequality is concerned, both these changes are equally significant.

Does this worsening of poverty support Mr Wade's conjecture about the underlying cause – and so about the perils of globalisation? To answer this, one needs to ask, where did poverty increase and why? Apparently, it increased especially in Africa, in rural China and in rural India. It seems odd to regard such regions as victims of globalisation. On the face of it, they are rather the opposite: victims of a lack of globalisation. Their geographical and economic isolation is surely their salient characteristic. It makes better sense to think of extending the scope of globalisation – which means addressing the causes of their isolation – than to think of limiting or somehow re-engineering the processes of global growth.

Good evidence, as discussed before in this space, suggests that growth reduces poverty. There is evidence, too, that poor economies can put themselves on a development path that causes their incomes to converge with incomes in rich countries. The plight of countries, or regions within countries, that fail to get on that path is indeed a matter of the gravest concern. It would be unforgivable to ignore them – and, as Mr Wade points out, their condition may be even more desperate than had been previously supposed. It would also be wrong to sit back and hope that globalisation, left to itself, will somehow sweep them up in due course. But, having said all this, the challenge is still to engage these regions in economic growth and technological progress, not to find some way of protecting them from it.

None of this addresses another of Mr Wade's arguments: that inequality is a bad thing in itself, regardless of the extent of poverty. Many people would agree with that – though it has some strange implications. One is that you could regard a country with more equality as a greater success than another, even if the egalitarian country had not merely lower incomes on average, but also more people in absolute poverty. Mr Wade's points about inequality and social stress are well taken. Yet pulling up the poor still seems a nobler calling than pulling down the rich.

The material on pages 223–25 first appeared in an Economics Focus in *The Economist* in April 2001.

What's good for the poor is good for America

Jeffrey Sachs on where Uncle Sam should be more generous, and why

ALTHOUGH ITS PROSPERITY depends on a worldwide network of trade, finance and technology, the United States currently treats the rest of the world, and especially the developing world, as if it barely exists. Much of the poorer world is in turmoil, caught in a vicious circle of disease, poverty and political instability. Large-scale financial and scientific help from the rich nations is an investment worth making, not only for humanitarian reasons, but also because even remote countries in turmoil become outposts of disorder for the rest of the world. The biggest priority of the July 2001 Genoa G8 Summit should be for the rich countries, above all the United States, to get serious about contributing to global economic development.

During the cold war, the United States and its allies provided the global public good of containment, investing trillions of dollars to stop the spread of communism. The task now is vastly more complicated. The principal goal of foreign policy is now almost containment's opposite: helping to ensure that all parts of the world, including the poorest, are integrated into global economic and ecological networks in mutually beneficial ways.

Unfortunately, American presidents in recent times have not acknowledged that this goal requires massive foreign-policy investments. America's foreign aid is 0.1% of GDP, a derisory shadow of what it used to be, and roughly one-third of the European level (see charts 1 and 2). Following America's lead, most of the large economies have allowed their own foreign-assistance programmes to shrink since the end of the cold war. Even when the United States reaped a peace dividend of more than 2% of GDP in reduced defence spending after 1990, it cut, rather than increased, foreign-assistance spending as a share of national income.

The lessons of state failure

Traditional diplomacy deals with risks of conflict between nation states.

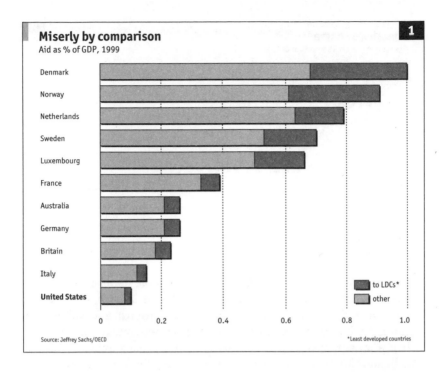

Miserly by comparison
Aid as % of GDP, 1999

1

Denmark
Norway
Netherlands
Sweden
Luxembourg
France
Australia
Germany
Britain
Italy
United States

to LDCs*
other

0   0.2   0.4   0.6   0.8   1.0

Source: Jeffrey Sachs/OECD   *Least developed countries

These risks are of course still present, but a more pervasive danger is that states will simply collapse. Of the dozen or so conflicts in Africa in recent years, few, if any, have involved cross-border aggression. Instead, bankrupt and impoverished states have imploded, the vacuum filled not by regimes with newly consolidated power but by brutal violence engulfing civilians. The disaster then fans out to neighbouring countries, and eventually much farther afield.

A special "task-force on state failure" set up by America's CIA has found that three variables are most predictive of state stability or instability: the openness of the economy (closed economies carried an increased risk of state collapse); democracy (authoritarian regimes were less stable); and infant mortality (a high incidence of disease raised the risk of collapse). In sub-Saharan Africa, where much of the population lives on the edge of subsistence, poverty and slow economic growth, or outright decline, increased the likelihood of future state collapse, thereby trapping the countries in a vicious circle of poverty and political instability. Rich countries, on the other hand, tend to maintain political stability which, in turn, promotes further economic development.

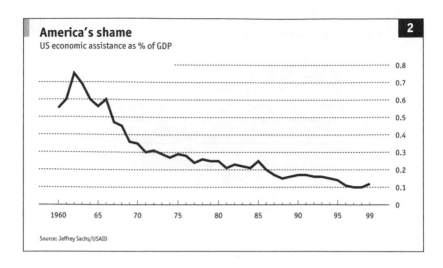

America's shame
US economic assistance as % of GDP

Source: Jeffrey Sachs/USAID

When countries were classified in 1990 by their status in the United Nations Human Development Index (an index of income, literacy and health), high-development countries achieved robust and stable economic growth during 1990–98, with average growth rates of around 2.3% a year and with 35 out of 36 countries enjoying rising living standards. Middle-development countries achieved a slightly lower growth rate, 1.9% a year, but seven out of 34 countries experienced outright declines in living standards. The poorest countries averaged no economic growth at all, with 15 out of 39 experiencing falling living standards. The flip-side to the poverty trap, however, is that the gains of development tend to be sustained, once countries break through to sufficient levels of income, health and literacy.

Conservatives in America often ask why it matters if an impoverished country collapses. The answer is that, aside from humanitarian concerns, crises in such far away places often suck the United States into crisis as well. Since 1960, America has been dragged into military conflicts in Cuba, Thailand, Laos, Congo, Vietnam, the Dominican Republic, Cambodia, Cyprus, Lebanon, Zaire, El Salvador, Libya, Lebanon, Honduras, Nicaragua, Chad, Liberia, Bosnia, Somalia and, more recently, Kosovo and Colombia.

State failures, or even milder state instability, have also undermined American and global interests through globally transmitted financial crises, drug-trafficking, money-laundering, terrorism, the spread of diseases such as AIDS and mass refugee flows. On the positive side, sustained economic development would create new and potentially large gains from trade, as well as much-needed co-operation in science and culture.

Even when a problem is correctly identified, there is a stunning disconnect between risk and action in America's foreign economic policy. The global AIDS epidemic, for example, has recently and wisely been identified as a risk to the security of the United States. What action has been taken? President George Bush has called upon Americans to give just $200m, or 70 cents each, to the new global fund to fight the disease.

The failure to make even basic investments in foreign policy has been pervasive, and the examples are legion. Eleven years ago, the last prime minister of unified Yugoslavia, Ante Markovic, launched a last-ditch plan for economic stabilisation. He appealed to Europe and the United States for a reduction in debt-servicing and other modest financial support, but was turned down by the creditor governments. Economic stabilisation was undermined, and this helped Slobodan Milosovic to get the upper hand. The rest, as they say, is history.

Recently America and European countries have made the same mistake in Nigeria, an impoverished and unstable country emerging from years of corrupt despotism. Although Nigeria's oil earnings, net of production costs and income to foreign oil companies, amount to around only $90 per Nigerian a year, the United States and Europe continue to prevaricate over urgently needed debt-reduction because the oil earnings are easy to squeeze for debt-service payments. The new democratic regime of President Olesegun Obasanjo is put at risk, and Libya's leader, Muammar Qaddafi, does not miss a chance to inflame matters in Nigeria's Islamic northern states.

Area after area of neglect can be catalogued, from the strife-torn Andes to regions around the world undermined by climate change. Through all of it, the United States barely lifts a finger. It somehow thinks that sending the impoverished and unstable governments down Pennsylvania Avenue to get loans from the IMF and the World Bank will do the job, but even some staff of those organisations now publicly acknowledge that they have failed: making loans when grants are needed, imposing excessive austerity by collecting rather than cancelling debts, and failing to find partner-institutions with the scientific expertise to tackle underlying problems of disease, low food production, climatic stress and environmental degradation.

Re-inventing foreign aid

The Bush administration and Congress must find their way to a renewal of American foreign policy and the sensible international investments that will be needed to back it up. The president's core team knows the world and its risks. The March 2000 Meltzer Commission, on which I served, demonstrated that there could be a bipartisan consensus on the need for much more American help for the poorest countries. The chairman of the Senate Foreign Relations Committee, Joseph Biden, is ideally suited by knowledge and temperament to help lead a bipartisan foreign-policy effort with the Bush administration. Here are some guidelines for investing in foreign policy in today's global economy.

First, we must identify the areas where money can really make a difference. Keenest attention should be paid to the world's poorest regions, the ones most likely to fall prey to the vicious circle of poverty, disease and state collapse. Remarkably, only around one-sixth of American aid is currently directed to the 48 least-developed countries, most of which are in Africa. Help for these countries should come in two ways: as direct support for national programmes to fight disease, malnutrition and illiteracy, when those programmes make sense and are honestly administered; and through programmes to develop new technologies to overcome barriers to long-term economic development.

Second, the United States should end its decade-long war against the United Nations agencies. Specialised organisations such as the World Health Organisation, the Food and Agriculture Organisation, the Consultative Group on International Agricultural Research, UNAIDS and the United Nations Development Programme need to be bolstered with more money and administrative reforms, not squeezed financially to the point of collapse. These agencies would be greatly strengthened by closer and properly financed links with America's own top-rank institutions, such as the National Institutes of Health and the Centres for Disease Control.

Third, and surely most important, the Bush administration must explain to Americans that a big increase in budgetary outlays on behalf of economic development in the world's poorest and most unstable regions is an investment in core American interests and values. All serious professional estimates show that the fight against AIDS in the developing countries will require at least $2 billion-3 billion a year from the United States government for the global fund – rather more than the $200m so far promised. External assistance for Africa will require not the current miserly $1 billion from America, but a several-fold increase, if profound problems have a chance of being overcome. Sub-Saharan Africa, neglected by the United States, has routinely received a sum equivalent to around one-sixth of the American aid given to the Middle East.

As a minimum, realistic target, the Bush administration should pledge to raise foreign assistance to at least 0.3% of GDP. This would not only bring the world's richest country back into line with the average of other donor nations, but would make available an extra $20 billion a year to invest in economic development. Such a turnaround in America's role could harness much larger contributions from the European Union, Japan, and other potential donors both public and private.

A Powell Plan?

Fifty years ago a soldier-statesman, General George Marshall, then secretary of state, explained to Americans that urgent financial support for Europe would stabilise societies destroyed by the second world war and the post-war economic crises. Such aid would unleash Europe's potential for recovery to everyone's mutual benefit. His vision was exactly on the mark. Winston Churchill called the resulting Marshall Plan "the most unsordid act in history".

The United States once again has a soldier-statesman, Colin Powell, as secretary of state. A new Powell Plan to mobilise American technology and finances, both public and private, on behalf of the economic development of the world's poor countries would be a fitting follow-up to the Marshall Plan. The world, and America, would be enormously safer and more prosperous as a result.

The material on pages 226–31 first appeared in a By Invitation in *The Economist* in July 2001.

The truth about the environment

Environmentalists tend to believe that, ecologically speaking, things are getting worse and worse. Bjorn Lomborg, once deep green himself, argues that they are wrong in almost every particular

ECOLOGY AND ECONOMICS should push in the same direction. After all, the "eco" part of each word derives from the Greek word for "home", and the protagonists of both claim to have humanity's welfare as their goal. Yet environmentalists and economists are often at logger-heads. For economists, the world seems to be getting better. For many environmentalists, it seems to be getting worse.

These environmentalists, led by such veterans as Paul Ehrlich of Stanford University, and Lester Brown of the Worldwatch Institute, have developed a sort of "litany" of four big environmental fears:

- Natural resources are running out.
- The population is ever growing, leaving less and less to eat.
- Species are becoming extinct in vast numbers: forests are disappearing and fish stocks are collapsing.
- The planet's air and water are becoming ever more polluted.

Human activity is thus defiling the earth, and humanity may end up killing itself in the process.

The trouble is, the evidence does not back up this litany. First, energy and other natural resources have become more abundant, not less so since the Club of Rome published *The Limits to Growth* in 1972. Second, more food is now produced per head of the world's population than at any time in history. Fewer people are starving. Third, although species are indeed becoming extinct, only about 0.7% of them are expected to disappear in the next 50 years, not 25-50%, as has so often been predicted. And finally, most forms of environmental pollution either appear to have been exaggerated, or are transient – associated with the early phases of industrialisation and therefore best cured not by restricting economic growth, but by accelerating it. One form of pollution – the release of greenhouse gases that causes global warming – does appear to be a long-term phenomenon, but its total impact is unlikely to pose a devastating problem for the future of humanity. A bigger problem may well turn out to be an inappropriate response to it.

Can things only get better?

Take these four points one by one. First, **the exhaustion of natural resources**. The early environmental movement worried that the mineral resources on which modern industry depends would run out. Clearly, there must be some limit to the amount of fossil fuels and metal ores that can be extracted from the earth: the planet, after all, has a finite mass. But that limit is far greater than many environmentalists would have people believe.

Reserves of natural resources have to be located, a process that costs money. That, not natural scarcity, is the main limit on their availability. However, known reserves of all fossil fuels, and of most commercially important metals, are now larger than they were when "The Limits to Growth" was published. In the case of oil, for example, reserves that could be extracted at reasonably competitive prices would keep the world economy running for about 150 years at present consumption rates. Add to that the fact that the price of solar energy has fallen by half in every decade for the past 30 years, and appears likely to continue to do so into the future, and energy shortages do not look like a serious threat either to the economy or to the environment.

The development for non-fuel resources has been similar. Cement, aluminium, iron, copper, gold, nitrogen and zinc account for more than 75% of global expenditure on raw materials. Despite an increase in consumption of these materials of between two- and ten-fold over the past 50 years, the number of years of available reserves has actually grown. Moreover, the increasing abundance is reflected in an ever-decreasing price: The Economist's index of prices of industrial raw materials has dropped some 80% in inflation-adjusted terms since 1845.

Next, **the population explosion** is also turning out to be a bugaboo. In 1968, Dr Ehrlich predicted in his best selling book, *The Population Bomb*, that "the battle to feed humanity is over. In the course of the 1970s the world will experience starvation of tragic proportions – hundreds of millions of people will starve to death".

That did not happen. Instead, according to the United Nations, agricultural production in the developing world has increased by 52% per person since 1961. The daily food intake in poor countries has increased from 1,932 calories, barely enough for survival, in 1961 to 2,650 calories in 1998, and is expected to rise to 3,020 by 2030. Likewise, the proportion

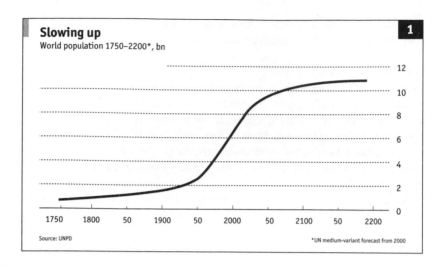

Slowing up `1`
World population 1750–2200*, bn

Source: UNPD   *UN medium-variant forecast from 2000

of people in developing countries who are starving has dropped from 45% in 1949 to 18% today, and is expected to decline even further to 12% in 2010 and just 6% in 2030. Food, in other words, is becoming not scarcer but ever more abundant. This is reflected in its price. Since 1800 food prices have decreased by more than 90%, and in 2000, according to the World Bank, prices were lower than ever before.

Modern Malthus

Dr Ehrlich's prediction echoed that made 170 years earlier by Thomas Malthus. Malthus claimed that, if unchecked, human population would expand exponentially, while food production could increase only linearly, by bringing new land into cultivation. He was wrong. Population growth has turned out to have an internal check: as people grow richer and healthier, they have smaller families. Indeed, the growth rate of the human population reached its peak, of more than 2% a year, in the early 1960s. The rate of increase has been declining ever since. It is now 1.26%, and is expected to fall to 0.46% in 2050. The United Nations estimates that most of the world's population growth will be over by 2100, with the population stabilising at just below 11 billion (see chart 1).

Malthus also failed to take account of developments in agricultural technology. These have squeezed more and more food out of each hectare of land. It is this application of human ingenuity that has boosted food production, not merely in line with, but ahead of, population growth. It has also, incidentally, reduced the need to take new land into cultivation, thus reducing the pressure on biodiversity.

Third, that **threat of biodiversity loss** is real, but exaggerated. Most early estimates used simple island models that linked a loss in habitat with a loss of biodiversity. A rule-of-thumb indicated that loss of 90% of forest meant a 50% loss of species. As rainforests seemed to be cut at alarming rates, estimates of annual species loss of 20,000–100,000 abounded. Many people expected the number of species to fall by half globally within a generation or two.

However, the data simply do not bear out these predictions. In the eastern United States, forests were reduced over two centuries to fragments totalling just 1–2% of their original area, yet this resulted in the extinction of only one forest bird. In Puerto Rico, the primary forest area has been reduced over the past 400 years by 99%, yet "only" seven of 60 species of bird has become extinct. All but 12% of the Brazilian Atlantic rainforest was cleared in the 19th century, leaving only scattered fragments. According to the rule-of-thumb, half of all its species should have become extinct. Yet, when the World Conservation Union and the Brazilian Society of Zoology analysed all 291 known Atlantic forest animals, none could be declared extinct. Species, therefore, seem more resilient than expected. And tropical forests are not lost at annual rates of 2–4%, as many environmentalists have claimed: the latest UN figures indicate a loss of less than 0.5%.

Fourth, **pollution** is also exaggerated. Many analyses show that air pollution diminishes when a society becomes rich enough to be able to afford to be concerned about the environment. For London, the city for which the best data are available, air pollution peaked around 1890 (see chart 2). Today, the air is cleaner than it has been since 1585. There is good reason to believe that this general picture holds true for all developed countries. And, although air pollution is increasing in many developing countries, they are merely replicating the development of the industrialised countries. When they grow sufficiently rich they, too, will start to reduce their air pollution.

All this contradicts the litany. Yet opinion polls suggest that many people, in the rich world, at least, nurture the belief that environmental standards are declining. Four factors cause this disjunction between perception and reality.

Always look on the dark side of life

One is the lopsidedness built into scientific research. Scientific funding goes mainly to areas with many problems. That may be wise policy, but

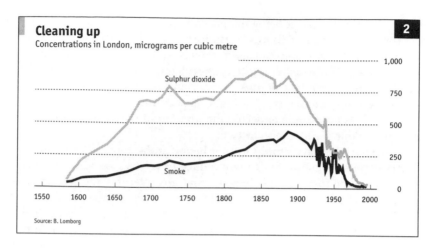

Cleaning up   **2**
Concentrations in London, micrograms per cubic metre

Sulphur dioxide

Smoke

Source: B. Lomborg

it will also create an impression that many more potential problems exist than is the case.

Secondly, environmental groups need to be noticed by the mass media. They also need to keep the money rolling in. Understandably, perhaps, they sometimes exaggerate. In 1997, for example, the World-wide Fund for Nature issued a press release entitled, "Two-thirds of the world's forests lost forever". The truth turns out to be nearer 20%.

Though these groups are run overwhelmingly by selfless folk, they nevertheless share many of the characteristics of other lobby groups. That would matter less if people applied the same degree of scepticism to environmental lobbying as they do to lobby groups in other fields. A trade organisation arguing for, say, weaker pollution controls is instantly seen as self-interested. Yet a green organisation opposing such a weakening is seen as altruistic, even if a dispassionate view of the controls in question might suggest they are doing more harm than good.

A third source of confusion is the attitude of the media. People are clearly more curious about bad news than good. Newspapers and broadcasters are there to provide what the public wants. That, however, can lead to significant distortions of perception. An example was America's encounter with El Niño in 1997 and 1998. This climatic phenomenon was accused of wrecking tourism, causing allergies, melting the ski-slopes and causing 22 deaths by dumping snow in Ohio.

A more balanced view comes from an article in the *Bulletin of the American Meteorological Society*. This tries to count up both the problems and the benefits of the 1997–98 Niño. The damage it did was

The price of a life `3`
Cost of saving one year of one person's life
1993$

Passing laws to make seat-belt use mandatory	69
Sickle-cell anaemia screening for black new-borns	240
Mammography for women aged 50	810
Pneumonia vaccination for people aged over 65	2,000
Giving advice on stopping smoking to people who smoke more than one packet a day	9,800
Putting men aged 30 on a low-cholesterol diet	19,000
Regular leisure-time physical activity, such as jogging for men aged 35	38,000
Making pedestrians and cyclists more visible	73,000
Installing air-bags (rather than manual lap belts) in cars	120,000
Installing arsenic emission-control at glass-manufacturing plants	51,000,000
Setting radiation emission standards for nuclear-power plants	180,000,000
Installing benzene emission control at rubber-tyre manufacturing plants	20,000,000,000

Source: T. Tengs et al, *Risk Analysis*, June 1995

estimated at $4 billion. However, the benefits amounted to some $19 billion. These came from higher winter temperatures (which saved an estimated 850 lives, reduced heating costs and diminished spring floods caused by meltwaters), and from the well-documented connection between past Niños and fewer Atlantic hurricanes. In 1998, America experienced no big Atlantic hurricanes and thus avoided huge losses. These benefits were not reported as widely as the losses.

The fourth factor is poor individual perception. People worry that the endless rise in the amount of stuff everyone throws away will cause the world to run out of places to dispose of waste. Yet, even if America's trash output continues to rise as it has done in the past, and even if the American population doubles by 2100, all the rubbish America produces through the entire 21st century will still take up only the area of a square, each of whose sides measures 28km (18 miles). That is just one-12,000th of the area of the entire United States.

Ignorance matters only when it leads to faulty judgments. But fear of largely imaginary environmental problems can divert political energy from dealing with real ones. Table 3, showing the cost in the United States of various measures to save a year of a person's life, illustrates the danger. Some environmental policies, such as reducing lead in petrol and sulphur-dioxide emissions from fuel oil, are very cost-effective. But many of these are already in place. Most environmental measures are less cost-effective than interventions aimed at improving safety (such as installing air-bags in cars) and those involving medical screening and vaccination. Some are absurdly expensive.

Yet a false perception of risk may be about to lead to errors more expensive even than controlling the emission of benzene at tyre plants. Carbon-dioxide emissions are causing the planet to warm. The best estimates are that the temperature will rise by some 2–3°C in this century, causing considerable problems, almost exclusively in the developing world, at a total cost of $5,000 billion. Getting rid of global warming would thus seem to be a good idea. The question is whether the cure will actually be more costly than the ailment.

Despite the intuition that something drastic needs to be done about such a costly problem, economic analyses clearly show that it will be far more expensive to cut carbon-dioxide emissions radically than to pay the costs of adaptation to the increased temperatures. The effect of the Kyoto Protocol on the climate would be minuscule, even if it were implemented in full. A model by Tom Wigley, one of the main authors of the reports of the UN Climate Change Panel, shows how an expected temperature increase of 2.1°C in 2100 would be diminished by the treaty to an increase of 1.9°C instead. Or, to put it another way, the temperature increase that the planet would have experienced in 2094 would be postponed to 2100.

So the Kyoto agreement does not prevent global warming, but merely buys the world six years. Yet the cost of Kyoto, for the United States alone, will be higher than the cost of solving the world's single most pressing health problem: providing universal access to clean drinking water and sanitation. Such measures would avoid 2m deaths every year, and prevent half a billion people from becoming seriously ill.

And that is the best case. If the treaty were implemented inefficiently, the cost of Kyoto could approach $1 trillion, or more than five times the cost of worldwide water and sanitation coverage. For comparison, the total global-aid budget today is about $50 billion a year.

To replace the litany with facts is crucial if people want to make the best possible decisions for the future. Of course, rational environmental management and environmental investment are good ideas – but the costs and benefits of such investments should be compared to those of similar investments in all the other important areas of human endeavour. It may be costly to be overly optimistic – but more costly still to be too pessimistic.

The material on pages 232–38 first appeared in a By Invitation in *The Economist* in August 2001.

7

The uses of technology

The "digital divide" has been the subject of much hand-wringing. Rich countries, with 15% of the world's population, account for some 90% of global IT spending. It has become commonplace to worry that this technological imbalance will only widen. This chapter, published as a survey in The Economist *just before this book went to press, takes a more optimistic view. Robert Guest argues that many poor countries are catching up, and that almost all benefit from technologies developed in rich countries. Innovations in the fields of medicine, agriculture and telecommunications are making poor people's lives longer, healthier and less poor.*

Getting better all the time

Developing countries are widely thought to be losing out from ever-faster technological change. Not so: science is rapidly improving the lives of poor as well as rich people

AN ANGOLAN refugee camp is not a happy place. Tired and hungry families huddle for shade under black plastic sheets. Amputees limp by on makeshift wooden crutches. The smell of human waste hangs thickly in the hot, dry air.

Angola is arguably the most wretched place on earth. Three decades of civil war show little sign of easing. A pitiless rebel army makes the countryside too dangerous to farm, so peasants flee to the cities in search of food and safety. Every rubbish skip has ragged children in it, foraging for lunch. Twentieth-century technology has caused terrible harm. Armour-piercing bullets keep evil men in power. Plastic explosives shred limbs.

Yet despite war and poverty, Angolans now live almost twice as long as their great-grandparents. By western standards, a life expectancy of 45 sounds pitifully short. But a century ago, Angolans, like most people throughout human history, survived for an average of only 25 years.

The reason is 20th-century medicine. Even the sad souls in Luanda's refugee camps have access to drugs. Antibiotics clear up infections that would previously have been fatal. Vaccines prevent countless children from dying before they can walk. In Angola as a whole, two-thirds of one-year-olds are immunised against tuberculosis. This is one of the lowest rates on earth, but it is a vast improvement on nobody 100 years ago.

The conventional wisdom is that as rich countries innovate with ever-increasing speed, the 5 billion people who live in developing countries are left behind. This survey is more optimistic. Of course technology makes the rich richer. But it also makes the poor richer, not to mention healthier, better-fed, longer-lived and supplied with more entertainment.

Consider the most basic indicator of well-being: staying alive. If people are living longer even in Angola, it should come as no surprise that the gains are even greater elsewhere. Angus Maddison, an economic historian, estimates that life expectancy in 1900 in what we now call the developing world – roughly speaking, everywhere apart from Western Europe, North America, Australasia and Japan – was 26. In the West, it was 46, about the same as in Angola today. Westerners now live 70% longer than they did a century ago, to an average of 78. People from developing countries can now expect to live two-and-a-half times longer than in 1900, to 64. These figures are astonishing. In the millennium before 1900, lifespans in Asia, Africa and Latin America barely budged.

People are living longer for many reasons: better food, cleaner water, more effective medicines. How did they get these things? It helps that the poor are getting richer: average annual incomes in developing countries doubled between 1975 and 1998, from $1,300 to $2,500 (in 1985 dollars at purchasing-power parity). It does not hurt, either, that their rulers are getting less despotic: since the collapse of the Soviet Union, 100 developing countries have ended military or one-party rule. (Angola was an exception to both these trends.)

The strongest force propelling human progress, however, has been the swift advance and wide diffusion of technology. Bread has been around for thousands of years, but the hybrid wheat seeds, chemical pesticides and fertilisers that have allowed food production to outstrip population growth are recent inventions. Water is older than mankind, but no one thought to add chlorine to it until the 20th century. And the medical advances of the past 100 years far surpass those of the previous million.

Countries vary hugely in their ability to produce new technology. According to a report by the United Nations Development Programme (UNDP), the 29 industrial nations that make up the Organisation for Economic Co-operation and Development (OECD), with 19% of the world's population, accounted for 91% of the patents issued in 1998. That year, those countries spent $520 billion on research and development (R&D) – more than the combined economic output of the world's 30 poorest countries.

Many people worry that the "digital divide" is unbridgeable. Rich countries grow richer from their high-tech industries, which allows them to invest in the next generation of high-tech products. High salaries in Silicon Valley suck the best brains out of poor countries. The West gets wired, enabling its researchers and businessmen to swap ideas and sign deals at Internet speed. Poor countries, excluded from these opportunities, fall ever further behind.

Sunnier folk argue that for rich countries to be pushing out new technologies at an unprecedented rate must be a good thing. Knowledge does not wear out, and American and Japanese inventions eventually get cheap enough for Africans to buy them. It still takes too long, but it is happening faster now than ever before.

The first three articles in this survey look at three fields where technology holds particular promise for the poor. The first is agriculture: the controversial science of genetic modification could feed the world, if only environmentalists would let it. The second is medicine: startling advances continue, but the fight against AIDS and tropical diseases will require more public money. The third is information and communication technology (ICT). Despite the pessimists' dire predictions, ICT is spreading more rapidly than anyone imagined, and is spawning and spreading other technologies, too. Most of the rest of the survey deals with how developing countries are trying to catch up and start innovating for themselves.

Feeding the five billion

New agricultural techniques can keep hunger at bay

SHRIMPS ARE MESSY creatures. When scrubbed, shelled and served with lime leaves and lemon grass in a hot Thai *tom yam koong* soup, they taste wonderful. But while alive, they excrete large amounts of toxic sludge.

On Thai shrimp farms, the traditional way of dealing with this sludge is to toss it in the nearest river. Land used for shrimp farming soon becomes polluted and unusable, so shrimp farmers keep cutting down fresh forest to build new shrimp pools. Since farmed shrimps live in their own waste, they often fall sick. So farmers stuff them with antibiotics, which could end up in your *tom yam koong*.

Fortunately, there is a technological fix. Bio Solutions, a Thai firm, has developed a pill containing bacteria that eat shrimp excrement. Throw the pill in the pool, and the bacteria multiply until they run out of food. Then they obligingly starve to death, in a tidy, biodegradable way. "If Asia is going to feed itself," says Charles Liu, the president of Bio Solutions, "agricultural biotechnology has to be part of the answer." That is what you would expect him to say – but he has a point.

Predictions that people would multiply beyond their capacity to feed themselves, like those Thai bacteria, have repeatedly been proved wrong. In 1798, Thomas Malthus foretold famine just as farm yields were taking off. To his credit, he later admitted that he was wrong. Not so Paul Ehrlich, an American biologist who wrote in 1969: "The battle to feed humanity is over. In the 1970s hundreds of millions of people will starve to death." They didn't.

The world's population grew much as expected, but food output more than kept pace. During the 1960s and 1970s, a "green revolution" swept the developing world. Millions of farmers started using higher-yielding hybrid seeds, chemical fertilisers, pesticides and weed-killers. The results were remarkable. For example, Mr Ehrlich had predicted that by the mid-1970s, India would be so obviously beyond hope that America would stop sending food aid. Yet by 1990, India was exporting surplus grain. Chinese rice farmers, using similar techniques, raised production by two-thirds between 1970 and 1995. By one estimate, the green revolution saved a billion people from starvation.

There were some side-effects. Governments subsidised the new chemicals, which encouraged their over-use. This damaged the environment in many parts of the developing world. But the main worry about the green revolution is that it has run out of steam. There are still areas – mainly in Africa – where its techniques have yet to be tried (see table 1). But in most of the developing world, the gains in productivity from it are tailing off.

Globally, 800m people are still malnourished. Heavily subsidised farmers in rich countries produce enough surplus food to feed the hungry, but not at a price the hungry can afford. Even if the rich world's surplus were simply given to the poor, this would not solve the problem. Most poor people earn their living from agriculture, so a deluge of free food would destroy their livelihoods. The only answer to world hunger is to improve the productivity of farmers in poor countries.

New seeds				1
% of permanently cultivated land sown with modern crop varieties				
Crop	1970	1980	1990	1998
Latin America				
Wheat	11	46	83	90
Rice	2	22	52	65
Maize	10	20	30	46
Cassava	–	1	2	7
Asia				
Wheat	19	49	74	86
Rice	10	35	55	65
Maize	10	25	45	70
Sorghum	4	20	54	70
Millet	5	30	50	78
Cassava	–	–	2	12
Sub-Saharan Africa				
Wheat	5	22	32	52
Rice	–	2	15	40
Maize	1	4	15	17
Sorghum	–	8	15	26
Millet	–	–	5	14
Cassava	–	–	2	18
Middle East				
Wheat	5	16	38	66

Source: UNDP

This will be difficult. The developing world's population is growing fast, but the amount of land available for cultivation is not. To feed the 2 billion new mouths expected by 2025, new ways must be found to squeeze more calories out of each hectare. But then more people means not just more stomachs to fill, but also more brains to figure out how to fill them.

There are plenty of good ideas available. The most powerful is biotechnology, and especially genetic modification (GM). It is a young science: biologists first found ways of manipulating recombinant DNA in the early 1970s. The first commercially available genetically modified organism (GMO) appeared a mere five years ago. Supporters of GM expect it to end world hunger. Opponents fear it may poison us all. It is worth stepping back for a moment to consider the evidence.

For and against GMOs

Farmers have been manipulating genomes since long before they knew about genes. For thousands of years, they sought to transfer desirable traits from one plant species to another by cross-breeding: this was how wild grasses were turned into wheat. They also selectively bred animals to make them fatter and tastier: this was how wild boars became pigs.

GM aims to achieve similar results, but faster. It typically takes 8–12 years to produce a better plant by cross-breeding. But if scientists can isolate a gene in one species that is associated with, say, the ability to grow in salty soil, they can sometimes transfer it directly into the genetic code of another species, without spending years crossing successive generations.

GM is more precise than cross-breeding, too. As any parent knows, sexual reproduction is unpredictable. The union of a brilliant woman and an athletic man does not always produce a brilliant and athletic child. In plants, as in people, some traits are inherited, others are not. At least in theory, GM solves this problem by transferring only the gene associated with the trait that the farmer wants.

The final advantage of GM is that it allows the transfer of traits between unrelated species. You cannot cross-breed cacti with corn, but you can take a cactus gene that promotes drought resistance and put it in a corn plant.

So far, scientists have produced GM crops that are more resistant to viruses and insects, and more tolerant of herbicides. In the future, GM could fill the world's larders with high-protein cereals, vegetables with extra vitamins, and all manner of cheaper, tastier and more nutritious foods than we currently enjoy. Researchers at Cornell University in America have even created bananas that contain a vaccine for hepatitis B. A single banana chip inoculates a child for one-fifteenth of the price of an injection, and with fewer tears.

Against these actual and potential benefits must be set the potential dangers. Shifting genes between different species could create health risks. For example, soyabeans given brazil nut genes have been found to express brazil nut proteins of the sort that might trigger allergic reactions. Soyabeans are used in thousands of food products, so if the problem had not been spotted this could have made life hazardous for people with nut allergies.

GM crops may also cause environmental problems. Their pollen might blow into fields of ordinary crops and fertilise them. There is no evidence that this has happened so far, but it is possible, with unknown effects. Also, crops genetically modified to repel pests might spur the evolution of super-pests or poison other species. Laboratory tests have shown that butterfly larvae are harmed when fed the pollen of plants genetically modified to express a toxin called Bacillus thuringiensis (Bt), which protects corn from corn borers and cotton from boll worms.

All these risks are rather speculative. As with any new technology, it is impossible ever to prove conclusively that GM foods are safe. It is essential to test GM products carefully before releasing them, and to keep monitoring them afterwards. But so far, there is no evidence that GM crops hurt either humans or the environment. Americans have been munching modified corn and soyabeans for six years without discernible harm. And so far it looks as though GM crops actually help protect the environment, by reducing the need for chemical pesticides.

In 2000, about 44m hectares of transgenic crops were planted, more than 20 times the area in 1996. Most of these fields, however, were in North America. Developing countries have yet to see much benefit from GM technology. But that could change. Among poor countries, the most enthusiastic adopter of GM technology has been China, where the government frets about food security. In 1997–99, China gave 26 commercial approvals for GM crops, including transgenic peppers, tomatoes, rice and cotton. The most commercially successful of these has been Bt cotton.

Cotton-chomping boll worms have grown resistant to pesticides. In 1992, these worms destroyed the entire cotton crop in some parts of China, ruining large numbers of farmers and bankrupting textile factories. So when Monsanto, a big American biotech firm, started selling boll-worm-resistant Bt cotton seeds, the Chinese government snapped them up. Bt cotton now covers half a million hectares of Chinese soil. Production costs have fallen by 14%, despite the hefty price that Monsanto charges for its seeds. Chinese scientists are now working on their own GMOs, and have already produced at least four new versions of Bt cotton.

The Chinese example is hopeful, but not unambiguously so. One reason that China's government was able to embrace GM technology is that the country is a dictatorship. Dissident voices are silenced or ignored. A few democracies, such as America, Canada and Argentina, have taken to GM food. But in Europe, although regulators say that GM products are safe, an energetic campaign by non-governmental organi-sations (NGOs) has convinced consumers that they are not, and dis-suaded supermarkets from stocking them. Through the Internet, the campaign has spread to the developing world.

India, like China, has lots of poor rural folk who must somehow be fed. Anything that raises rural incomes is likely to help. Indian field trials found that Bt cotton produced 40% more fibre than ordinary cotton, with five fewer chemical sprays for each crop. For a typical small farmer with five hectares, this would save $50 per season, a huge sum by local standards. The farmer would also inhale less pesticide. Despite these findings, the Indian government refuses to permit the commercial planting of Bt cotton, largely because of pressure from NGOs. Protesters have invaded field trials and burned GM crops. Some even blocked the delivery of American food aid to cyclone victims, arguing that it proba-bly contained GM products.

Some poor countries hesitate to plant GMOs for fear of upsetting Europeans. NGOs claim that GM crops may "contaminate" neighbour-ing fields with their pollen. It would be a short step to call for a boycott of all the food exports, modified and unmodified, of countries where GMOs are widely grown. Even for developing countries that allow GM crops to be planted only in isolated plots for research purposes, the risk of a boycott remains. The peasants who live near research centres often notice how good the new crops are and steal the seeds.

Unlike the techniques of the green revolution, GM technology was largely developed by private companies. In the eyes of many, this made it suspect, but such suspicion is largely misplaced. The profit motive gives companies a strong incentive not to poison their customers. But it gives them no incentive to cater for people who cannot afford their products. Better versions of poor people's staples, such as millet, sorghum and cassava, will probably appear only if governments pay for some of the research, but the current hysteria about GMOs makes this politically difficult. When the UNDP recently suggested that GM technology could help the poor, it was met with howls of outrage.

The many ways of fighting hunger

GM is not the only weapon in the war on hunger. Democracy is impor-tant too: famines usually occur only in dictatorships. And other tech-nologies can produce impressive results: using less controversial biotechnology, the UNDP and the Japanese government recently pro-duced a high-yielding hybrid rice that grows faster and contains more protein than ordinary varieties. But battles are easier to win if you have many weapons at your disposal. To remove the most powerful one from the arsenal seems unwise.

For the poor, GM appeared at an awkward time. After several people in Britain died of what was almost certainly a human version of mad-cow disease, Europeans lost faith in their governments' ability to keep dangerous food off their plates. Since people in rich countries rarely go hungry, they were not wildly excited about the promise of cheap and abundant food. Perhaps they will change their minds when scientists create better rather than simply cheaper foods: cholesterol-free bacon, perhaps. But in the meantime, it is sad that the priorities of the well-fed few should make it harder for the world's hungry billions to feed them-selves.

Brains v bugs

Poor people now receive better medicine than rich ones did a century ago. But diseases, old and new, still need fighting

IMAGINE A HOSPITAL where the water is dirty, where tuberculosis is rife, and where the doctors are so ignorant that a patient has only a 50-50 chance of benefiting from a consultation. Imagine too, that most of the drugs prescribed are useless, and some are poisonous. This is a fair description of what health care was like in America a century ago. One in four children died before the age of 14, mostly from infectious diseases. In the early 20th century, Oliver Wendell Holmes, an American judge, declared that if all the medicines of his day were tossed into the ocean, it would be better for mankind and worse for the fish.

Health care in the developing world today is rather better than that. Poor people are living longer, not because the natural human lifespan has increased, but because many of the horrors that prevent people from reaching old age are being tamed. A child born in the developing world today can expect to live eight years longer than one born 30 years ago. Even in the world's 40 poorest countries, infant mortality in the past 30 years has fallen by a third. A World Bank study found that technical progress was the biggest single cause of reductions in mortality, accounting for up to half the improvement between 1960 and 1990.

Important discoveries have included:

◪ **Vaccines.** Influenza, which killed around 20m people in 1918–19, is now largely under control. Smallpox was eradicated in 1979. Other foul diseases, including measles, whooping cough, rubella, diphtheria, tetanus and tuberculosis, have been curbed by vaccination. In recent decades, technology has made vaccines easier to deliver in poor countries. A droplet of polio vaccine can be swallowed: no need for needles. More heat-stable vaccines that do not need refrigeration have been created. Combination vaccines can be delivered in a single shot.

◪ **Antibiotics.** Penicillin was discovered in 1928, but a way to mass-produce it was invented only during the second world war. Since then, ever more sophisticated antibiotics have been marketed around the world. Infections that used to be fatal can now be cured in a trice.

▪ **Oral rehydration therapy (ORT).** This is one of the simplest and most effective medicines ever. Developed in Bangladesh, ORT has saved millions of babies from dying of diarrhoea. It is a mixture of sugar and salt dissolved in water that prevents dehydration and so keeps the child alive. Before ORT, the standard treatment was an intravenous drip, at a cost of $50 per baby. Packets of oral rehydration salts started being mass-produced in the 1980s, at a cost of less than 10 cents each.

Despite these and many other advances, ill health remains a huge problem for the poor. Thirty thousand children under five die each day from preventable causes. Debilitating parasites make multitudes too weak to work, or blind them. And in Africa, after a century of progress, the rise in life expectancy stopped after 1990. In much of the southern and eastern part of the continent, people started dying younger because of AIDS.

The easiest way to fight disease in poor countries is to keep extending current technology into regions it has not yet reached. Two-thirds of diarrhoea cases are now treated with ORT, but that still leaves a lot of dehydrated children. In some of the poorest countries, such as Ethiopia and Burkina Faso, under 20% of those who need ORT receive it. The proportion of children worldwide inoculated against the six main vaccine-preventable diseases soared from 5% in 1974 to 74% in 1998, but what about the other 26%? More comprehensive jabbing could eliminate diseases completely, as happened with smallpox and could soon happen with polio.

However, blanket coverage by existing technologies is not the whole solution. For diseases that are not yet curable, new drugs must be found. New drugs are also needed for bugs that develop resistance to old drugs. And new vaccines are needed for new diseases.

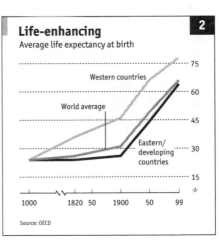

Life-enhancing 2

Average life expectancy at birth

Western countries

World average

Eastern/developing countries

75
60
45
30
15

1000   1820 50   1900   50   99

Source: OECD

Researchers have some handy tools. Biotechnology has spawned several useful drugs, including mass-produced insulin for diabetics and a vaccine for hepatitis B. More life-prolonging pills will follow. Genomics offers new ways to cure disease, by tampering with genes that contribute to cancer, for example, or by boosting genes that might fight it. Nanotechnology – fiddling with things as small as individual molecules – may allow the construction of robots small enough to remove blockages from capillaries.

Vaccines or Viagra?

The trouble is that most medical research is done in rich countries, for the benefit of rich people. The fattest profits are to be made from tackling chronic conditions that affect lots of westerners, such as heart disease and cancer. The ills of the poor are neglected: of the 1,223 drugs introduced between 1975 and 1996, only 13 were aimed at tropical diseases. In 1998, the world spent $70 billion on health research, but only $300m of this was directed at developing an AIDS vaccine, and a piffling $100m was devoted to malaria research.

When drug firms do produce pills that might help the poor, their patents allow them to charge monopoly prices which the poor cannot pay. The patented drugs that have curbed AIDS in rich countries can cost $10,000 a year. For most Africans, this is an impossible sum. Some AIDS activists cite that as evidence that "patents kill".

This is unfair. Without patents, there would be no incentive for private companies to invent new medicines. Drug firms spend $300m–500m on creating a single pill. They could never recoup this investment if others were allowed to copy their ideas and sell them at a thin margin over what they cost to manufacture.

Patent protection is temporary and conditional. To win it, an invention must be original, useful and non-obvious. The inventor must reveal how his invention works, and publish the information. He is then typically granted the sole right to sell the product for 17–20 years from the time the patent application was filed. For drugs, the effective monopoly period is shorter: it can take a decade to develop, test and bring a patented molecule to market.

Abolishing patents would more or less halt progress in pharmacology, but there is a strong argument for charging different prices for drugs in poor countries. A treaty signed by most countries in 1994 allows governments to override patent protection during a national emergency. AIDS in Africa clearly qualifies as an emergency. Several drug firms have started to offer AIDS drugs to Africans at as little as a tenth of their normal price, partly in response to international pressure and partly because they were not generating much profit in Africa anyway.

Although this is welcome, it will not make as much difference as many hope. In most poor countries the patents on the drugs that people need most have already expired. If people still do not get them, it is either because the drugs are still too costly, or because the country's health-care system is a mess. In most parts of Africa, AIDS cocktails are unaffordable even if sold at cost. Only a few countries are poor enough to qualify for discounts but rich enough to afford to buy discounted drugs. Of these, Brazil and Botswana have shown enthusiasm, but South Africa, despite having a larger number of HIV-positive citizens than any other country, has not. Public hospitals in South Africa rarely offer anti-retroviral drugs even to pregnant mothers to prevent their unborn children from contracting HIV, although this would save money as well as lives.

Differential pricing will not deal with the problem that drug firms' research concentrates mainly on ailments affecting rich people. Only public money can fill the gap. Foreign aid on this would be well spent. Malaria is estimated to cost Africa 1% of GDP every year: treating the symptoms is expensive, and few people can work while in the fever's grip. AIDS hurts southern and eastern Africans even more. Festus Mogae, the president of Botswana, has said that the virus threatens his country with extinction. Finding vaccines for these diseases would be a peerless public good. Some efforts are under way. For example, the International AIDS Vaccine Initiative (IAVI), launched by the Rockefeller Foundation, brings together states, academics and drug firms. One vaccine candidate started clinical trials in Kenya in January.

Big drug firms have heaps of know-how that could be harnessed to help the poor. One possible way, proposed by Jeffrey Sachs of Harvard University, would be for rich-country governments to promise to buy, at a reasonable price, any drug likely to bring about a big improvement in poor people's health. This should give drug firms an incentive to come up with an AIDS or malaria vaccine, or with better pills for tropical diseases. If they did not deliver, taxpayers would pay nothing.

Getting together

The more that developing countries themselves contribute to these efforts, the more likely they are to succeed. Not many can handle the whole process of drug discovery, development, testing and marketing on their own. But several have pockets of unique expertise, or a wide variety of potentially useful medicinal plants. For example, Vietnamese scientists extracted an effective malaria drug from a tree long used in traditional medicine.

Turning biodiversity into medicine is not easy, however. There has been only a handful of other recent triumphs. The Amazon jungle may well hide a cure for cancer, but no one has found it yet. The trouble is that countries with rainforests tend to lack pharmacological expertise, and the big drug firms that have the know-how are all based in countries without rainforests.

Unscrupulous western researchers sometimes solve the problem by stealing plants from poor countries. Some firms have learnt about the healing properties of plants from locals and patented the active ingredients without acknowledging the locals' contribution or rewarding them for it. Two cancer drugs, for example, were developed using a rose periwinkle plant found in Madagascar, but the country received no benefit.

Stopping "biopiracy" will be tricky, but multinational companies hate bad publicity, so many are striking fairer deals. The Brazilian government, for example, receives royalties from Novartis, a Swiss drug firm, for providing it with micro-organisms. Merck, an American drug firm, pays Costa Rica for samples of plants and insects, and promises a share of any future profits from them. Vanderlan Bolzani, the head of a public project to find bioactive compounds in Brazilian plants, approves of such deals. "In Brazil," she says, "we know how to find potential drugs, but we don't have the capability to develop and test them. So we have to co-operate."

Fishermen on the net

The digital revolution is helping the poor, too

THE GLOBAL great and good are obsessed with the "digital divide". Half the people in the world, they fret, have never made a telephone call. Africa has less international bandwidth than Brazil's city of Sao Paulo. How, ask dozens of inter-governmental task-forces, can the poor get connected? Amid all the attention paid to developing countries' lack of Internet access, some people feel that more fundamental problems are being ignored. Ted Turner, an American media boss, observed in 2000 that there was no point in giving people computers when they had no electricity.

He may be wrong. Indian scientists recently produced a prototype of a battery-powered device called the Simputer – short for "simple computer" – that is expected to cost only $200 a unit. Even at that price it may be too expensive for the truly poor. But computers can be shared. And the time may come when they will pay for themselves. Information and communication technology (ICT) may be overhyped, but it does matter. True, people in poor countries need food and medicine before they need Internet access, but ICT could help them lay hands on both of these more easily.

In several fishing villages on the Bay of Bengal, for example, an Internet link-up allows a volunteer to read weather forecasts from the US Navy's public website and broadcast them over a loudspeaker. For fishermen who work from little wooden boats, knowing that a storm is looming can mean the difference between life and death. The Internet also lets them know the market price for their catch, which helps them haggle with middlemen. And they can download satellite images revealing where fish shoals are.

Communication, as everybody knows, is getting cheaper. Any task that can be digitised can now be done at a distance, which creates all sorts of opportunities for developing countries. Fixing software for a London firm does not require Indians to travel to Britain. They can do it from Bangalore. That is why India's software industry has grown from almost nothing ten years ago into the most dynamic business on the subcontinent, employing 400,000 people and generating more than $8 billion in sales in 2000. The country has almost as many fluent English speakers as England, and universities that turn out hordes of computer-literate graduates. Charging a small fraction of what Californians demand, Indian programmers fixed a large chunk of the world's millennium-bug troubles, and take on a larger share of western companies' back-room operations each year.

And they are not the only ones. Dial a helpline for an American bank, and you may find yourself talking to someone in the Philippines or Puerto Rico. A computer screen tells the telephonist what the weather is like in whichever city the customer is calling from, and suggests appropriate responses to the customer's grumbles about the local baseball team's performance last night. Creepy? Maybe, but it lowers costs for consumers and creates jobs where none existed before.

Accurate, timely information is useful in almost any field. Take health care. The Internet is the quickest and cheapest way yet devised of disseminating medical research. Using websites such as Healthnet, doctors in poor countries can easily and cheaply keep up to speed with the latest developments in their field. In Bangladesh, the local Medinet system provides access to hundreds of expensive medical journals for less than $1.50 a month. Throughout Africa, outbreaks of meningitis are tracked over the Internet so that epidemics can be stopped early.

Yuppie toys in rural Bangladesh

Granted, these health-care schemes mostly depend on charity for their funding. And the lack of Internet content in languages other than English is a problem. But new websites in other languages pop up every day. And as the cost of ICT falls, it may not be long before poor people start clubbing together to buy time online with their own money. It has already happened with mobile telephones.

For many Bangladeshi women, the mobile phone provides upward mobility. Women in rural areas borrow money from Grameen Bank, a microlender, to buy a GSM phone. Handsets can cost a year's income for the whole household, but more than 90% of borrowers are able to service their loans because they earn money charging other villagers to make calls.

Everyone benefits. In Bangladesh as a whole, 97% of homes lack a telephone. In rural areas, practically no one has a phone. So when a Grameen-backed phone entrepreneur sets up shop, the whole village is suddenly connected to the outside world. Parents can call the nearest city, for example, to find out what has happened to the remittance from their son working on a construction site in the Gulf. A telephone call can

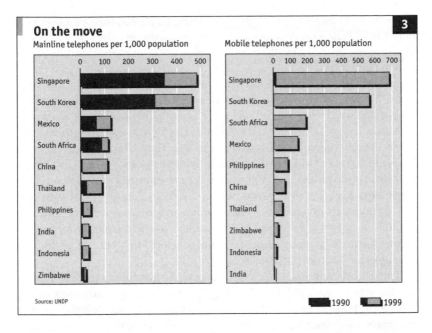

On the move

Mainline telephones per 1,000 population | Mobile telephones per 1,000 population

Source: UNDP

■ 1990   ▨ 1999

take the place of a long and expensive trip: one study found it typically saved between 3% and 10% of the caller's monthly household income.

The service also turns a profit. The callers may be poor, but because there are so many of them, rural phones in Bangladesh generate more revenue than urban ones. Grameen Phone, a Grameen Bank offshoot founded to provide services for the poor, now sells to everyone and has become the largest provider of mobile-phone services in Bangladesh.

Mobile phones are popular everywhere, but in poor countries they have extra advantages. It is quicker and cheaper to sell a poor person a mobile telephone than to install a payphone in a remote village. A phone in someone's house is constantly guarded, which makes it unlikely to be vandalised.

Mobiles are user-friendly, too. Fixed-line telephone services in most developing countries are provided by awful state-owned monopolies. Ask for a telephone line to be installed in your home in Zimbabwe, and you can choose between bribing someone or waiting for several years. But if you walk into a mobile-phone shop, your handset will be up and running in five minutes.

Nor is lack of a credit history a problem. Poor people are barred from opening accounts with traditional telephone companies because no one trusts them to pay their bills. With mobiles, however, they can buy pre-paid cards. When they have used up all their minutes, they buy another. There is no chance that they will receive an unmanageable bill at the end of the month.

Because the mobile-phone companies get paid in advance, they waste no time or money on chasing bad debts, as fixed-line firms do. So their cashflow is better and they are able to expand their networks faster. In many poor countries the number of mobile users has over-taken the number of land-line users in less time than it takes to get a land line installed. In Uganda, for example, it took two years for MTN, a private mobile-phone firm, to outstrip UTL, the clumsy state-owned tele-coms firm. Before it was privatised in 2000, UTL in a typical year lost 40% of revenues in bad debts, and another 30% because of "audit adjust-ments". In 1997–99, the number of land-line users in Uganda inched up from 54,000 to 59,000. Over the same period, the number of mobile users exploded from 7,000 to 87,000.

This still means that only one Ugandan in 240 has a mobile phone, but it's a start. And ICT is spreading faster than any technology in the whole of human history. In 1900, 24 years after the telephone was invented, only 5% of homes in America were hooked up to the tele-phone network. In most other countries, the figure was negligible. Com-pare this with the spread of the Internet. In 2000, 18 years after the creation of a rudimentary Internet and 11 years after the beginning of the World Wide Web, 6.7% of the world's population were logging on. In other words, the Internet is spreading around the whole world faster than the telephone spread around its richest country a century ago.

The poor are catching up

And poor countries, for once, are not missing out on this revolution. In 1998, according to the UNDP, only 12% of Internet users were in non-OECD (ie, less developed) countries. By 2000 this proportion had almost doubled, to 21%, when the cake itself had more than doubled in size over the same period.

The Internet is not only a marvellous technology; it is a tool that helps developing countries to adopt outside technology faster, and sometimes to develop their own. The makers of the Simputer used free open-source software, which they could not have downloaded without the Internet. Indeed, without the Internet, open-source software would not exist, as it depends on large numbers of volunteer programmers swapping ideas online.

In developing countries scientists are thin on the ground. A decade ago, if a researcher from a poor country wanted to bounce ideas off lots of other experts every day, he probably had to move to a rich country. Now he simply logs on. Cheaper communications mean more north–south collaboration, and indeed more south–south collaboration. In 1995–97, American scientists co-wrote papers with colleagues from 173 other countries. Kenyans published papers with scientists from 81 other nations.

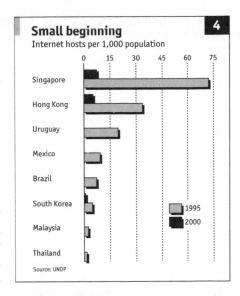

Small beginning 4

Internet hosts per 1,000 population

Source: UNDP

The Internet also allows more collaboration within countries. Brazilian biologists work with colleagues at opposite ends of the Amazon river and on both sides of the equator. Some of them surprised the world in 2000 by sequencing the genome of a bacterium that shrivels oranges. It was the first time that a free-living plant pathogen had been sequenced anywhere, a breakthrough for southern-hemisphere science. According to Andrew Simpson, one of the project's leaders and an old Brazil hand, this would not have been possible without the Internet. "It's a godsend," he says. "It gives us confidence that what we are doing is as good as what is going on in America, because we can see what is going on in America."

Wired schools, wired nations

Growing up with technology makes it easier to embrace

SOMETHING UNHEARD-OF is happening in South Korea: students are starting to challenge their teachers. They would never have dreamt of it in face-to-face encounters, but electronic communications are a different matter. Now that all the schools have been wired, once-shy pupils have begun to bombard their teachers with questions and even complaints. Older teachers find the change disturbing, but younger ones see it as necessary preparation for life in the 21st century.

The habits of hard work and self-discipline that South Korean schools have long drummed into their charges remain useful, as do the high standards of literacy and numeracy for which their pupils are envied. But if the country is to move beyond taking other people's inventions and manufacturing them more cheaply, its youngsters will need to think more creatively. It's a daunting task, but one that the Internet makes a little easier.

The drive to foster more creativity pre-dates the arrival of the Internet, and South Korean schools have been wired for only four years, so it is too early to be sure what difference ICT is making to the country's education system. But anecdotal evidence suggests that the change is already noticeable, and mainly to the good.

Schools share teaching ideas online. Parents can keep track of what their children are going to study by visiting school websites. Students have more opportunity to try things: to conduct simulations of scientific experiments, for example, rather than simply learning the results by rote. "Multimedia makes classes more fun," says Kim Jun Hyung, director of information technology at the Ministry of Education in Seoul. "And parents approve. Most families have PCs now, and they all cite their children's education as the reason for buying them."

Are the kids learning new skills? It seems they are. The amount of hacking soars during the school holidays. New viruses appear, school records are broken into and some pupils' grades are retrospectively improved. A number of bright students have dropped out of college – something that would have been considered shameful only a decade ago – to start software companies.

Getting the basics right

In classrooms all over the developing world, ICT is proving useful. In some countries, "distance learning" helps to compensate for teacher shortages. In Botswana, for example, a sparsely populated desert country where many teachers have died of AIDS, a free three-month Internet-based course evaluated by the University of Botswana boosted students' test scores by half. But computers and modems cannot magically make bad schools good. If the teacher is drunk or absent, or if parents send their daughters to work in the fields rather than pay school fees, the fix must be institutional, not technological.

There is a lot of encouraging evidence that education is improving in most places. In the early 1920s, under 25% of children born in poor countries learned to read. By 1999, three-quarters of adults in developing countries were literate. In every country for which the UNDP could find data, literacy in the past 15 years has improved or at least remained constant. Against that, countries for which no data are available, such as blood-soaked Angola and Sierra Leone, are bound to have done worse than the rest, so the average is probably not as good as it looks. What is more, with the world changing so fast, literacy is not enough. To take advantage of technology, developing countries need better scientific and mathematical skills.

Poor countries have too often tried to build education systems from the top down. In Latin America and Africa, funds and attention were lavished on universities before there were enough adequately prepared schoolchildren to fill them. East Asian countries, by contrast, have tended to put first things first. Japan introduced universal and compulsory primary education in 1872, when its citizens, on average, were no richer than the people of Djibouti are today. Other East Asian countries achieved universal primary schooling in the 1970s. Secondary education initially lagged behind Latin America, but it surged ahead in the 1980s, as the "tiger" economies boomed and demand for skilled workers soared. Tertiary enrolments rose last: in South Korea, from 16% of the relevant age group in 1980 to 68% in 1997.

East Asian schools show that how much you spend on education is less important than the way you spend it. Spending on public education in East Asia was only about 2.5% of GNP in 1960, inching up to 2.9% by 1997. Other developing countries spent far more – 3.9% on average – while African governments shelled out a hefty 5.1%. As East Asia grew richer, the absolute level of spending rose, but not nearly to the levels common in Western Europe or North America. And yet East Asian

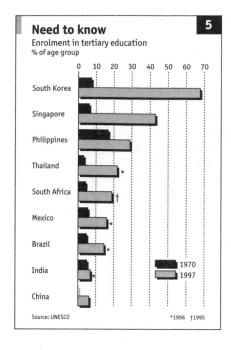

Need to know 5

Enrolment in tertiary education
% of age group

South Korea
Singapore
Philippines
Thailand
South Africa
Mexico
Brazil
India
China

1970
1997

Source: UNESCO   *1996 †1995

students consistently thrashed everyone else in internationally comparable tests. How did they do it?

What went on outside school made a big difference. For example, mothers nagged children to do their homework, and the job market put a premium on a good education. But what went on in the classroom was important, too. The state saw its role as making sure that every child learnt to read, write and work with numbers. Calculators were forbidden until students could do sums in their heads. Laggards were coached until they reached the required standard.

Teachers addressed the whole class at once, sometimes quizzing individual students to make sure everyone was following. Classes were large. This is usually considered a bad thing because students get less individual attention. However, given a limited budget, there is a trade-off between class size and teachers' pay. Because it had fewer teachers, South Korea was able to pay them more, relative to average income, than any other OECD country, which helped recruit better teachers.

Higher learning

The benefits of primary education accrue to society at large; those of higher education go mainly to those individuals who receive it. That is why most East Asian countries (except Singapore) make advanced students pay for their tuition. Poor but bright students can win scholarships. For most young people, however, university is a costly venture, which may help to explain why so many South Koreans opt for the kind of technical subjects that lead to reliably well-paid careers.

No country produces enough technically skilled people to match demand, but some developing countries do fairly well on this score. China, India and the four Asian tigers (South Korea, Hong Kong, Taiwan and Singapore) between them have about 3m college students enrolled in technical subjects. The trouble is that many of the best will emigrate.

The "brain drain" is a problem for all developing countries. South Africa loses 15–20% of its skilled technical workers each year. By one estimate, more than half of college students from developing countries who study abroad never return. More liberal American visa rules for ICT professionals introduced in 2000 were expected to attract 100,000 Indians a year before the bubble burst.

The Indian government naturally resents paying up to $20,000 per head to educate these people only to see them take their skills to a rich country, but in the short term there is not much it can do about it. Taxes on emigrants would be easy to dodge. Governments such as South Africa's and Malaysia's, which discriminate against ethnic minorities with technical skills, might slow the exodus of such people if they stopped discriminating, but show no inclination to try. In the long run, the best bet is to create an environment where such people can find challenging and adequately rewarded jobs at home.

How countries go high-tech

Policy makes all the difference

IN MOST COUNTRIES, selling alcohol to motorists is discouraged, but service stations in Brazil sell it by the litre – to put in people's cars. When the price of oil jumped in the 1970s, the Brazilian government decided to develop an alternative that did not rely on imports. It chose ethanol, made from home-grown sugar.

The intentions were noble. Besides reducing the country's vulnerability to OPEC price hikes, the alcohol-fuelled car was supposed to cut pollution and stimulate research in Brazil. From a technological perspective, the plan worked. Domestic manufacturers successfully produced cars that ran on ethanol. The trouble was that ethanol was both more expensive and less efficient than petrol. Motorists would not use it unless they were given a financial incentive.

The government duly provided one by subsidising ethanol to sell at 60% of the price of petrol. Before long, most of the cars sold in Brazil were ethanol-powered. Unfortunately, ethanol subsidies helped to get the public finances in a mess. The government printed money, thereby sparking hyperinflation. Among other things, this crippled Brazilian science. Researchers could win a government grant to build a laboratory, only to find that by the time the money was disbursed it was barely enough to buy a pair of protective goggles. Long-term planning became pointless. Businesses that might otherwise have invested in R&D did not bother.

Politicians in poor countries all want their countries to become more technologically competent but, as Brazil's story illustrates, it is hard for governments to pick winners in technology. If a developing country is to start coming up with inventions of its own, it needs the kind of political, social and economic arrangements that foster innovation. But what might these be?

Naturally, the example that most people look to is America. Politicians everywhere want to build a Silicon Valley in their own country, but they can't. America's thriving high-tech industries were not planned. Silicon Valley is what happens when thousands of scientists and entrepreneurs migrate to a sunny rich state with tough patent laws, a sophisticated financial system and a culture of inventing things and making money out of them. All these things take time to evolve. Governments can remove obstacles and push things in the right direction, but when they start making detailed plans they tend to come unstuck. Public investment in basic science is useful, for those who can afford it. But public investment in developing high-tech products is usually wasteful.

Many of the things that governments can do to promote technology are worth doing anyway. An obvious one is maintaining peace and stability. Clever people are mobile, and mostly prefer not to live in war zones. Other important factors include an open attitude to trade and investment, a sound infrastructure, a sensible approach to intellectual property and a flexible financial system.

Isolating yourself from the rest of the world is a sure way to stay technologically backward. At an exhibition in North Korea, your correspondent was shown a computer with a "North Korean" operating system. It did not seem to do much. Asked why, the party functionary in charge said it was "in display mode". Your correspondent furtively rebooted it and discovered that the software was made by Texas Instruments. "Self-reliance" as practised in North Korea used to be a popular concept in poor countries. In Africa, Latin America and India, many governments made a virtue of shutting out foreign goods and investment. Inevitably they shut out ideas, too. With no foreign competition, local firms had no one to learn from and little incentive to make their own products better.

Give a little, take a little

In the past decade or two, most developing countries have opened up a bit. Freer trade has brought in new products, which can be taken apart and copied. Foreign direct investment (FDI) has spread skills and technology. When Motorola builds a factory in China, it trains Chinese engineers. When BMW and DaimlerChrysler build cars in South Africa, they transfer know-how to their local suppliers.

Big countries can lure foreigners with the prospect of, say, putting their personal organisers in a billion Chinese palms. China uses the carrot of its potentially huge domestic market to persuade foreigners to share their technology with local partners. Small countries do not have this option, so many of them, controversially, offer fiscal incentives instead. In Costa Rica, for example, Intel was given a bundle of tax concessions to build a factory. Other high-tech firms followed, transforming the tiny Latin American country from a banana plantation into a microchip exporter.

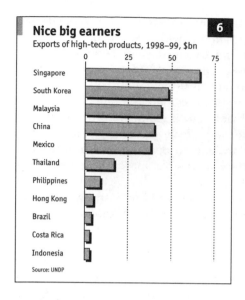

Nice big earners | 6
Exports of high-tech products, 1998–99, $bn

	0	25	50	75
Singapore				
South Korea				
Malaysia				
China				
Mexico				
Thailand				
Philippines				
Hong Kong				
Brazil				
Costa Rica				
Indonesia				

Source: UNDP

Ethnic ties can help, too. Much of the money pouring into China comes from the 50m-strong Chinese diaspora. Israel's software and biotech industries thrive on links with Jews in Europe and America. India's brain drain sometimes turns to gain when Indians working in Silicon Valley use their cash and contacts to set up new ICT firms back in Bangalore.

Besides its other benefits, high-tech trade makes people richer. In 1985–98, developing countries' exports of high-tech products grew 12-fold. Over the same period, their exports of things grown in the ground or dug out of it rose by a paltry 14%. By 1999, high-tech goods made up a larger proportion of the exports of developing countries than of industrial ones.

A decade ago, scientists in Bangkok wasted hours each day seething and choking in stationary traffic. Many left the city. Now the Thai capital has an air-conditioned overhead railway, and some journeys that used to take all morning can be made in ten minutes. The city is still congested, but it's a start.

The joys of leapfrogging

Countries with poor infrastructure need not despair. Like Thailand, they can leapfrog to the next technology. In building a railway network, they do not have to go through the steam age first. When setting up a telephone system, they can go straight to fibre optics and mobile telephones. Some developing countries have built a better communications infrastructure than many rich countries enjoy. Brazil, for example, which stopped trying to be self-sufficient in the 1990s, now has more broadband DSL lines per head than Britain. In South Korea, 40% of households have broadband Internet connections, and most share trading is done online.

But are all these good things too expensive for struggling developing countries? Not necessarily. The great thing about a telephone network is that you do not have to build it yourself. The firms that know how to wire countries are usually willing to do so at no cost to the public purse, so long as they can then charge people to make calls. In fact, they will often pay good money for the privilege. In 2001, Nigeria raised $570m by auctioning licences to set up mobile networks.

In most developing countries, the national telephone monopoly is an object of ridicule and rage. Slow, expensive connections are the main reason why monthly Internet access charges are six times the average monthly income in Madagascar, and nearly three times in Nepal. (In America, the figure is more like 1%.) Some monopolies block progress with an energy their customers can only wish they brought to bear on their main business. In Kenya, for example, the state telephone firm had the country's only Internet exchange-point shut down, forcing local surfers to use overseas links at 15 times the cost.

But things are improving. Twenty years ago, competitive telephone markets were almost unheard of. In 2000, the International Telecommunications Union (ITU), in a survey of 183 countries, found that 38 enjoyed a competitive market for fixed-line international telephone calls. Sixteen countries had a duopoly. The remaining 129 endured monopolies, but many plan to end them. Where competition is allowed, service invariably improves, bandwidth expands and prices fall. In South Korea, where five mobile-telephone firms are at each other's throats, handsets are given away and the number of new subscribers has soared.

Trade and telephones stimulate innovation by linking clever people with other clever people anywhere in the world. In promoting growth, these things are probably more important than education. A World Bank study found that average incomes in countries where people were free to trade and had easy access to telephones grew swiftly even if the education system was not much good. In well-educated countries with restricted trade and few telephones, per-head incomes grew more slowly. Not surprisingly, countries that scored well on both counts did best.

Until recently, the forms that Chinese bureaucrats filled in when buying computer systems did not contain a space for the cost of software. Why pay for something that can easily be copied? Steal a cow in a Zambian market, and you may get killed before the police arrive. But set up a stall selling pirated Madonna CDs, and probably no one will mind. Poor countries rarely protect intellectual property. Some say they are right not to bother. Most patents are held by rich westerners. Poor countries, runs the argument, will never scale the technology ladder if Merck and Microsoft extract royalties at every rung.

The counter-argument goes like this. Piracy is a cheap way to climb the lower rungs, but it takes you only so far. Failure to respect intellectual property rights deters high-tech FDI. Firms will not bring technology to countries where it can be stolen with impunity. Furthermore, if poor countries do not reward innovation, their people will have no incentive to innovate. Several Indian biotech firms that export their products are wary of selling them at home for fear of piracy.

Many developing countries are now trying harder to uphold intellectual property rights. In 1994, 141 countries signed TRIPS, an agreement to tighten patent protection. Royalties need not always flow from poor to rich. Brazil and India, for example, are considering laws to oblige foreign companies to make payments to indigenous people if they turn local plants into drugs or other commercial products.

One area where poor countries can free-ride with impunity is in regulation. It takes time, money and expertise to determine whether a drug or foodstuff is safe. Agencies such as America's Food and Drug Administration have huge budgets and make few mistakes. Poor countries could save millions, and get valuable medicines on the shelves more quickly, if they simply decided that a product safe enough for Americans was safe enough for them, unless there was good reason to assume that, for example, it might work differently in a tropical climate. This is already happening: a dozen East European countries now recognise rulings by the European Union's drug-approval agency.

Putting money where the brains are

Scientists must eat. They also need money for computers, test tubes and bits of pig to experiment on. Developing countries have two difficulties in funding their own R&D. One, obviously, is lack of money. The other is that even if they have spare cash, they do not usually have flexible and efficient mechanisms for directing it to useful research.

In many developing countries, science is almost entirely state-funded. In the Philippines, for example, public spending on R&D accounts for 98% of the total. There is nothing wrong with public funding, but on its own it is never enough. In all advanced countries, public and private research complement each other. Taxpayers' dollars paid for the basic research that underpinned the Internet, but it took private companies to enable users to access the web. Public laboratories helped sequence the human genome, but it will be profit-driven pharmaceutical firms that turn genomic data into drugs.

In America, people with good ideas can usually find the cash to put them into practice. American venture-capital funds have bundles of the stuff to invest in risky projects. High-tech firms can raise yet more money by listing their shares on Nasdaq. In the late 1990s, investors grew

More venturesome		7
New venture capital, $m		
	1995	2000
United States	4,566	103,170
Hong Kong	245	769
Singapore	5	651
India	3	342
China	–	84
South Korea	1	65
Philippines	2	9
South Africa	–	3
Source: UNDP		

absurdly over-enthusiastic about technology stocks and caused a bubble. When it burst in 2000, many start-ups died. The booms and busts of Californian capitalism can be alarming. But no other system yet devised channels so much money into technology so quickly, nor pulls the plug so quickly when an idea proves to be a dud.

In the developing countries that have caught up fastest, private investment has played a crucial role (see chart 7). No poor country has capital markets like America's, of course. Bio Solutions, the Thai biotech firm mentioned earlier, could not lay its hands on venture capital, because there are hardly any venture capitalists in Thailand. Instead, it secured seed money in the traditional way: from the founder's family. This method works admirably if you have wealthy parents. However, a young Thai with a good idea but no connections will probably fail to get any funding.

As capital flows more freely across borders, developing-world entrepreneurs can increasingly tap rich countries' savings. And some developing countries are copying aspects of western capital markets at home. The transformation in South Korea has been striking. In the 1970s, only a fifth of Korean R&D was privately financed; now the proportion is four-fifths. The Asian economic crisis of 1997 prompted a further shake-up. Before then, most private R&D was done within huge conglomerates, or chaebol, that were financed by bank loans. Lenders assumed that the government would never let the biggest chaebol fail, and so let them over-borrow. Small firms, meanwhile, found it almost impossible to raise money.

Climate change

In 1997, South Korea nearly defaulted. The most indebted *chaebol* went bankrupt and were broken up. Those that were left realised they had to change. They cut their workforces and their debts, and started outsourcing more high-tech work to small companies. At the same time, the government rushed to stimulate high-tech start-ups. Hefty tax breaks and subsidies for venture capital (vc) created a new market, and vc investments shot up from $1m in 1995 to $65m in 2000. *Chaebol* employees left what they had always assumed were jobs for life to set up firms making things like mobile-phone components. University students got funding to design and market computer games. New firms scurried to list on Kosdaq, the Korean Nasdaq, whose market capitalisation soared from $7 billion in March 1999 to $113 billion a year later. Kosdaq slumped at the same time as Nasdaq, and in late 2001 was capitalised at a more modest $25 billion.

Good Korean ideas now get the backing they deserve, according to Yoo Hyang Sook, director of the state-funded Centre for the Functional Analysis of the Human Genome in Taejon, south of Seoul. "If your idea has obvious commercial applications, you can easily get money from a venture-capital fund," she says. "If you are pursuing basic research, the government helps as much as it can." Others think the state has wasted a fortune. Richard Kim, president of Venture Source, a firm that matches local entrepreneurs with foreign investors, reckons that only a small fraction of recent start-ups are making profits, and that many simply took the government subsidy and disappeared.

It is too early to say who is right, but no one could fail to be impressed by the speed at which South Korea keeps adapting to a changing world. Koreans will tell you that this is because Korean culture welcomes change. But that is not a uniquely Korean trait. When the benefits of something new are obvious, people are usually quick to embrace it. And since the benefits of many recent inventions are indeed obvious, many staid, traditional societies are changing in whatever ways are necessary to take advantage of them.

Keep it simple

High tech is not the only tech

GOOD IDEAS are not always complex. Take the Hippo Roller, a South African invention, which in essence is a plastic barrel with a handle. Placed on its side, it can be filled with water and pushed along like the wheel of a wheelbarrow. Women find they can roll four times as much water in a Hippo Roller as they used to carry in buckets on their heads, so they make fewer ten-mile treks to the water hole. In some South African villages, young men think the Hippo so cool that they have started fetching the water themselves.

Technologies that improve people's lives do not have to contain microchips, nor do they have to cost hundreds of millions of dollars to develop. Clay ovens, for example, are more fuel-efficient than cooking pots balanced on stones, saving poor families hours of gathering firewood each day. Plastic syringes with ratchets to prevent re-use stop infections from being spread by dirty needles. Simple products can be hugely successful: think of the fortunes made from cardboard milk cartons and Post-It notes. If a new device fills an unmet need, people will buy it.

In poor countries, however, the connection between demand and supply is sometimes lost. When a country relies on foreign aid to pay for poverty-relief programmes, it often has to spend the money in ways that reflect the donors' priorities rather than the recipients' needs. Aid is sometimes tied to the purchase of goods from the donor country, which is why so many African villages have broken-down tractors they do not know how to repair. Big donors sometimes have a bias in favour of big projects with obvious results, which is why so many third-world peasants have had to make way for dams.

Big dams and power stations tend to supply the national electricity grid, which often does not extend to poor people's homes. Many national grids in developing countries are publicly owned and broke, and therefore unlikely to bring electricity to rural homes in the foreseeable future. But there may be an alternative: micropower. Small turbines on small rivers can provide enough energy for medium-sized villages in Sri Lanka or Peru. The poor are prepared to pay for electricity, even though most micropower schemes still need to be subsidised.

271

Deregulation could help. The abolition of public power monopolies would leave micropower generators free to sell surplus electricity to the national grid, raising money and perhaps easing power shortages elsewhere.

Fewer buffaloes, livelier democracy

Technology is shaking up culture, society and politics, mostly for the better

THE KING of Thailand is campaigning to save the water buffalo. These sturdy animals once pulled every plough in Thailand, but they are being replaced by tractors. The rhythm of country life has changed. Man and beast no longer toil together in harmony. The king worries that a valuable part of Thai culture is vanishing.

Thai farmers, however, like their new machines. They don't have to be fed before dawn, or mucked out. They don't try to escape, or trample the neighbour's crops. Most important, they get the job done faster and with less effort, so the farmer can put his feet up and watch television.

Technology makes many people uneasy. They wonder if it is safe, and they have trouble coping with constant change. Such worries are understandable. Many new inventions are indeed dangerous. Aeroplanes can crash, chemical factories can leak and smart bombs are expressly designed to kill. But these dangers should be measured against those of the past. Aeroplanes are much safer than any previous method of travelling long distances. Chemicals keep food free of lethal germs. And wars fought with primitive weapons are just as bloody: think of Rwanda.

Nothing is perfectly safe, and safeguards themselves have costs. Insisting on longer trials for drugs or GM foods might reduce the risk that people will ingest something harmful, but it also delays potentially life-saving medicines reaching patients, or higher-yielding seeds reaching Peruvian peasants. Stricter safety standards can cut short more lives than they save, and make things more expensive.

When electric light bulbs were introduced, the *New York Times* gave warning that they might cause blindness. In 17th-century Europe there was a movement to ban coffee, which was feared to cause paralysis. When humans first learned to make fire, some doubtless got burnt, but meat is tastier and more wholesome roasted than raw.

Even if new gadgets will not harm our bodies, what of our souls? What if television kills traditional songs and festivals, or persuades people to swap ancient religious principles for the empty materialism glamorised in American soap operas? It is a worry. But a glance at the world's most technologically advanced countries suggests that the new does not necessarily drive out the old. As America has grown more sophisticated technologically, it has not grown noticeably less religious. Television in Japan has not killed *kabuki* theatre; instead, it has projected it to a wider audience. People tend to preserve the traditions they value, and ditch the ones they do not care about. Many Chinese scientists respect *feng shui*, and many Africans pray to their ancestors. But foot-binding has ceased, and witches are lynched only in the most backward villages.

Power to the individual

The most important way that technology shapes culture is by increasing the power of individuals. If rural life seems oppressive, buses make it easier to go to the city and get a job. Modern contraceptives give women more control over their own fertility. Drudgery-relieving devices free up time for more rewarding activities.

Technology can also shift the balance of power between ordinary people and their rulers. In January 2001, for example, text messages swapped among mobile telephones helped to topple a corrupt and incompetent Philippine president. Joseph Estrada outwitted an attempted impeachment, but was overthrown in a bloodless coup after hundreds of thousands of protesters massed in Manila to demand his removal. The crowds were raised with the message: "Full mblsn tday Edsa". It was short for "full mobilisation today at the Edsa shrine in Manila". Opposition leaders sent it to every mobile number they knew. Recipients buzzed it to every number stored in their handsets. Within minutes, millions knew what was afoot.

Modern communications can make dissent safer. In 1986, when Fil-ipinos threw out an even worse president, Ferdinand Marcos, it took months to organise rallies. Messengers had to catch ferries between the archipelago's 2,000 inhabited islands to spread the word. If the secret police caught them, the message did not get through. This year the mes-sages were unstoppable, and their senders were untraceable. Most were using prepaid cards to charge their phones, which allowed them to remain anonymous. Authoritarian regimes from China to Saudi Arabia still silence subversion, but they cannot always stop people from visit-ing banned websites. Technically skilled dissidents can download soft-ware that routes them around government firewalls.

In more democratic countries, the web lets civic groups organise and swap information. Four years ago, most South Koreans barely knew what an NGO was. Now there are thousands of them: blacklisting corrupt politicians at election time, lobbying for friendlier (or more hostile) ties with North Korea, networking with foreign NGOs and, of course, campaigning against globalisation.

Electronic communications help make societies less hierarchical. "When you send an e-mail," says Sakiko Fukuda-Parr, the main author of a recent UNDP report on technology and development, "no one can see the cut of your suit, and no secretary blocks your path to the minister's office." Within companies, too, junior employees who would never have dared knock on the chief executive's door might send him an idea electronically.

The decline of deference is both a cause and a consequence of technological progress. In pre-industrial societies, authority generally derived from age or genealogy. In 18th-century France or 20th-century rural Malawi, sons deferred to fathers and ordinary folk to hereditary chiefs. Such traditional attitudes had their uses, but they did not foster innovation. Scientific inquiry requires people to question received wisdom, and to draw conclusions based on evidence. This was how the West first overtook the older and then more technologically advanced civilisations of China and India. According to Mohamed Hassan, director of the Third World Academy of Sciences in Trieste, deference still slows research in many third-world laboratories. When young researchers are afraid to challenge their professors, precocious insights are sometimes lost.

It's your choice

Young Thai men used to spend years in Buddhist monasteries, cultivating their spirituality. These days they cannot spare so much time. Typically, they spend only a few weeks shut away studying the *sutras* before they rush back to the city. No one forced them to change their priorities. If they choose, they can spend their whole lives in a monastery. But for the most part, they choose not to.

No one is forced to take part in our modern, technology-adoring society. Anyone who would rather go and live on nuts and berries in the forest is free to do so. But most people like what modern technology has to offer, and fret only that they cannot get enough of it.

Developing countries are making the same transition that Europe, America and Japan made earlier, only faster. This causes strains. In Britain, the upheavals of the industrial revolution were spread over several generations. The East Asian tigers packed an equally momentous change into a single generation. Future catch-ups may be even quicker and more traumatic.

Failure to adapt is bound to hurt some people. The invention of synthetic indigo dyes bankrupted indigo farmers in El Salvador. As more countries lay fibre-optic cables, Zambian copper miners are laid off. But the winners will greatly outnumber the losers. Thanks to technology, people in developing countries today have fuller stomachs, longer lives and fewer nasty illnesses than ever before. They are also less poor and have many more choices about how they want to live.

There is no reason why, in 50 years' time, the average citizen of the developing world should not be as comfortably off as Americans are today. As current technologies get cheaper, they will spread. As the Internet keeps scientists in Africa, Asia and Latin America abreast of the latest developments in their field, they will start to produce more breakthroughs themselves.

Predatory and incompetent governments will doubtless continue to hold some poor countries back. But taken as a whole, the developing world has one great advantage that rich countries can never match. They can call on five times as many brains, and the gap is getting wider.

Sources

Among the sources the author found most helpful in researching this survey were the UNDP's Human Development Report 2001, *Making New Technologies Work for Human Development*; the World Bank's World Development Report 1998/99, *Knowledge for Development*; and a cheerful book by Stephen Moore and Julian Simon, *It's Getting Better All the Time: 100 Greatest Trends of the Last 100 Years*, Cato Institute, 2000. More sources are list on *The Economist's* website, www.economist.com.

The material on pages 241–76 first appeared in a survey written by Robert Guest in *The Economist* in November 2001.

IV
GOVERNING THE GLOBAL ECONOMY

8

Reform of international financial architecture

Whither the International Monetary Fund and World Bank? This is a perennial question around Washington. The right thinks the two institutions do too much for too many countries (usually the wrong ones); the left, with few obvious successes to point to, gives ground uneasily. In the survey that opens this chapter (January 1999), Zanny Minton Beddoes offers broad thoughts about what shape both institutions might take in future, stressing that reform will not come easily. Two additional articles cover subsequent developments. One is a widely-discussed report to the American Congress of March 2000, which recommended cut-backs to both institutions; the other is the work by Horst Köhler, the IMF's energetic head, to streamline the conditions attached to the Fund's loans. Another player in global economic governance is of course the World Trade Organisation. For a critical view on the WTO, see the article on pages 52–57 of chapter one.

Time for a redesign?

The world's financial system has serious flaws. Unfortunately, so do the alternatives

EVERY JANUARY, THE world's top bankers, businessmen and politicians gather in the Swiss ski resort of Davos for the "World Economic Forum", the global equivalent of an office brainstorming session. In recent years this has been a rather complacent occasion, a celebration of globalisation. This weekend's gathering [in January 1999] should be different. The turbulence of the past year is forcing a reappraisal of the stability of the international financial system.

The Davos dream – greater prosperity for all as global integration advances – is under attack.

Turmoil in Brazil, the depth and spread of Asia's crisis, Russia's chaotic default on its debt and the resulting investor stampede away from risky markets, and the collapse of the hedge fund Long-Term Capital Management are merely the highlights – or rather low points – of an extraordinarily precarious 12 months. Capital markets proved volatile and susceptible to contagion, and emerging economies suffered the painful consequences. Two-fifths of the world economy is now in recession. Except for Japan, most of the misery is concentrated in the developing world.

The sense of crisis is now receding. A global economic meltdown, which seemed possible for a few nail-biting weeks in October 1998, has been avoided. Yet it is widely agreed that this was a narrow escape, and that "something must be done" to make the global financial system safer, particularly for emerging economies.

Everybody who is anybody has opined on the matter. President Clinton wants to "adapt the international financial architecture to the 21st century"; Tony Blair, Britain's prime minister, wants "a new Bretton Woods for the new millennium"; Alan Greenspan, head of America's central bank and a man not given to hyperbole, has called this once-boring subject "a cage-rattler". He, too, wants to change the "patchwork of arrangements" governing global finance.

Thinking about it

All this interest brought forth a plethora of suggestions on how the system should be redesigned. A mammoth website on the Asian crisis and international financial reform has about 50 links under the heading of "reform of the architecture of the international financial system". There is an abundance of "blueprints", "frameworks", "action plans" and "agendas", as well as working groups, councils and committees.

But will all this effort achieve much? History suggests not. Financial crises occur with monotonous regularity, and are followed just as regularly by demands for a new architecture. In the half-century since the foundations of today's system were laid at the Bretton Woods conference in 1944, there have been numerous calls for new institutions, new rules or a "Bretton Woods II". When the fixed-exchange-rate system broke down in the early 1970s, an official committee debated a successor regime at length and without success. Again, during the debt crisis of the 1980s, several new organisations were mooted. Yet none of these deliberations brought dramatic change. Once the crisis receded, so did the appetite for a big fix.

Instead, the Bretton Woods blueprint evolved organically in response to changing circumstances. Its central institutions took on new tasks. When the fixed-exchange-rate system broke down, the IMF simply began to monitor the new system of floating rates, and shifted the bulk of its activity to developing countries. After the collapse of communism, the Fund became the chief architect, and financier, of the transition from communism to capitalism. Since Mexico's crash in 1994, it has shifted gear again, providing more money more quickly to countries hit by capital-market crises.

Other rules and procedures evolved too. Regulators in rich countries, prompted by the impact of the Herstatt Bank collapse in 1974, pledged to co-ordinate supervision of international banks. More than a decade later, they came up with the Basle Capital Accord, now the globally accepted minimum standard of bank health. Since 1997 it has been complemented by a broader set of core principles of banking supervision. Other, looser, standards have also emerged as financial markets have integrated. For example, IOSCO, the international federation of securities regulators, has agreed on a set of standards for cross-border offerings. The International Accounting Standards Committee has developed a set of global accounting standards. Thanks to such evolutionary changes, the financial architecture in 1999 looks rather different from that in 1969, let alone 1949.

But global finance has changed even more radically. In rich countries, the 1970s and particularly the 1980s saw a widespread liberalisation of

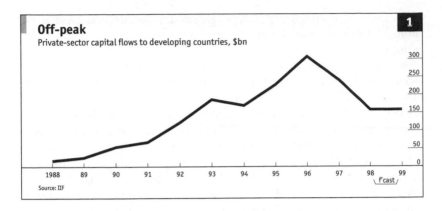

Off-peak **1**
Private-sector capital flows to developing countries, $bn

Source: IIF

domestic finance. Freed from suffocating regulation, banks innovated, creating junk bonds, mortgage-backed securities and other new instruments. Computers made it possible to unbundle risks into a complex array of securities. Turnover on foreign exchange, equity and debt markets rose dramatically.

The ideological shift towards free markets in the developing economies, coupled with their need for external capital, drew new participants into the international financial arena. During the 1990s, governments, banks and companies from an ever more exotic range of emerging economies raised money abroad. Private-sector financial flows to developing countries shot up (see chart 1). Even so, the "emerging-market" asset class remains a tiny share of overall financial assets.

Today's capital markets are international, yet they are supervised and regulated largely on a national basis. The world they operate in is wholly different from that which the Bretton Woods institutions were designed to support. In boom times this discrepancy did not seem to matter. Commentators simply suggested that the machinery of the Bretton Woods financial architecture – especially the World Bank – was redundant. What was the point of a huge bureaucracy doling out public money, they asked, if the private sector was perfectly capable of building dams, bridges and hospitals? The old framework was outmoded, but as long as capital sloshed easily around the world there was little urge to build a new one.

This complacency was first challenged by Mexico's spectacular financial crash in late 1994. It was further dented when the Asian crisis hit in mid-1997. And it was truly shattered by the turbulence of 1998 (at least until the next boom begins). The world has therefore embarked on one of its periodic searches for radical reform. But before it can come up with solutions, it must identify the problems with today's global architecture.

It is easy to draw up a checklist of what went wrong. Financial systems in many emerging markets were weak, badly supervised and inadequately regulated, and exchange-rate regimes were inappropriate. Mexico, Thailand, South Korea, Indonesia and Russia all hit trouble because their firms, banks or governments borrowed too much short-term money, lulled into a false sense of security by stable exchange rates. Once crisis struck, the reaction of today's interconnected financial markets was vehement, and their ills proved highly contagious. Unrelated markets fell as investors sold securities to maintain their overall risk profile or raise cash to make good their losses elsewhere.

More traditional panic also played a part. After Russia's default, in particular, investors eschewed all kinds of risk. As in every financial crash since the 17th-century tulip crisis, greed suddenly turned to fear. The difference this time was that the effect was global, not just local. When markets panicked after Russia's crash, the impact was felt everywhere, from Brazil to American municipal bonds. Moreover, the mechanisms for resolving the crisis were found wanting. The IMF, in particular, lacked the resources, mandate and expertise to deal with a global capital-market problem.

Impossible trinity

Listing the problems may be easy; finding solutions is not. Should there be more or less global regulation, more or less public financial support, looser or tighter exchange-rate regimes? There are no simple answers, because the problems of modern economic policy are maddeningly interlinked. A policymaker trying to design the ideal financial system has three objectives. He wants continuing national sovereignty; financial markets that are regulated, supervised and cushioned; and the benefits of global capital markets. Unfortunately, as Larry Summers, America's deputy treasury secretary under Mr Clinton, has argued, these three goals are incompatible. They form the "impossible trinity" that underlies the instability of today's global architecture.

Any coherent reform proposal must favour two parts of the trinity at the expense of the third. For instance, those who wish to regulate markets and maintain national sovereignty must do so at the expense of capital-market integration. Those who wish to maintain sovereignty and yet allow capital markets to integrate must accept an entirely free market at the global level. Those who want capital-market integration and global regulation must forfeit national sovereignty.

This impossible trinity renders most radical architectural blueprints Utopian, since politicians are not prepared to choose only two out of the three objectives. The best hope in the short term, therefore, lies in improving the trade-offs between them. There is plenty of scope. Transparency can be improved; global (voluntary) standards can be developed across a broader range of institutions and products; incentives can be devised to make market participants stick to the regulatory rules. Such improvements will reduce the risk of financial crises even in a world of sovereign states.

Broadly, this is what the various official bodies charged with "redesigning the global architecture" are trying to do. The language is over-ambitious; "a spot of modest interior redecoration" would be nearer the mark. Yet, since no one can agree on anything more radical, for the moment that is all that can be hoped for.

Eventually, more dramatic change is bound to come. This survey will argue that in a couple of decades the global financial architecture will look substantially different from today, not because a more enlightened set of politicians has designed a Bretton Woods II, but because the system has naturally evolved along a different route: regional integration. By 2020, the world will see at least two big regional currency blocks, maybe more. And although there will be global regulatory standards, supervision – and, more importantly, crisis-management – will increasingly take place at the regional level. The IMF will still be there, but mainly for countries that have remained outside regional blocks. An implausible idea? Not compared with some of the other blueprints around.

A wealth of blueprints

The more radical, the less likely to succeed

THINK OF A financial-reform idea, and you will find that someone got there first. Proposals include the abolition of the IMF, the reintroduction of broad capital controls and the creation, respectively, of a global central bank, a global financial regulator and a world currency. To be taken seriously, such ideas must pass two tests. They must be an improvement on the status quo, and they must stand a chance of being implemented. Most radical blueprints fail on both counts.

The idea of controlling capital flows is currently enjoying a vogue. A swelling chorus of politicians and academics, inspired by nostalgia for the Bretton Woods era – when capital mobility was limited and governments were free to follow their own (usually Keynesian) economic policy – wants to reassert control over international financial flows, especially those generated by short-term "speculators". George Soros, a speculator himself, has become convinced that capitalism will collapse unless speculation is curbed. Malaysia's prime minister, Mahathir Mohamad, in September 1998 imposed stringent exchange controls and restricted portfolio flows out of Malaysia. Eminent academics have spoken in favour of capital controls. Paul Krugman advocates controlling capital outflows in a crisis, while Jagdish Baghwati, a well-known free-trader from Columbia University, has criticised the objective of free capital flows.

The theoretical benefits of the free movement of capital are well known: it enhances economic welfare by channelling savings to their most productive uses. Moreover, capital mobility allows countries to insure themselves against risk. If, say, Mexico suffered a temporary economic downturn, it could, in theory, borrow abroad to compensate. But, argue the opponents of capital mobility, these benefits must be weighed against substantial risks. Trade in dollars, they reckon, is not the same as trade in widgets, because capital markets suffer from a number of market failures. In the absence of perfect information, investors tend to move in herds, rushing in and out of markets on rumour. Hence markets overshoot, at considerable cost to the real economy.

These theoretical deficiencies, say the sceptics, explain why capital mobility has not only failed to provide tangible economic benefits but also imposed large costs. A favourite statistic is that the developed world grew by 4% a year between 1945 and 1973, the halcyon days of the Bretton Woods regime, when trade was gradually liberalised but capital remained fettered. Now that it has become much more mobile, average economic growth has dropped by a third and instability reigns. The past two decades have seen more than 90 serious banking crises, each of which resulted in bank losses that, in proportion to GDP, exceeded the costs of America's banking collapse during the Great Depression. True, correlation does not prove causality, so some economists have tried more formal techniques. For example, Dani Rodrik, of Harvard University, has used regression analysis to examine the impact of capital mobility on growth. He finds no evidence that it has helped.

The sociological case against capital mobility echoes an argument first made by Karl Polanyi, an Austrian economic historian, who wrote in 1944 that unregulated markets, outside a web of social relations, would eventually have dire consequences. Plainly, there are regional variations of capitalism. Footloose financial flows without a cultural underpinning, it is claimed, are a recipe for disaster. The aim, instead, should be to ensure that national variations of capitalism can co-exist, which implies some control over capital flows.

Mr Krugman makes a different case. He argues that at times of economic crisis, the sudden outflow of foreign capital leaves policymakers with two equally unpalatable choices. Either they must raise interest rates sky-high to defend their exchange rate, so harming the domestic economy, or they must let their exchange rate collapse, which will be equally detrimental. Capital outflows deprive them of the ability to stimulate the economy through lower interest rates. To retain that option, Mr Krugman advocates capital controls as the least bad response to a crisis.

These arguments cannot be dismissed out of hand. Capital mobility combined with weak financial systems has clearly caused big problems. True, Asian countries might not be in such a mess if they had liberalised more sensibly (by, for instance, opening up to long-term capital flows before short-term ones). But the case against capital mobility ducks one obvious question: if it is so bad, why do governments pursue it?

The case for capital mobility

The answer is equally obvious: because they see real benefits from it. These include the transfer of technology and know-how from foreign direct investment, the increase in efficiency from deepening stock and bond markets, and the ability to tap sizeable external sources of finance.

The fact that they have not so far shown up on economists' regressions may well be due to measurement problems (remember that a decade ago economists were still deeply divided over whether countries got any benefit from free trade).

Moreover, would-be capital controllers need to avoid rose-tinted nostalgia when looking back on the Bretton Woods era. For most of that time, domestic as well as international finance was tightly regulated. Indeed, domestic financial restrictions are a prerequisite for effective international controls. Yet no one doubts that these restrictions had their costs: in poor countries, in particular, profligate governments routinely helped themselves to their citizens' savings through inflation and negative real interest rates.

Most important, consider how implausible it is in today's networked world that strict regulation of capital flows could be reimposed. No democratic government could contemplate the restriction of personal liberty that would be needed to return to the Bretton Woods blueprint. Draconian regulation would invite corruption on a vast scale, and anything less draconian would soon be circumvented. Many Latin American countries reinstated controls during the 1980s debt crisis, but found they scared off foreign investors and produced few benefits. "Capital controls didn't avoid any of the costs of the debt crisis, and postponed a few of them at a premium," says Ricardo Hausmann, chief economist of the Inter-American Development Bank.

That is not to deny that individual countries, such as Malaysia, can temporarily buck the trend and restrict capital flows, though they will probably pay a price. More importantly, it is perfectly possible for countries to reduce their controls only gradually, and to retain prudential regulations on short-term capital inflows (of which more later). But reform efforts designed to stop or reverse the overall trend of capital-market integration are non-starters.

Free-market hitches

Equally doomed, however, are those blueprints which aspire to a wholly free international market. Extreme liberalisers want to abolish the IMF. In the United States, they include George Shultz, a former treasury secretary; Anna Schwartz, an eminent economic historian; numerous conservative Republicans; and editorial writers on the *Wall Street Journal*. They argue that today's financial woes are caused by bail-outs of both countries and investors. The demon that must be exorcised is moral hazard.

Moral hazard means that investors and borrowers may behave recklessly because they believe they will be bailed out when trouble hits. The IMF, argue the free-marketeers, creates moral hazard in two ways: by rescuing governments from the consequences of stupid policies, it encourages them to repeat their mistakes; and by rescuing incautious investors, it rewards their recklessness. This criticism has gained considerable voice in recent years as the size of IMF support packages has increased. Mexico's $40 billion rescue in 1995, those critics charge, has greatly increased the risk of future crises.

Like the capital-control lot, the anti-IMF brigade has some silly and some serious arguments. It is hard to see how IMF bail-outs can create much moral hazard for governments, since IMF money comes with arduous conditions attached. For investors, on the other hand, moral hazard is a distinct possibility. They did lose a lot of money in some of the recent crises, including Mexico and Asia, but in Russia, for example, they openly admitted to a "moral-hazard play" as they bought highly lucrative but risky short-term government debt. Russia, they assumed (wrongly), would never be allowed to fail.

Even if moral hazard is a problem, it is not clear that a free market can provide the solution. Its advocates point to the American financial system in the late 19th century when there was no central bank, no securities commission and no deposit insurance. Banks held high capital ratios, and leverage was far lower than it is today. Although there were huge and costly banking failures, the system as a whole survived. Many free-marketeers view this era as a model for today's international markets. But in reality it shows why such proposals will not work.

In the course of the 20th century, as the vote was broadened, democratic governments chose to soften the edges of the free market at the national level by introducing central banks, deposit insurance and their regulatory underpinnings. The same political considerations are now beginning to influence the debate at the international level. As capital markets integrate, voters will demand the maintenance of such safety nets, whatever the risk of moral hazard. A completely unfettered international capital market is politically unacceptable.

What about the third side of the triangle: building the global institutions and regulations to match the global capital market? This is the idea that gets aspiring global architects most excited. They would like to replicate at the global level the institutions that already regulate and support capital markets at the national level. There are essentially three ideas, which come in different versions: a global lender of last resort, a global bankruptcy court and a global financial regulator.

At a national level, central banks act as a lender of last resort. Since they can print money, they can lend freely in an emergency to prevent the banking system from collapsing. The most radical reformers would like to replicate this role at the global level with a global central bank and a global currency. This idea is not new: it was famously floated by Harvard University's Richard Cooper in an article in Foreign Affairs in 1984. But any proposal that calls for a global currency clearly does not pass the feasibility test.

Not everyone believes that an effective international lender of last resort demands a global currency. In a paper[1], Stanley Fischer argues that historically lenders of last resort have been crisis managers and crisis lenders. You don't have to be a central bank to do either, he reckons. Provided that the lender of last resort had enough resources, it could stem panic even without the ability to create money.

Other would-be architects have elaborated ideas for just such a limited global central bank. George Soros would like an "international central bank" that would "act as lender of last resort with regard to a select group of countries". Jeffrey Garten of the Yale School of Management wants an independent global central bank that could "inject more money into the system to spur growth" and oversee the operations of shaky financial institutions. However, in his view it should not be able to override the decisions of the Federal Reserve. Yet if its powers were severely limited, such a global central bank would be little different from today's IMF (and hence hardly a radical proposal). If, on the other hand, it were able to inject a significant amount of liquidity globally, such a bank would clearly compromise the authority of national central banks.

Similar dilemmas plague proposals for global regulation. Henry Kaufman, a Wall Street financial consultant, would like to see a "Board of Overseers" of international financial markets which would develop global financial standards and supervise and evaluate institutions under its purview. John Eatwell of Cambridge University and Lance Taylor of the New School in New York have put forward similar ideas.

In principle, the idea of a global regulator for global markets makes sense. The problem, again, is feasibility. To whom would such "global regulators" be accountable? Who would ensure that they did not become unwieldy bureaucracies? And, most important, would there be sufficient political agreement to set them up, and to subordinate national regulators to them? In an environment where America cannot even agree on a single overarching national financial regulator, the notion of a powerful global regulator who would nibble away at national sovereignty is hardly realistic.

Proposals for an international bankruptcy court also seem sensible but infeasible. The efficient functioning of domestic financial markets depends crucially on effective bankruptcy law. When firms go bust, national bankruptcy courts play a central role in sorting out the mess. Many commentators, notably Jeffrey Sachs of Harvard University, suggest that something similar is needed at the international level to deal with countries rather than companies. The trouble is that the parallel is far from perfect. A domestic court can fire a bankrupt firm's management, reducing the risk of moral hazard. But even the most ardent globalist is unlikely to recommend that an international bankruptcy court should be able to fire a country's government. On a more mundane level, countries have vastly different types of bankruptcy codes (the Americans, for instance, favour debtors far more than the Europeans), so they will find it hard to agree on an international code they would be prepared to observe.

In short, all the radical blueprints are flawed. The current financial problems are simply not severe enough to overcome large political obstacles to radical change. Remember that the Bretton Woods agreement – an inspiration for radical reformers – was concluded towards the end of a world war and soon after the Great Depression. The Bretton Woods conference, although attended by 700 people, was dominated by two countries (Britain and America) and two people (John Maynard Keynes and Harry Dexter White). Today, a broader array of rich countries would want their say, and so would the developing world. They all have vested interests and their own agenda. That means there is little chance of radicalism. The best hope of progress lies in trying to improve today's messy trade-offs. A good place to start is crisis prevention.

Notes

1 "On the Need for an International Lender of Last Resort", by Stanley Fischer. January 1999.

A stitch in time

Prevention is much better than cure

IMAGINE YOURSELF TAKING a business-school exam in international financial management. The test is a case study. It concerns Opacia, an emerging economy which is in a bit of a mess. Corporate financial statements mean little as firms routinely lend to each other off balance sheet. You have no idea how big the country's foreign liabilities are, though you know that its banks and companies like to borrow dollars short-term, usually to finance long-term local investment projects. There is no effective bankruptcy law, and corruption is rife. Question: is this a safe place to invest money?

Clearly it is not. But that did not stop international investors, between 1993 and 1997, pouring more than $500 billion into Asian economies that bore a remarkable resemblance to Opacia. When times were good, investors seemed oblivious to the lack of transparency and the regulatory shortcomings; when crisis hit, there was a stampede for the exits. This neatly illustrates the importance, as well the difficulty, of making today's financial system safer. Not only must emerging economies be given an incentive to clean up their act, but investors, for their part, must be given an incentive to be more prudent.

How can this be done? Some financial architects, aware that strict global rules would offend against national sovereignty, have come up with something they hope will be more acceptable. In place of rules, they advocate more international "standards" for everything from bank supervision to corporate governance. Many such standards already exist – for example, the Basle capital-adequacy accord and IOSCO's principles of securities regulation – and many more are being developed. The OECD is drawing up international standards of corporate governance; the International Bar Association is developing a model bankruptcy code. Such standards, it is hoped, will ease the trade-off between sovereignty and global regulation.

Perhaps; but they are not a panacea. Internationally agreed standards are often too vague to mean much. The Basle core principles of sound banking, for instance, may be useful as a broad political statement, but they are not much use as a detailed guideline for bank supervisors. Even the most specific standards can be evaded in spirit, if not in letter. To be effective, standards must be closely aligned with incentives.

Transparency standards are a case in point. No one could possibly disagree on the benefits of disclosure: everybody accepts that more information makes markets work more efficiently. Mexico and South Korea might both have avoided sudden exchange-rate crises if investors had had a more accurate idea of the country's foreign-reserve levels. Indonesia might have steered clear of the abyss if its firms had been forced to disclose the size of their unhedged foreign liabilities.

Standard solution

Hence the rush to produce disclosure standards. In addition to the international accounting standards developed by the International Accounting Standards Committee, the Basle Committee is working on standards of transparency for banks. The IMF has set up a "Special Data Dissemination Standard" – a checklist of countries' financial and economic data – on the Internet. It has also developed a code of good practices on fiscal transparency, and is preparing a similar code for monetary policy. At this rate, there will be transparency standards for every aspect of government and corporate activity within a couple of years.

But will anyone observe them? Rich countries like to push disclosure for others, but are not so keen on it for themselves. For example, of all the G7 countries Britain is still the only one that routinely publishes its official reserves' forward position. The IMF's special data standard seems to have made little impression so far. Only 47 countries meet the requirements, and investors seem to take little notice of it anyway. "We don't trust it, and we don't use it," says David Folkerts-Landau, head of global research at Deutsche Morgan Grenfell, and a former IMF official.

The moral is that setting standards alone is not enough. Whether they are for transparency, corporate governance, auditing procedures, bank supervision or anything else, it is only the first step. To ensure that firms, banks and governments comply with them, you need either better supervision or better incentives.

Unsurprisingly, the bureaucrats have put most emphasis on supervision. They have spent long hours debating how to co-ordinate the work of different supervisory organisations. Hans Tietmeyer, the boss of Germany's central bank, prepared a report on this for the G7; the British have already proposed a permanent "Standing Committee for Global Financial Regulation" to do the job.

Equal energy has been spent discussing how much of a part the supervision of standards should play in the IMF's annual health-check of member economies. The G22 group thought the IMF should produce a regular transparency report on every country. Others suggest the IMF should spend more time monitoring bank supervisors. Yet others want bank supervisors to keep an eye on each other's standards through a system of peer review.

Yet these debates have an Alice-in-Wonderland quality to them. The IMF does not have nearly enough people to track how far countries comply with a broad array of financial-market standards. And even if it did, IMF bureaucrats are notoriously reluctant to blow the whistle on a laggard country. Likewise, banking supervisory agencies in rich countries have no surplus trained staff to send off to emerging economies. Unless and until regulators are trained in far greater numbers, detailed international supervision of all emerging economies' financial standards is impossible. That means the onus lies with incentives.

The IMF could itself create the right kind of incentives by tying the amount of money a country could borrow directly to its standards of disclosure and the safety of its financial sector. But since countries turn to the IMF only in times of crisis, a more useful source of incentives is the regulators themselves.

Market access is a big carrot, and banishment a big stick. Already the Federal Reserve must be sure that a foreign bank is subject to "comprehensive consolidated supervision" by its home-country regulator, or at least is moving towards it, before such a bank will be granted permission to establish an office in the United States. Similarly, British financial regulators carry out more frequent and detailed inspections of the British subsidiaries of banks from countries whose supervisory standards are considered lax. Such incentives could be broadened and strengthened.

Beyond Basle

Regulators could also improve the incentives available to their own financial institutions, and particularly the Basle capital-adequacy standards. In a global capital market, the Basle standards are a crude way to measure a bank's health. For instance, they measure the riskiness of a loan by whether it is made to a country inside or outside the OECD. Commercial lending to governments of OECD countries carries a zero risk-weighting, that to non-OECD countries a 100% weighting. So when Mexico joined the OECD in 1994 (just before it crashed), a Mexican loan suddenly became an apparently much less risky asset. Another example of the Basle standards' shortcomings is that short-term lending requires less provisioning than long-term loans.

Such crude distinctions have encouraged international banks to bypass the Basle requirements by securitising their debt portfolio. They have also encouraged them to indulge in reckless behaviour, lending short-term to Asian borrowers because such loans carried a lower risk-weighting. Of the $380 billion in interna-

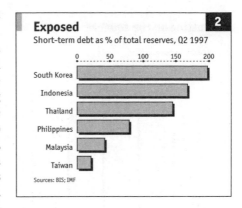

Exposed — 2

Short-term debt as % of total reserves, Q2 1997

Sources: BIS; IMF

tional bank lending outstanding to Asia at the end of 1997, 60% had a maturity of less than one year.

Fortunately the Basle standards are being updated. The proposals will be an important indicator of where reform is heading. In particular, they will show how far regulators are prepared to rely on market incentives for supervision.

Interesting ideas abound. Some regulators suggest that loans to emerging markets with poor financial systems should carry a higher risk weighting. Others prefer to make more direct use of the market to gauge risk, for example by basing a loan's risk-weighting on an average of the borrower's score from major credit-rating agencies. The difficulty is to ensure that market signals (such as a credit rating) do not increase the rush to lend to risky countries in boom times.

Do-it-yourself

A more radically market-oriented option is self-regulation by the banking industry. Charles Calomiris of Columbia University has reworked an idea first mooted by the Chicago Federal Reserve in the late 1980s: that bank regulation should depend on banks policing themselves. Under his proposal, each bank would finance a small proportion of its assets by selling subordinated debt to other institutions. The yield on this debt would not be permitted to rise above, say, 50 basis points over Treasury bills or equivalent risk-free assets. Because these subordinated debt holders would have only downside risk (they would not benefit from the profits of a reckless lending spree, but would share in the losses), the holders of subordinated debt would be rigorous monitors of the banks' behaviour. Banks rather than supervisors would be in charge.

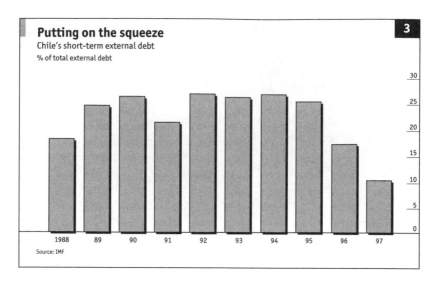

Putting on the squeeze | 3
Chile's short-term external debt
% of total external debt

1988 89 90 91 92 93 94 95 96 97

Source: IMF

The idea has gone down well in high places, at least in America. It enjoys the public support of one Federal Reserve governor, and has fans in the Treasury department and Congress. In principle, self-regulation makes sense both for sophisticated banks from rich countries, where regulators have a hard time keeping up with technical innovation, and for banks in poor countries, where supervisors are weak and often politically influenced. So far, Argentina is the only country that has the beginnings of such a system, though it does not set a maximum yield on its debt. But if the United States introduced the idea, others might well follow.

Yet even if market-based supervision is adopted, it will not happen overnight. For several years at least, emerging economies will be stuck with the status quo: too few supervisors trying to regulate weak banks. That means they must pay particular attention to overall macroeconomic stability, but also rely on some short-cuts to financial safety.

The most fashionable quick fix is prudential controls (or taxes) that discourage the most dangerous behaviour: short-term borrowing abroad. Even the most ardent champions of capital mobility, including the IMF, concede that such prudential regulations are worth having. Chile is everybody's favourite example. In 1991, it introduced a one-year mandatory non-interest-bearing reserve requirement on all foreign borrowing, first set at 20% and then raised to 30%. This meant that anyone who borrowed money abroad had to put 30% of it in the central bank for a year and got nothing for it. Chile also insisted that only firms and banks with a credit rating as high as that of the government itself could borrow abroad.

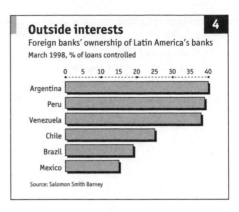

Outside interests 4

Foreign banks' ownership of Latin America's banks
March 1998, % of loans controlled

Source: Salomon Smith Barney

The reserve requirement did, eventually, reduce the share of short-term inflows (see chart 3), but at a price. Interest rates in Chile are higher than they would otherwise be. The capital market is divided between big firms that can borrow abroad and small ones that are stuck with high domestic interest rates. And when capital inflows dry up, as they have done in the recent past, the reserve requirement acts as a further deterrent. In response, Chile has reduced its reserve requirement to zero. All the same, its experience suggests that in the right circumstances such regulations can be helpful.

The mirror image of reducing short-term liabilities is boosting short-term assets. Emerging economies, especially those with weak financial systems, need big foreign-exchange reserves. Their banks have to keep a sizeable share of their assets in liquid form. Governments with heavy debt burdens (that is, most of Latin America) need to adopt what Mr Hausman of the Inter-American Development Bank calls the "skin-diver strategy": they must plan their finances to be able to withstand a sudden panic among foreign investors. That requires a large cushion of cash and a well spread out repayment schedule: emerging economies that allow repayments on their debt to fall due in large chunks are asking for trouble.

Foreign watchdogs

Lastly, one of the best ways to increase domestic financial stability quickly is to encourage foreign banks to come in. Their presence reduces the risk of a banking panic; the competition they provide will also spur domestic banks to improve their performance in a way supervision alone could not achieve. Especially in the wake of a crisis, a foreign presence can be built up quickly. Argentina now has only one bank of any size that is not owned or controlled by a large international bank. Four out of Mexico's big six are owned, or at least partly controlled, by foreigners. Outsiders are looking hard at Indonesian and Thai banks. As more countries recognise the benefits, foreign ownership of banks could become one of the most effective paths to financial security.

But it is no guarantee against future crises, even if emerging economies, and investors, radically change their behaviour. So crisis prevention alone is not enough. Financial architects must also produce blueprints for dealing more effectively with the inevitable crashes.

Pity the firemen

What to do if the worst happens

TODAY'S CURRENCY CRISES differ from those of the 1970s and 1980s in four crucial ways. They spread more quickly; they involve bigger sums of money; they are often caused by private, rather than government, profligacy; and they are devilishly difficult to diagnose. In particular, it is often hard to tell whether a crash is a crisis of liquidity or solvency; yet the difference is crucial.

A liquidity crisis is usually due to market panic. When investors exit *en masse*, a solvent government, or bank, or firm, becomes unable to raise money to pay its short-term bills. This is best dealt with by lending money until the panic subsides. A solvency crisis, by contrast, occurs when investors find out that a government, or firm, or bank, has fundamental problems. The proper response is to accept that debts need to restructured, but also to insist that whatever caused the problem in the first place is tackled, by attaching tough conditions to any assistance. Unconditional help would be disastrous, allowing investors to recoup their money and thereby encouraging further reckless investment.

Liquidity and solvency can be hard to tell apart. The 1980s debt crisis, for instance, was first treated as a liquidity crisis. Latin American debtors, it was thought, would be able to overcome their problems with the help of temporary loans, provided they ended their spendthrift ways. Only several years later was the problem accepted as one of solvency, and much of the debt written down. The recent growth of private-sector lending (sometimes with government guarantees) has made the distinction even less obvious. When crisis strikes, it is hard to know whether investors are panicking wildly or exercising sensible caution, whether a country needs unconditional support or tough reforms.

A mixed record

In recent crashes, the IMF has steered a much-criticised middle course. In 1995, together with and at the behest of the American government, the Fund bailed out investors by lending huge amounts to Mexico, in return for tough macroeconomic policy changes. The country suffered a severe recession, but private-sector confidence was rapidly restored.

The Asian crisis got a different treatment. Partly for fear of causing moral hazard, and partly because it did not have the money, the IMF made no attempt to pay off all of Thailand's, South Korea's or Indonesia's short-term liabilities. Instead, it optimistically assumed that some of these debts would be rolled over by the lending bankers. Moreover, much of the money on offer was more apparent than real. It was a "second line of defence" to be provided by individual countries, many of which had no intention of coughing up. To restore market confidence, the IMF once again demanded tough monetary and fiscal policy, as well as measures against crony capitalism.

In Russia, the IMF started with a version of its approach in Asia: tough conditions and a big loan package. When this failed to restore market confidence, the Fund stood aside, and a desperate Russia unilaterally announced a devaluation and default. The ensuing international chaos prompted the IMF to try yet another tack when Brazil first hit trouble in autumn 1998. Together with a number of individual countries, the Fund tried to prevent a crisis by pledging $41 billion to boost Brazil's reserves, much of it up front. That strategy held only for a couple of months: Brazil failed to deliver on promised fiscal reform, so investor confidence continued to wane, and on January 15th 1999 Brazil was forced to float its currency.

Few are happy with the IMF's record of advice and assistance. Martin Feldstein, an economist at Harvard University, argues that its demands for far-reaching structural reforms to resolve Asia's liquidity crisis were unnecessary and counterproductive. Jeffrey Sachs, also from Harvard, likewise reckons that the Asian market panic required more money and fewer conditions. Joseph Stiglitz, chief economist at the World Bank, was a vocal critic of the IMF's high-interest-rate policy in Asia. Free-marketeers lamented the use of public money to bail out "crony capitalists".

Bail them in

A year ago [1998], most architectural reform proposals concentrated on making sure that the private sector took a hit: investors had to be made to "pay a price" for their reckless lending. The bureaucrats also agreed that procedures were needed to create "orderly" debt workouts. An international bankruptcy court, they felt, would be unfeasibly radical, but smaller innovations might make crises less chaotic. A first step would be to ensure that creditors co-operate in a restructuring, rather than cut their losses and run. This is particularly tricky with bondholders. In America, under most existing bond contracts any restructuring requires the unanimous consent of all creditors. If one bondholder disagrees, he can sue the issuer, making the crisis worse.

One sensible innovation therefore would be to change bond contracts to include "collective action" clauses, which would allow them to be restructured by majority vote. Similar provisions already exist under English law. With luck, access to key international capital markets will be made conditional on such clauses. Although existing bonds would not be affected, bond crises would gradually become easier to deal with.

Superficially, bank loans pose fewer problems, since they involve fewer players. The main bankers can be assembled and bullied into restructuring their loans. During the 1980s debt crisis, the IMF made its lending conditional on debt-restructuring agreements by commercial banks. It used a version of this approach in South Korea in 1998. Foreign banks with outstanding short-term credit lines to Korean banks were persuaded to roll over their debts "voluntarily" (against a handsome return).

It is harder to force bankers to take a loss. Since a sudden withdrawal of interbank loans could cause the collapse of a debtor country's banking system, foreign bankers are in a strong position. Under a proposal put forward by Robert Litan of the Brookings Institution, emerging economies should let it be known that any bank which deserts them in a crisis will automatically be subjected to a "haircut" (a reduction of the principal) on its loan. But that would serve only to scare off bankers.

More usefully, the IMF's role in restructurings should be better defined. Since the late 1980s, the Fund has been able to lend to countries that were late with their payments to banks, and has done so on about 40 occasions. By "lending into arrears", it provides a country with working capital while it is negotiating with its creditors. In September 1998, the IMF agreed to consider "lending into arrears" for bonds. Once it starts doing so, it is bound to become a more central figure in debt restructurings.

Some reformers would like to go even further. They want to give the IMF the explicit power to declare a debt moratorium, thereby making it more like an international bankruptcy court. Leaving aside questions of sovereignty, this could dramatically increase the cost of capital to emerging economies. Investors would demand a high risk-premium as they fretted about the prospect of a moratorium that may well be politically motivated.

Watch them run

Today's architects also talk loosely about forcing banks to contribute to rescue packages. The idea of "bailing in banks" is attractive: it would make sure that private investors stake some of their money on the success of a crisis-prevention package. But in practice this presents huge problems. When crisis looms, it is hard to persuade creditors not to flee. Forcing them to stay in could precipitate the panic the measure is intended to prevent. In October 1998, for example, there was much talk of a private-sector contribution to the $41 billion support package for Brazil, but in the end there was none because the banks, fearful that they might be forced to contribute to a bail-out, had been frantically reducing their exposure to Brazil, making things worse.

In September 1998, the Clinton administration stopped talking about haircuts for bankers and suggested the IMF should have a "contingency financing facility". Countries in good economic health could draw on IMF loans in advance of any crisis to head off trouble. Although the principle was accepted by the G7, it is not yet clear exactly what it implies. Many IMF officials favour a minimalist interpretation. Other reformers see this facility as the first step towards making the IMF a true lender of last resort. Countries in good standing would automatically be allowed to draw on this money. Eligibility might be determined by, say, the transparency and the strength of a country's financial sector.

Not enough in the kitty

The idea has two drawbacks. The first is money, or rather the lack of it. Despite its recent capital increase, the IMF still has puny resources compared with the amount of private capital sloshing around the world. At present, this facility could help only a couple of countries such as Argentina or Mexico. In principle, the IMF's coffers could be replenished more comprehensively, or it could borrow from the world's central banks. But a large pot of IMF money would inevitably encourage reckless behaviour unless its use was tightly controlled.

The inventive Mr Calomiris, among others, has drawn up a complete blueprint for global reform that recasts the IMF as a provider of liquidity. Only countries that fulfilled a strict set of conditions would be eligible for any IMF money at all. All IMF lending would be short-term, say for 90 days, and would have to be backed by government bonds. If a country did not pay back on time, it would be ineligible for IMF money for five years.

But these restrictions are so stringent that hardly any country could meet them. And as an essentially political body, the IMF is unlikely to stand aside while all but a handful of countries are hit by crisis. Moreover, it would be hard to remove a country from the list of eligible recipients without actually causing a crisis. If the IMF cannot bring itself to blow the whistle on countries for lack of transparency, there is little chance that it will become the disciplinarian Mr Calomiris wants it to be. The IMF's Mr Fischer – who supports the idea of pre-emptive financing – suggests that countries which do not qualify might pay higher interest rates. But that seems a weak precaution against reckless behaviour. In reality, the IMF can be only a limited lender of last resort.

Other would-be architects have suggested different solutions. George Soros thinks that mandatory insurance, issued by an international credit insurance corporation, is the answer. Just as deposit insurance averts the danger of depositor runs, so the credit insurance issued by such an international institution would avert the danger of a sudden loss of creditor confidence. The IMF would set a ceiling on the amount of loan finance a country could issue, leaving any loans over and above that uninsured. This idea suffers from many flaws, the biggest of which it shares with Mr Calomiris's blueprint: ultimately, it is inconceivable that a large country would be left to fail, even if it had borrowed above its ceiling.

A more plausible option is the limited provision of liquidity through private-sector credit lines, guaranteed in advance. For an up-front fee, Argentina has set up a contingent repurchase facility with 13 commercial banks, thus securing guaranteed access to $6.7 billion of cash (equivalent to about 10% of bank deposits), with government bonds as collateral. Argentina secured $1 billion from the World Bank and the Inter-American Development Bank to guarantee part of this repurchase facility. More such multilateral guarantees would enable more countries to set up private liquidity lines more cheaply. But there are limits even to this plan. Private banks are unlikely to provide huge credit lines, and in a general panic they will refuse to renew them.

Optimists reckon that these reform efforts will produce a financial system modestly better than the present one at dealing with crises. The IMF, in particular, will end up with a more useful tool kit. But pessimists conclude that today's international financial architects are hopelessly confused. They want to punish investors and stem panic at the same time. One moment they talk of giving banks a haircut, the next of establishing new lines of credit. They refuse to recognise trade-offs. Unfortunately the sceptics appear to have the better case. That would help explain why the official architects are strangely silent about another crucial aspect of global financial reform: exchange rates.

Fix or float?

It all depends

A T A CASUAL glance, the IMF's attitude towards exchange rates seems extraordinarily erratic. In 1997 the Fund urged Asian countries to devalue or float their currencies. In 1998 it lent billions to Russia and Brazil to try to help them maintain their exchange rates. It has praised Hong Kong for its super-strict currency board, and feted Singapore for its flexible managed float. Given that exchange-rate regimes are by definition central to currency crises, such different approaches cannot all be ideal.

They are not, but the IMF's inconsistency reflects deep divisions about exchange-rate regimes among economists. Tellingly, the official international financial architects (the G7, G22 and so forth) have steered clear of the subject. That is because the exchange-rate issue, more obviously than any other, is mired in the impossible trinity that prevents reform of international finance. It is one area where the trade-offs cannot be fudged.

In a world of increasingly mobile capital (see chart 5), countries cannot fix their exchange rate and at the same time maintain an independent monetary policy. They must choose between the confidence and stability provided by a fixed exchange rate and the control over policy offered by a floating rate. Traditionally, the deciding factor in a country's choice has been its vulnerability to external shocks, such as sudden shifts in commodity prices. A floating currency allows a country to adjust to external shocks through the exchange rate. In countries with a fixed currency, domestic wages and prices will come under pressure instead.

But floating exchange rates have a big drawback: they can overshoot and become highly unstable, especially if large amounts of capital flow in and out of a country. That instability carries real economic costs. Moreover, floating rates can reduce investors' faith in a currency, thus making it harder to fight inflation. To get the best of both worlds, many emerging economies have tried a hybrid approach, loosely tying their exchange rate either to a single foreign currency, such as the dollar, or to a basket of currencies. Until the recent bout of crises, many academics agreed that such "limited flexibility" was a good compromise.

But that consensus has been shattered. Most academics now believe that only radical solutions will work: either currencies must float freely, or they must be tightly tied (through a currency board or, even better,

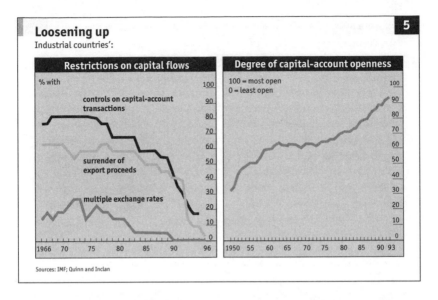

Loosening up
Industrial countries':

Restrictions on capital flows

% with

controls on capital-account transactions

surrender of export proceeds

multiple exchange rates

1966 70 75 80 85 90 96

Degree of capital-account openness

100 = most open
0 = least open

1950 55 60 65 70 75 80 85 90 93

Sources: IMF; Quinn and Inclan

currency union). Unfortunately the academics rarely agree on the best solution. Take the remedies suggested for Brazil's ills. Harvard's Mr Sachs had long been arguing for a floating exchange rate, which the country introduced on January 15th 1999. Rudi Dornbusch, of MIT, is equally adamant that a currency board remains best.

Policymakers prefer to play down exchange rates. Any regime can work, they argue, provided it is backed by sound economic fundamentals. That is true but trite. Of course a country will benefit from sound fiscal and monetary policies; but, as recent events have shown, a country's choice of exchange-rate regime clearly affects its vulnerability to crises. Asian countries got into trouble because of their exchange-rate pegs, and were then thrown into chaos by the volatility of floating rates.

On the face of it, in a world of capital mobility a more flexible exchange rate seems the best bet. A floating currency will force firms and investors to hedge against fluctuations, not lull them into a false sense of stability (as they were in most of Asia). It will also make foreign banks more circumspect about lending. At the same time it will give policymakers the option of devising their own monetary policy. History, too, is on the side of greater flexibility. Since the mid-1970s the number of countries with flexible exchange rates has increased steadily (see chart 6). All this suggests that the global architects should be promoting, and preparing for, a world of floating currencies. In an excellent book[1]

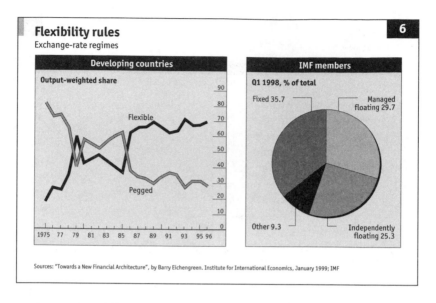

Flexibility rules 6
Exchange-rate regimes

Sources: "Towards a New Financial Architecture", by Barry Eichengreen. Institute for International Economics, January 1999; IMF

on international financial reform, Berkeley's Mr Eichengreen suggests that the IMF should push countries to adopt floating exchange rates rather than wait until a currency crisis obliges them to.

But on closer inspection, the choice is not quite so clear. According to the World Bank, over the past 30 years more crises have befallen countries with flexible than with fixed exchange rates, though they have been more severe for fixed-rate countries. Moreover, monetary independence may be more apparent than real, at least for developing countries with small-scale financial systems. Confronted by sudden market panic, emerging economies dependent on foreign capital have to raise interest rates sky-high to prevent their currency from collapsing.

Mexico is a good example. It has a floating currency, which depreciated by more than 10% in response to the investor panic after Russia's meltdown. Even so, Mexico's interest rates were far higher than those of Argentina, which has a super-fixed currency board. In other words, Mexico paid a hefty price to reassure investors that its currency would not go into free fall.

Beware volatility

But the biggest problem with a floating currency remains the risk of volatility. As Paul Volcker, a former chairman of the Federal Reserve, likes to point out, the entire banking system of many an emerging country is no bigger than a typical regional bank in the United States (the sort now considered too small for global financial markets, and merging furiously). For many emerging economies, small financial markets mean that exchange-rate volatility will be a structural, not a temporary problem. If a couple of mutual funds suddenly decided to make a serious investment, the country's exchange rate could rocket, starting an unsustainable boom in the property and banking sector, and causing havoc for exporters.

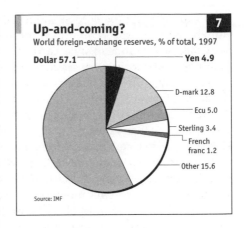

Up-and-coming?   7
World foreign-exchange reserves, % of total, 1997

Dollar 57.1 — Yen 4.9
D-mark 12.8
Ecu 5.0
Sterling 3.4
French franc 1.2
Other 15.6

Source: IMF

The more pragmatic proponents of floating rates recognise the risks of volatility. Mr Eichengreen, for instance, wants emerging economies to discourage short-term capital inflows to minimise exchange-rate volatility. He thereby acknowledges that – at least for economies with small financial sectors – floating exchange rates are feasible in the long run only if capital-market integration is slowed down.

Others argue that floating exchange rates make no sense for small emerging economies. Rigidly pegged rates, they reckon, would be far more sensible. Mr Volcker, for instance, has suggested that small emerging economies should seek financial safety and currency stability in "size" and "diversity". By diversity, he means a good dose of foreign ownership in the financial sector; by size, regional currency arrangements. Emerging markets, he thinks, should link up with the leading regional currency, such as the dollar in the Americas.

This can be done in a number of ways. Currency boards are one option. Hong Kong and Argentina, which both have boards, have shown that they can withstand huge swings in investor confidence – mainly because a currency board forces prudence in the banking system and encourages foreign ownership. A more dramatic step is currency union. Either individual countries can pool their currencies to create a new one (as the Europeans have done), or they can simply adopt the currency of another (Panama, for instance, uses the dollar).

Are such regional currency unions a plausible option for emerging economies? In Europe, the answer is surely yes. Poland, Hungary, the Czech Republic and others now queuing up to join the European Union seem sure to adopt the euro at some point. Only the timing is at issue. Elsewhere the prospects are much more uncertain. Although there has been talk of a European-style currency union for the Latin American countries in Mercosur, they are more likely to adopt the dollar.

Not long ago, the idea that any economy would voluntarily give up its currency in favour of the dollar was political dynamite. Today the mood is different. Argentina's president, Carlos Menem, has asked his technocrats to examine the idea of using the US dollar throughout Latin America. In Mexico, a poll in October 1998 found that nine out of ten people preferred dollarisation to a floating peso. In private, senior financial officials in Washington suggest that regional dollarisation is a sensible long-term goal. Whether regional currency unions are co-operative (as in Europe) or hegemonic (as they would most likely be in the Americas), they raise tough questions of sovereignty and regulation. In Europe, for instance, responsibility for bank supervision, and the provision of liquidity in the event of a bank panic, will officially remain with national regulators and national central banks. But many national regulators admit that in the event of a serious crisis the European Central Bank would have to step in, and that bank supervision will eventually be handled at the regional level.

In the Americas, it is most unlikely that the Federal Reserve would come to the rescue of an individual Argentine or Mexican bank, so each country would have to build up a safety fund of its own for such purposes. But if a large regional crisis erupted, particularly one that threatened the health of American banks, currency union would make assistance from the Federal Reserve much more likely.

Regional reservations

Although regional currency unions will not be formed overnight, they are likely to become an increasingly attractive option in Europe and for some countries in the Americas. Further afield, however, they present more of a problem. Though Asia's small (and very open) emerging economies would benefit greatly from regional currency stability, nationalist sentiments and mutual suspicion, especially between China and Japan, seem to rule out regional unions.

The yen, despite Japan's current economic difficulties, is clearly the leading Asian currency. But predictions of a "yen block" in Asia seem off the mark. This is partly because Japan's stifling regulation has frustrated the growth of bond and derivatives markets that might have encouraged other Asians to do business in yen. But political reasons also play a part. Back when the Asian crisis was still a local affair, the Japanese suggested an Asian monetary fund: a regional self-help group that might provide liquidity for the area's cash-strapped economies, and perhaps a precursor to a regional currency regime. The idea was firmly squashed by the Americans (who feared a loss of influence), with the support of many South-East Asian countries (which trust Americans more than they trust the bureaucrats in Tokyo). Although Japanese policymakers have recently been talking up the international role of the yen and have even referred again to an Asian monetary fund, this still seems a remore possibility.

The best guess at the moment is that emerging economies will divide into two groups: those with flexible exchange rates and a relatively low level of integration into global capital markets; and those that bind their economies tightly through currency boards or currency unions, and as a result have heavily integrated financial systems with strong foreign ownership. Within a couple of decades, this division could result in two sizeable currency blocks, the dollar and euro zones, together with a large number of countries with floating exchange rates. Different countries will have taken different routes to achieving the "impossible trinity" of integration, regulation and sovereignty. Those in regional unions will have given up sovereignty for integration; those with floating rates will have maintained sovereignty, but often at the cost of restricting integration with the rest of the world.

As part of this evolution, some aspects of international financial organisation will become easier. Global financial regulation, for instance, will become more feasible once regional supervision and regulation have been established within currency blocks. Reaching global agreement will become less cumbersome as the number of participants in negotiations falls. The IMF's job, in principle, might become simpler if regional central banks played a larger role in providing emergency liquidity within their blocks. Economies remaining outside regional currency unions would have floating exchange rates, reducing the likelihood of large-scale liquidity crises.

Clearly, exchange-rate regimes are central to the debate about global architecture. Emerging economies' choices between fixed and floating currencies can make a huge difference to the way the international financial system develops. The architects ignore them at their peril.

Notes

1   *Toward a New International Financial Architecture: a Practical Post-Asia Agenda*, by Barry Eichengreen. Institute for International Economics, Washington DC, January 1999.

From architecture to action

As long as it is not too ambitious

THE MORE THE rich world's leaders bang on about the urgent need for a new global financial architecture, the clearer it becomes that the grand talk will achieve little and may even be counterproductive. The impossible triangle – achieving a global capital market, with appropriate regulation and supervision, while maintaining national sovereignty – is simply impervious to rhetoric. By demanding new blueprints, politicians raise expectations that will inevitably be dashed. Worse, by talking up the prospects for sweeping global financial reform, they may actually reduce the chances of constructive and modest change. By making a grand plan seem realistic, they may intensify squabbles over which country sits on which committee, and channel energy away from serious efforts such as the ill-fated G22 meetings.

As it happens, there are many less ambitious things that can be done right now. First, and likely to produce the quickest results, rich countries can lead by example. From improving their standards of financial disclosure to including collective-action clauses in their foreign-bond contracts, industrial countries can begin to change the norms of international financial markets. If an emerging market unilaterally changed its new bond contracts to make restructuring easier, the market would suspect that this would entail higher risk, and would require higher interest rates to make up for it. But if several industrial countries jointly led the way, such contracts would soon become standard.

Second, industrial countries can remedy the distortions that encourage their own financial institutions to behave recklessly in emerging markets. Top of the list should be a revision of the Basle capital accords. With the best will in the world, it will take years for many emerging markets to improve their bank supervision, and even longer for them to strengthen their banks. The quickest way to safer finance, therefore, is to change creditors' behaviour. Nonetheless, financial architects could be much more creative in improving incentives for emerging markets to get their house in order. For instance, what better way to ensure that bankruptcy laws are passed than making access to the New York or London capital markets conditional on having such legislation in place?

Third, the architects should encourage international institutions to innovate. Argentina's contingency-finance arrangement with private banks seems to be working well; if the World Bank or other multilateral organisations were to guarantee a portion of such emergency credit lines, more banks would be prepared to offer them to more countries. This would not solve the question of providing liquidity in a crisis, but it might help at the margin.

Silence and confusion

As well as implementing such modest changes (rather than just talking about them), the international architects need to become more open about some of the trade-offs involved. Two issues stand out: exchange-rate management and the role of the IMF. The official international architects are virtually silent about exchange rates. And they want the IMF to respond to a crisis in two opposite and incompatible ways: by stemming panic as well as by punishing reckless investors.

Since the development of exchange-rate regimes around the world will help to determine the direction of architectural reform, it seems odd for the architects to ignore them. Even without a consensus on whether fixed or floating currencies are best, it is important to understand the consequences of choosing one or the other. If you dislike the prospect of regional currency zones, for instance, then you need to know exactly what effect floating regimes will have.

Similarly, it is vital to be clear about what the IMF can, and cannot, do. It is not a true lender of last resort, because it does not have the resources to provide limitless liquidity to stop a financial panic. Nor does it ever seem likely to acquire such resources, unless the world goes for global regulation, a global currency and a global central bank – which is highly unlikely. The IMF, therefore, will always be constrained by limited funds. So when trouble hits, it should not attempt to provide huge amounts of money, but concentrate on its role in overseeing countries' negotiations with creditors.

In the aftermath of crisis, this agenda sounds modest. It will not satisfy the radicals who want to redesign global finance. It will not remove the tension between national sovereignty, capital-market regulation and global financial integration. But it may make the next global financial panic a little less alarming for investors and regulators, and a bit less painful for emerging economies.

The material on pages 281–311 first appeared in a survey written by Zanny Minton Beddoes in The Economist in January 1999.

Slimming the Bretton Woods duo

Is America's Congress out to revitalise the IMF and the World Bank, or to ruin them?

WHEN A REPORT sponsored by America's Congress, and embraced by senior Republicans, argues that the IMF and the World Bank should be radically scaled back, but that foreign aid to the poorest countries should be dramatically increased, it is hard not to be cynical. America is one of the world's stingiest donors of foreign aid. It spends a measly 0.1% of GDP on development aid a year, by far the lowest of any industrialised country. In countless budget battles Republicans have masked their parochialism with rhetoric about international bureaucracies and contempt for corrupt foreign countries.

Put aside that cynicism. Does this report (known as the Meltzer report, after the committee's Allan Meltzer of Carnegie-Mellon University, and signed by Jeffrey Sachs, a well-known development economist at Harvard) offer sensible principles for reforming international financial institutions and for rebuilding a consensus for foreign aid in America?

The report, published in March 2000, argues that the IMF should concentrate on one big market failure: financial panics in which solvent economies cannot borrow. It should stop having detailed loan agreements with economic strings attached. To be eligible for IMF support, countries should pass four preconditions, including adequately capitalised banks and a yet-to-be-determined criterion for fiscal prudence. The money should be lent short-term and at penal rates. Only in systemic crises should non-eligible countries receive Fund bail-outs. And it should not lend at subsidised rates to the poorest countries.

This vision of the IMF providing liquidity to healthy countries as a central bank might provide it to healthy banks is not new; a small library of academic papers is devoted to the subject. It is, nonetheless, appealing. How much better to have a clearly focused IMF than today's grubby combination of geopolitical slush fund and emerging-economy schoolmaster. Unfortunately, the appealing principle does not translate easily into practice.

It is, first of all, impossible to devise preconditions ensuring that basically sound but strapped-for-cash countries get IMF money. Make eligibility conditions too stringent and too few countries would qualify; but bail-outs of big countries would be justified because of "systemic risk". Make them too loose and moral hazard would increase because investors would expect bail-outs of too many countries. But the Meltzer report is, nonetheless, a sensible direction for IMF reform. Countries with better banking systems and more prudent economic policies should have easier access to money at lower interest rates than those that do not. The IMF should provide incentives for countries to aspire to better financial standards.

Developing principles

Underlying the report's vision for the development banks such as the World Bank is a similarly attractive principle. In a world where private capital flows to poor countries dwarf official assistance, development banks should do what markets cannot or will not do. They should provide international public goods (such as research into the treatment of tropical diseases) and should transfer resources to alleviate poverty in the very poorest countries, and those that do not have access to private capital.

That hardly seems today's practice. According to the report, some 70% of the Bank's non-concessional lending over the previous seven years went to 11 countries (including China, Argentina, Mexico and Brazil) that had access to capital markets. And, it says, almost half of the Bank's lending to countries with access to capital markets in the 1990s went to activities from which the private sector can profit.

Given that poverty alleviation is the Bank's ostensible goal, this is odd. It is true that the Bank's lending has become more focused on social sectors recently, and it is also true that the majority of the world's poor people live in countries such as China or Brazil, which do have access to capital markets. But, as the report points out, the fact that there are poor people in a country with such access does not self-evidently justify lending by the Bank.

Often, such countries' failure to spend on the poor is down to bad budgeting. That is why the report recommends phasing out all development-bank lending to countries with investment-grade ratings, or an income per head of over $4,000. Instead, resources should focus on the poorest: countries with income per head of less than $2,500. Those in between, and those with erratic access to capital markets, would get limited aid. Again, however, the attractive principle faces a murky reality. Countries' access to private capital is more limited than aggregate figures would suggest.

On occasion, the Bank can be a catalyst for private-sector money. In the aftermath of Asia's crisis, Bank guarantees helped to speed up countries' return to the capital markets. And with the advice and conditions it attaches to its loans, World Bank lending arguably fosters good economic policy better than the private sector. But even these qualifications do not undermine the basic direction of sensible reform: not to concentrate resources on countries with access to capital markets.

The real risks of refocusing the Bank more explicitly on the poorest countries are political. The Bank itself is a mechanism to raise resources for the poorest. Roughly a third of the Bank's profits are spent on debt relief and subsidised loans. In principle, as the Meltzer report suggests, it might be more efficient just to spend the money directly. The danger, however, is that the Bank's shareholders would use this as an excuse to cut their own foreign-aid budgets still more. Then you would lose the Bank's benefits for middle-income countries and also have less money for the poorest. To expect such an outcome would, of course, be much too cynical.

The material on pages 312–14 first appeared in an Economics Focus in *The Economist* in March 2000.

Huff, puff and pay

There is plenty of support for the principle of simplifying IMF
conditionality. Putting it into practice is another matter

LIKE ANY NEW boss, Horst Köhler, who became managing director of
the International Monetary Fund in May 2001, wants to make his
mark. From the outset, Mr Köhler wanted to bring more focus to what
the IMF does, and to set clear priorities. His approach can be summed up
as less means more: smaller rescue packages for countries needing IMF
help, and fewer, but more effectively applied, conditions for those packages. He wanted the Fund to be better both at crisis management and at
crisis prevention.

So far, it has not gone as smoothly as Mr Köhler had hoped. The
reforms he brought in to make the Fund better at spotting trouble ahead
are only now being implemented. It is too soon to know how effective
they will be (the sceptics are, well, sceptical). On crisis management, too,
the jury is out: Turkey, for instance, has been in almost continuous nego-
tiation with the Fund since autumn 2000, and Mr Köhler has admitted
that, if the Turkish government fails to deliver on its promises to the IMF
for a third time, his reputation could be damaged. Nor are IMF packages
noticeably smaller. The bail-outs agreed for Turkey and Argentina
seemed pretty big to most people.

On conditionality, though, Mr Köhler seems to be making some head-
way. At the spring 2001 meetings of the World Bank and the IMF, he
secured backing for his proposed changes in the way conditionality is
applied. Countries getting financial support from the Fund cannot be
expected to do everything at once, says Mr Köhler. It is necessary to
decide on priorities, and to focus conditionality on measures that are
critical to the macroeconomic objectives of recipient-country programmes, leaving those countries some scope to make policy choices for
themselves. One benefit of this more streamlined approach, in Mr
Köhler's view, is that it gives debtor countries the chance to build political support at home for their reform programmes – a vital element
whose absence has, on occasion, caused IMF-sponsored programmes to
collapse in the face of local opposition.

This new approach was endorsed by the main policymaking body of
the IMF, the International Monetary and Financial Committee, when it

met on April 29th 2001. Its communiqué noted that streamlining conditionality shifts "the presumption of coverage from one of comprehen-
siveness to one of parsimony." This echoes what some Fund-watchers
have been urging for some time. Morris Goldstein of the Institute for
International Economics (IIE), a Washington think-tank, has long argued
that the approach of IMF staff to conditionality has got out of hand. Mr
Goldstein is not suggesting that IMF funds should be disbursed without
strings. But he has questioned the sharp rise in the number of conditions
attached to programmes (140 at its peak in the case of Indonesia, for
example). Efforts to include in conditionality everything but the kitchen
sink, says Mr Goldstein, have brought legitimate charges of "mission
creep".

One of the consequences of this is that monitoring compliance
becomes more difficult. For instance, is a country compliant or non-
compliant when it observes 30 out of 50 conditions? It is hard to tell,
says Mr Goldstein, in an updated paper published by the IIE[1].

Mr Goldstein is no enemy of the IMF, rather a constructive critic. He
was, indeed, an IMF staff member for nearly 25 years, and deputy director of the research department for seven. Yet the prickly reaction that his
views on conditionality have drawn from some Fund staffers shows
that Mr Köhler needs support from below, as well as above, if the new
policy is to be effective. At a seminar in Washington, for instance, one
IMF official asked whether it was wrong to include measures aimed at
poverty reduction.

Of course it is not. Even so, such efforts may be misguided. They may
also be over-ambitious, given the finite resources and expertise within
the Fund for monitoring compliance. After all, most IMF funding is not
directly aimed at poverty reduction *per se*, but at helping countries to
achieve the macroeconomic and financial stability that are the foundations of prosperity. Better, surely, to limit the number of conditions that
countries seeking assistance should be asked to meet, and then to ensure
that they do indeed meet them.

If eliminating mission "creep" is going to be a struggle, so too is cutting back on mission "push" – the desire of the IMF's biggest shareholders to get the Fund to take on extra responsibilities, sometimes even as
they are voicing support for streamlining conditionality. The IMF, for
instance, is now expected to play a leading role in combating money-
laundering and financial abuse. The communiqué also endorsed the
idea that the Fund should deal with corruption and poor governance.
These are important aspects of sustainable economic reform. But they

could imply an extension, not a reduction, of Fund involvement in domestic policymaking.

The fact is that it often suits the rich countries that largely dictate IMF policies to tack on specific conditions to individual country packages. They may talk about giving more focus to the Fund's activities, but in practice they find them useful policy tools, especially if they want to avoid the expense and bother of bilateral help. This is true, above all, for America – much the biggest shareholder in the Fund with, in effect, right of veto. The new Bush administration came into office amid expectations that they would be tougher on countries in trouble, and that they would oppose big bailouts. So far, though, their approach has been wholly pragmatic: after much huffing and puffing, the packages for Turkey and Argentina won strong American backing.

For the time being, at least, this has put the IMF in a stronger position than it might have hoped. Whether Mr Köhler can exploit this to make what the Fund does more effective will be a good test of his mettle.

Notes

1   "IMF Structural Conditionality: How Much Is Too Much?". Institute for International Economics working paper, April 2001.

The material on pages 315–17 first appeared in an Economics Focus in *The Economist* in May 2001.

Index